THE ROOTS OF RUSSIAN COMMUNISM

A Social and Historical Study of Russian Social-Democracy 1898–1907

Also by David Lane

POLITICS AND SOCIETY IN THE USSR (1970)

THE END OF INEQUALITY? SOCIAL STRATIFICATION UNDER STATE
SOCIALISM (1971)

SOCIAL GROUPS IN POLISH SOCIETY (1973) *with George Kolankiewicz*

DAVID LANE

THE ROOTS
OF
RUSSIAN COMMUNISM

A SOCIAL AND HISTORICAL STUDY
OF RUSSIAN SOCIAL-DEMOCRACY 1898–1907

THE PENNSYLVANIA STATE UNIVERSITY PRESS

UNIVERSITY PARK

First published in 1969 by Royal Van Gorcum Ltd., The Netherlands. This edition
published 1975 by Martin Robertson & Company Ltd., 17 Quick Street, London
N1 8HL.

Published in the United States of America by Pennsylvania State University Press, 215
Wagner Building, University Park, Pennsylvania 16802.

ISBN 0-271-01178-5
LC 74-15196

Printed in Great Britain

CONTENTS

INDEX OF TABLES

INDEX OF CHARTS

INDEX OF MAPS

ABBREVIATIONS

References when first used are given in full and thereafter abbreviated. Dates in the text are of the Russian Julian calendar. References to the 'party' refer to the Russian Social-Democratic Labour Party. Place of publication is London, unless otherwise stated. The following abbreviations for journals and periodicals have been used.

K.A.	*Krasny arkhiv*
P.R.	*Proletarskaya revolyutsiya*
K.L.	*Krasnaya letopis'*
V.I.	*Voprosy istorii*
V.I. KPSS	*Voprosy istorii KPSS*
L.S.	*Leninski sbornik*
L.R.	*Letopis' revolyutsii*

PREFACE

Though I am responsible for the inadequacies of this book, they would have been more numerous had I not received criticism and advice from many people. I am indebted to Mr H. T. Willetts, who guided me for several years as a post-graduate student at the University of Oxford and who read the whole manuscript; to Professor R. W. Davies of Birmingham University, who has always given me encouragement and help. Mr David Shapiro, Professor R. E. F. Smith, Mr Leo van Rossum and Miss Janet Duckworth have read all or parts of the book and have made many useful suggestions. Mr. Charles B. Timmer of the International Institute of Social History expeditiously saw the book through the press.

My work would not have been possible but for the support of Nuffield College, Oxford and for leave of absence and other assistance generously given by the University of Birmingham. During some visits to the USSR in connexion with this work, I was greatly assisted by members of the Society for Cultural Relations who made many arrangements and by Soviet scholars who discussed my work with me. Last, but not least, I must thank my wife who has read innumerable drafts, has always offered encouragement and has helped me with various points.

University of Essex
England.

INTRODUCTION

'Every revolution bears the stamp of its own distinctive genius. It is a product of the historical forces that go before, of the leaders who shape its course, and of the problems with which they are confronted. It is a shallow view of Russian history which sees Bolshevism as an alien excrescence grafted on the Russian body politic by a handful of power lusting conspirators without roots in the past ... Bolshevism as a movement was an indigenous, authoritarian response to the environment of Tsarist absolutism which nurtured it. Autocracy generates its own authoritarian antibodies and endows them with its own peculiar contours.'

M. Fainsod, *How Russia is Ruled*, 2nd Ed. (1963), p. 3.

This book is concerned with the social composition, structure and political activity of Russian Social-Democratic groups from the end of the nineteenth century to the Russian Revolution of 1905. Primarily, it is neither concerned with the theory of the Russian socialist movement nor with the analysis of Russian economic and social change. It deals with the people who made up the movement and the meaning of Social-Democratic ideas to them. It considers the nature of the Social-Democratic movement in Russia, the strength of its membership and support, and the extent to which differences in social structures affected Social-Democratic activity. The general features of the history of Russian Social-Democracy and its development are well known and I shall not repeat the story in this book[1]. The split of the Russian Social-Democratic Labour Party into Bolshevik and Menshevik factions and the division of the party into two organisations will be investigated at the lower levels of the party to discover what differences existed in social support and political outlook. The economic and social differences between areas will be

---

[1] The best-known English sources are: L. Schapiro, *The Communist Party of the Soviet Union* (1960): J. L. H. Keep, *The Rise of Social Democracy in Russia* (1963).

examined to show whether they were related to the support of the two factions.

There is little work in English on Russian Social-Democracy. Some works which have dealt with the history of local organisations[1] do not give a picture of the nature of Russian Social-Democracy as a whole and do not systematically cover Russia. The general histories[2] are concerned less with the social than the political and philosophical study of the movement and its critical evaluation. Books written from the point of view of political theory fall into the same category[3]. These works have been concerned with Russian Social-Democracy as an organised political party whereas I shall consider it in wider terms, as a social movement.

In this book, the emphasis is on the local Social-Democratic organisations, their activity and support. An empirical study of the support of the RSDLP and its rôle in the localities is necessary before any generalisations may be made either about the nature of Russian Social-Democracy or about the kind of support a revolutionary movement attracts. Merle Fainsod, cited in the frontispiece, does not carry out his analysis of the connexion between Bolshevism and the social order: only in very general terms does he describe social forces in Russian history (the autocracy, the peasantry, the intelligentsia, the bourgeoisie) which preceded the revolution. One does not learn which particular factors were connected with the growth of Bolshevism, how wide a movement it was and among which strata it had support. L. H. Haimson's work[4] is concerned with the intellectual origins of Bolshevik ideas and sheds little light on the relationship of the social structure to the growth of Social-Democracy and the development of the Bolshevik and Menshevik factions.

Many writers[5] have pointed out the importance of the Populist movement as a precursor to Bolshevism. But no study has attempted to trace either continuity in membership from the Narodniks to the Bolsheviks or the ways local Bolshevik activity was built upon previous Narodnik groundwork.

Research into the history of Social-Democracy in the USSR has

---

[1] R. Pipes, *Social Democracy and the St. Petersburg Labor Movement, 1885-1897* (Harvard University Press 1963) and R. M. Slusser, *The Moscow Soviet of Workers' Deputies of 1905: Origin, Structure and Politics* (Ph. D. Columbia University 1963).

[2] For example, L. Schapiro, *The Communist Party of the Soviet Union* (1960) and J. L. H. Keep, *The Rise of Social Democracy in Russia* (1963).

[3] J. Plamenatz, *German Marxism and Russian Communism* (1954).

[4] *The Russian Marxists and the Origins of Bolshevism* (Harvard University Press, 1955).

[5] F. Venturi, *The Roots of Revolution* (1960); R. Pipes, 'Russian Marxism and its Populist Background: the Late Nineteenth Century', *The Russian Review* (October 1960), vol. 19, no. 4; and S. V. Utechin, 'Who Taught Lenin', *Twentieth Century* (1960), vol. CLXVIII.

concentrated mainly on the history of the Bolsheviks. Such work is immense in scale. Apart from deficiencies in the history of the Mensheviks, general party histories have only tenuously related Social-Democracy to the structure of the working class and have only briefly mentioned the composition of local groups[1]. Soviet work has not considered in any depth the social structure of the Social-Democratic movement. Local party histories vary much in quality – many are intended for party activists and are not very scholarly though others are[2] – and none give any indication of the scope of the whole movement. *Voprosy Istorii KPSS* (the main Soviet journal on party history) has printed much on local party groups but the bias against the Mensheviks and the exaggerated role of the Bolsheviks are apparent[3]. Generally, work in this journal is less reliable and more one-sided than the writings of the immediate post-revolutionary period. The more positive side of Soviet research has been the publication of much valuable archive material about the grass roots of Social-Democracy[4].

As the emphasis in this book is on the social composition and support of Russian Social-Democracy, it may be necessary to explain and justify the attention given to these phenomena. At the outset it is necessary to make clear that, on its own, the analysis of the social composition of a revolutionary movement may not explain its success. This is as much due to the increasing weakness of established authority as to the strength of the revolutionary party or movement, and the causes of such weakness may be, for example, economic, administrative or military. Success may also be due to the organisational structure of the revolutionary party, which may allow the 'right man, at the right time, to take the right decisions', as well as to the relevance of the political and social theories on which a political party may base its policies. Nevertheless, studies of social stratification have thrown much light on the development of political parties, and have shown how different policies were dependent on, and related to certain social conditions and social strata for support[5].

[1] For example, *Istoriya kommunisticheskoy partii sovetskogo soyuza*, vol. I (M. 1964).

[2] For example, A. N. Pyaskovski, *Revolyutsiya 1905-1907 gg. v Turkestane* (M. 1958).

[3] Some useful source material, however, has been collected, 'U istokov partii: materialy o sotsial-demokraticheskikh organizatsiyakh v Rossii nakanune II s'ezda RSDRP', V.I.KPSS Nos. 3, 9, 1963.

[4] A. M. Pankratova (ed.), *Revolyutsiya 1905-1907 gg. v Rossii: dokumenty i materialy* (M. 1955-).

[5] See, for example, the discussion in R. Bendix, 'Social Stratification and Political Power', *American Political Science Review*, No. 46 (1952), pp. 363-5; S. M. Lipset, 'Social Stratification and 'Right-wing Extremism'', *British Journal of Sociology*, Vol. X, No. 4 (Dec. 1959): R. Heberle, *Social Movements*, (N. Y. 1951).

Attention is directed at the social composition of a political party because it indicates the social and economic interests which the party promotes. This does not mean that there is a mechanical relationship between the actions of a party and its composition such that, for example, a party composed exclusively of manual workers or business-men acts always solely to satisfy the wishes of that social group. The identification of a social group with a party implies, on the one hand, that the group regards some (or all) aspects of party policy to be in its interest and, on the other, that the party's own actions are constrained by the group interest of its members (or supporters). It is true that the leaders may coerce or manipulate the membership to accept a policy which may perpetuate the power or interests of the leaders. There are, however, factors built into the political system and into political parties which limit this tendency – speci-fically, the existence of other political parties, or the growth of factions. In the case in point, not only were there the Socialist-Revolutionaries, Cadets and numerous national socialist parties but the RSDLP contained two major factions (the Bolshevik and Menshevik): the existence of a competing Social-Democratic group made it difficult for the leadership of either to diverge too far from the membership's wishes.

The policies of the party (or the factions of a party) must be related to the subjective needs of its membership and the factors which create these needs. The explanation of the growth of a revolutionary party must, therefore, lie in the nature of the perceivers. The theory of the party is quite distinct from the appeal of the theory, and the exploration of purely theoretical or logical aspects of party policies in no way helps explain who supports it, or why support comes its way. Party policy or philosophy or activity is a constant factor whose acceptance or rejection may only be explained in terms of the individual. A psychological investigation of individual motivation is impossible in historical study. Here we may examine the group formations and group allegiance of party supporters and from such data we may make inferences about individual perception and motivation. The amount and nature of support for a revolutionary party are not of merely academic interest, for the numbers involved are crucial to its success and the social background of its support helps to establish the nature of a successful revolution.

The appeal (or lack of it) of Marxist socialist parties to the prole-tariat has been generalised as follows: '...the working class became less radical politically in the country which was the farthest advanced economically. Radicalism...was a concomitant of economic back-wardness, also of a world-wide diffusion of ideologies, the acceptance of which in the receiving countries was not an outgrowth of their class structures though it had a major impact on these structures'[1]. While the first conclusion on the conservatism of the working class does not concern us here, the second is not sufficient to explain the growth of Social-Democracy, and especially of Bolshevism in Russia. Bendix and Lipset ignore both the ways the Russian social structure was receptive to socialist ideas and the endogamous development of radicalism in Russia. They cannot account for the success of the Bolshevik rather than Menshevik or Socialist-Revolutionary radicalism. Though it is sometimes held that Russian Social-Democracy, due to Tsarist repression and the small working class, was relatively unimportant as a social movement, political sociologists (like historians) have provided no empirical data to substantiate such general statements as the above, nor have they shown which social groups supported or opposed Bolshevism.

It is noteworthy that one of the most influential recent books on class and class consciousness makes no reference to the Russian proletariat, or to its role in the Russian revolutions[2]. Sociologists have tended to counterpose industrial or urban society to non-industrial society. Early twentieth century Russia is placed in the second category because of its large peasant population. This distinction may sometimes be analytically convenient but must be abandoned for the study of recent revolutionary movements which have developed in societies undergoing industrialisation. The attitude of the informed non-specialist historian with regard to Russian Social-Democracy may be summed up by Professor A. J. P. Taylor's view that '...the Bolsheviks before 1917 [were] a minor sect in a relatively unimportant party ... So far as the Bolsheviks had a background, it was to be found in the general history of European socialism, not in that of Russia'[3].

No thorough investigation of the support or membership of the RSDLP has been carried out, let alone of its social stratification. Many of the statements made are little more than good guesswork. Professor Schapiro has characterised 'the lines on which the Bolshevik party was developing [in 1905, as] a disciplined order of professional committee men, grouped round a band of conspirators who were all linked by personal allegiance to their chieftain, Lenin, and ready to follow him in any adventure, so long as his leadership appeared

[1] R. Bendix and S. M. Lipset, 'Political Sociology', in *Current Sociology*, Vol. VI (Paris 1957), p. 98.
[2] R. Dahrendorf, *Class and Class Consciousness in Industrial Society*, (1959).
[3] Review of Hugh Seton-Watson's 'The Russian Empire 1801-1917' (Oxford 1967), *The Observer*, 16 July 1967.

sufficiently radical and extreme'[1]. J. L. H. Keep has asserted that
'... the RSDLP, professedly a proletarian party, was in reality an
organisation of revolutionary intellectuals with only a modicum of
popular support'[2]. Such views have important implications for the
study of the revolutionary process, for they imply that the 1905
Revolution (and the October 1917 Revolution) could not have been
carried out to any extent by a politically-aware social movement[3].
The social composition of the two factions of the party has not been
systematically studied. A widely accepted view is Keep's, cited
above, that the party was mainly composed of intellectuals. Solomon
M. Schwarz asserts that '... in practice the *social composition* of the
organization led by the Bolsheviks and by the Mensheviks was about
the same'[4].

But these assertions leave many questions unanswered about the
social composition of the party. For example, how is party membership to be defined? At what levels of party organisation was the
social composition the same? Were the supporters of the two
factions the same? Were there any differences within the general
classification of 'intellectuals' or 'workers' who supported or who
took in the activity of the factions?

This book will attempt to answer these questions. The empirical
data should clarify the position of the party in Russia and may also be
utilized for comparative purposes. Primarily the formative years of
the RSDLP, from 1898 to 1907, will be considered.

The principal sources used on party history are: a) printed documents of the movement, b) Social-Democratic newspapers, c) the
reports or letters of activists, d) government records (especially
police reports), e) memoirs and reminiscences of active Social-
Democrats, f) histories of party organisations. The reliability of
sources on party history is often questioned[5]. There can be no doubt
of the authenticity of a) and b) above, when originals may be consulted.
Many of the sources, however, are reprints: one usually has no means
of checking whether such reports, documents and memoirs are
authentic, though no cases are known of documents used in this book
being wilfully forged. On the other hand, memoirs sometimes suffer

---

[1] L. Schapiro, *The Communist Party of the Soviet Union*, (1960), p. 61.
[2] J. L. H. Keep, *The Rise of Social-Democracy in Russia*, (1964), p. 287.
[3] Professor Plamenatz has argued that the victory of the Bolsheviks in 1917 was unrelated to
their support and he rules out *a priori* the growth of a class-conscious proletariat in Russia
before the Revolution. *German Marxism and Russian Communism* (1954) pp. 209, 219-21, 236-38.
[4] Solomon M. Schwarz, *The Russian Revolution of 1905* (University of Chicago Press, 1967) p. 211.
[5] For example, it is said that some documents on Stalin and Beria are forgeries. These are
exceptional and a more important cause of distortion is the suppression of archive material.

editorial cuts, and sources may be withheld from publication which damage the reputation of political leaders. Impartiality and detachment, if at all possible, are not to be expected from those who were, or are, actively involved in a political movement. Soviet historians explicitly reject a detached 'objectivity': this must be borne in mind when dealing with f) above – as must the compensating anti-Bolshevik antidote developed in other quarters. I shall attempt, wherever possible, to give alternative statements of facts; secondly, to rely on sources published close to the events and thirdly, to use statistical tests and grouped data to minimise reliance on individual statements. For the RSDLP as a whole there can be no doubt that the sources available are more plentiful for the Bolshevik than for the Menshevik faction.

The sources on the social composition of the movement may suffer from the biases which the victory of the Bolsheviks made inevitable: allegiance to anti-Bolshevik factions may be omitted from the biographies of those wishing to exculpate themselves in the eyes of the authorities and class or social origin may be misrepresented. The main sources here used are the biographies of revolutionaries published in the nineteen-twenties or early nineteen-thirties.

On the social and economic structure of the Russian empire there are no special problems apart from the location of sources. The main primary sources are the 1897 census, and various official reports; some excellent Soviet secondary sources have been consulted on these general topics.

The study is arranged in two parts which are complementary. Part One is divided into two chapters. The first deals with the size and social composition of Russian Social-Democracy and the social background of the members. The second chapter measures social support comparatively by considering the performance of the party in the elections to the Second Duma.

Part Two is in seven chapters, each containing a local study in which I consider the features of the areas, the early history of Social-Democracy, the structure of party groups and their activity in the revolution of 1905. Moscow and St. Petersburg are studied because of their importance; Tver, to show activity in a small town in a rural area. Otherwise, the Committees have been selected on a regional basis: Ekaterinoslav in the Ukraine and Baku in the Caucasus because in both towns there were Bolshevik and Menshevik circles and for both source materials were known; Ivanovo-Voznesensk was the largest town outside Moscow in the central economic region and the home of the first Soviet; of the Siberian centres Omsk was chosen because again source materials were readily available. In the treatment of these Committees I show their relationship to the region of which they were a part. The studies are not comprehensive: Poland and the Baltic are excluded, mainly because the RSDLP was not the main Social-Democratic party there; the Urals, the extreme north, and the Volga basin are also ignored. The Bund[1] has not been dealt with because it was not part of the RSDLP for much of the time between 1903 and 1907 and because of its special character. While work on these topics would, of course, make the study more complete, I believe that it would not substantially change the picture.

Many of the topics cannot be dealt with in full. For example, of the complex local history of Social-Democracy before the Second Congress only an outline can be attempted and its salient features be described. The study of the Soviets which arose in 1905 is necessarily incomplete: the full histories of the individual Soviets would fill many books. I shall deal with their structure as fully as possible paying particular attention to the role of the Social-Democrats.

The conclusion brings together the empirical data and relates them to theories attempting to explain the rise of the revolutionary movement in Russia.

---

[1] The Bund (The General Union of Jewish Workers in Russia and Poland) formed in 1897, had a large membership of Jewish workers in the western areas of Russia. It left the RSDLP in 1903 over the issue of its authority over the Jewish working class in its ranks. It rejoined the RSDLP as a constituent part in 1906. The relations between the Bund and the RSDLP are dealt with in detail by H. Shukman, *The Relations between the Jewish Bund and the RSDLP 1897-1903*, D. Phil. Thesis (Oxford 1961).

PART ONE

Chapter one

THE MEMBERSHIP AND SOCIAL COMPOSITION
OF RUSSIAN SOCIAL-DEMOCRACY

1. The Size of Membership

In the absence of well authenticated party lists, the 'membership' of a revolutionary party is open to many definitions. Even in relatively stable societies, the definition of party membership is highly ambiguous: some parties include indirect subscribers (say men paying a trade-union levy), others restrict it to members of a select group or caucus. I intend to consider Russian Social-Democracy as a social movement. This has been defined as a group of individuals 'united and held together by a sense of belonging together and conscious of sharing the same opinions, values and goals, not necessarily with a formal organisation'[1]. An alternative formulation is that of Turner and Killian: 'A social movement is a collectivity acting with some continuity to promote a change or resist a change in the society or group of which it is a part. As a collectivity, a movement is a group with indefinite and shifting membership, with leadership whose position is determined more by the informed response of the members than by formal procedures for legitimizing authority'[2].

The party as a formal organisation was a relatively smaller group which fluctuated in membership. As a movement, however, Russian Social-Democracy included a much wider range and number of participants than the formally registered members. There are, clearly, differences in the intensity of attachment of given groups of individuals. Later, an attempt will be made to distinguish between different levels of party membership but here the generic difference between members and supporters needs to be clarified. A 'member' is any person who agrees with the aims of a party, and who persistently performs some service (other than voting) on behalf of the party. By performing a service, I mean spreading the message (agitating) formally or informally, besides attending party meetings and carrying

---

[1] R. Heberle, *Social Movements* (N. Y. 1951) p. 269.
[2] Ralph H. Turner and Lewis M. Killian, *Collective Behaviour* (New Jersey 1957) p. 308.

out the usual obligations of party activists (distributing literature, collecting subscriptions and participation in policy making). Such a person need not, of course, be formally 'enrolled' – he may have no party membership card; in underground political activity such members may even be typical. A 'supporter' is one who sympathises with the aims of the party but who commits no act to ally himself to it except perhaps to vote or pay a subscription.

Unfortunately, party sources are not generally based on such categories and the conditions of an underground party also make organisers' estimates less reliable. Even formal membership figures may be underestimated by taking the numbers of adherents at a given point in time, because the collapse of revolutionary cells through the arrest and imprisonment of many members means that quite a large number of men who would normally be regarded as 'members' are omitted from the count. The sending-in of returns may also be incomplete. On the other hand, some reports by local Committees may be over-optimistic and 'membership' may include what I have defined as 'support'. Also, as members were often on the move, they may have been counted by two or more Committees. Whilst official membership figures have many drawbacks, they are still an important source of information and it behoves us to consider, in detail, the data available.

On the basis of reports presented to the Second Congress[1], membership of the Committees of the RSDLP in Russia in 1903 could not have been more than a few thousand, excluding the membership of the Bund. Whilst not a great deal as a proportion of the population, it is sufficient to provide a basis for a conspiratorial revolutionary party. The Bolsheviks' party census in 1922 of 22 gubernias and oblasts shows that 1,085 men had joined the party before 1905[2] a considerable continuity of memberships between the pre- and post-revolutionary periods. A rough extrapolation would be to double this figure to allow for the areas excluded from the census, and to add another 1,085 as an estimate (a one-third loss) of men leaving or dying between 1904 and 1922: this gives us a total of 3,255. Though some would have been Bundists or Mensheviks in 1904, this figure fits in well with my earlier estimate. For 1905, S. G. Strumilin has estimated that there were about 8,400 'organised Bolsheviks'[3]. Probably the Mensheviks had about the same. By the

[1] II S'ezd RSDRP (Protokoly) (1959), pp. 514-685.
[2] Vserossiyskaya perepis' chlenov RKP 1922 g. (M. 1922), p. 19.
[3] 'Sostav Rossiyskoy kommunisticheskoy partii' (pp. 32-3), cited in E. Smitten, Sostav vsesoyuznoy kommunisticheskoy partii (bol'shevikov) (M. L. 1927), p. 5. It is worth pointing out here that a

Fourth Congress in April 1906, membership had grown, it is estimated, to 13,000 for the Bolsheviks and 18,000 for the Mensheviks[1]. Another estimate (for October 1906) was 33,000 Bolsheviks, 43,000 Mensheviks[2].

A regional breakdown of membership appeared in *Vpered* (No. 5, 11 Dec. 1906) which gave the following figures: St. Petersburg 6,000, Moscow 6,700, central region 13,500, Kazan, Samara and Saratov 3,000, south Russia 25,000, Caucasus 16,000, north-west Russia 3,000, Turkestan 1,000, Urals 6,000, and Siberia 1,500: a total for the RSDLP of 81,000 men. We may note the high membership figures for the south and the Caucasus, together 41,000 – just over half the total – and for the central economic region, including Moscow, 20,200. By 1907 the total membership had increased to 150,000: Bolsheviks – 46,143, Mensheviks – 38,174, Bund – 25,468, and the Polish and Latvian parts of the party 25,654 and 13,000 respectively[3].

On the basis of these statistics one may fairly safely conclude that both factions had about 40,000 men in 1907, a very large increase in membership from 1903. Though some of these newly registered members may have been men who previously had some revolutionary experience, had sympathised with, or even taken a small part in Social-Democratic activities before 1905, many others would not have been 'members' as I have defined them. From the above figures one cannot deduce much about the nature of their allegiance to the party.

A second way to measure the membership is to consider the number of men actively involved in Social-Democratic activities over a period of a few years. Here I shall attempt to estimate the 'active' membership, as I have defined it earlier, from 1898 to 1905. I have, therefore, tried to calculate, on the basis of biographies of revolutionaries, the number of men in the Social-Democratic movement between these dates. Biographical sources concerned with the activists of the Russian revolutionary movement suffer from the biases which the victory of the Bolsheviks made inevitable:

hard core of the estimated 8,400 men in the party in 1905 were still members in 1927: of the 1927 membership, 3,768 had joined in 1905 or before (and another 1,024 had joined in 1906-07). (E. Smitten *op. cit.* p. 56).

1 V. I. Lenin, 'O sozyve ekstrennogo partiynogo s'ezda' (10 Nov. 1906), in *Sochineniya* (IV Ed), Vol. XI, p. 235.

2 'Tovarishch' (11 Oct. 1906), cited by Lenin, *loc. cit.* p. 236.

3 M. Lyadov, 'Londonski s'ezd RSDRP v tsifrakh' in *Itogi Londonskogo s'ezda*, (St. Petersburg 1907), p. 84. The detailed numbers suggest an accurate census, but many of the Committees' estimates were a basis for the numbers of delegates to party conference and one would expect these to be on the large side.

allegiance to anti-Bolshevik groups may be omitted from the biographies of those wishing to exculpate themselves in the eyes of the authorities, and class or social origin may be misrepresented. One of the most reliable sources is *Deyateli revolyutsionnogo dvizheniya v Rossii*[1] which was discontinued after the publication of the first two parts covering the surnames beginning with the letters A,B,V, Gm. This source collected together from numerous archives (including police files) data of men who had been actively involved in revolutionary activity.

I have counted all the entries of this series beginning with the letters A and B. The sampling bias involved is that A's and B's may contain a higher proportion of certain social or national groups than of the population as a whole (though no one has shown this). Many of the entries, especially of the men not playing leading roles, are based on police reports which reflect the efficiency or inefficiency of the security authorities and may, therefore, represent some regional biases – no sampling procedure can remedy such deficiencies in the original sources. The method makes it possible to estimate the parameters of the movement which is what concerns us here and has the advantage that it includes only men who were 'activists' – that is 'members' by my definition. The total number of entries beginning with the letters A and B is 1,442. Many of these, however, are people who were in the movement in the 1880's and 1890's and who, as far as records go, played no part in the movement after 1897. I must, therefore, exclude from the sample such entries, which number 214, leaving 1,228. We must now discover what proportion of the total this sample represents.

The first two letters of the alphabet account for one tenth of the entries in the *Brokgauz and Efron* encyclopedia but the Russian names in the *ukazatel' imen* of the party congress reports are probably a better guide to the distribution of names in the Social-Democratic movement. The Russian names beginning with A and B account for 12%, 14% and 11% of the entries in the II, IV, and V Congress reports (the editions are of 1959, 1959 and 1963 respectively). Taking a figure of only 10%, therefore, one may estimate the total actively involved in Russian Social-Democracy from 1898 to 1905 to be 12,280[2]. It may underestimate the total because of incomplete police reports, or of sources inaccessible to the compilers of the

---

[1] *Deyateli revolyutsionnogo dvizheniya v Rossii: bio-bibliograficheski slovar'*. Ed. V. Vilenski-Sibiryakov et al, (M. 1927-33) Tom V, Sotsial-Demokraty 1880-1904. Vypusk I, A-B; Vypusk II, V-Gm.
[2] The editors of *Deyateli revolyutsionnogo dvizheniya v Rossii* claim that the biographies are of men joining the party up to and including 1904, but the dividing lines are blurred and the volumes may include others – though the 'mass membership' of 1907 is most certainly excluded.

biographies, while, on the other hand, a few may have been wrongly included. Assuming that the members split equally between the factions, the number of Bolsheviks compares closely with Strumilin's estimates (p. 12). The figures, though approximate, show that, for a revolutionary underground movement, a large number of people had been actively involved in Russian Social-Democracy before 1905. One ought not to view Russian Social-Democracy as something centred on the cafes of Geneva and composed of an élite mostly in exile[1].

If the party was composed of some twelve thousand men, most of whom were working in the Russian 'underground', then the task of defining their social composition is a formidable one. For the party itself carried out no social survey of membership during this time. Of course, accounts of active Social-Democrats, as that of Schwarz cited above[2], often refer to the social origin of their associates. Such reminiscences are unreliable: at best they can only refer to a relatively small number of activists; at worst, the passage of time completely distorts the actual picture.

2. Class, Estate, Social Status: Definitions

Here it is not possible to discuss at length theoretical aspects of social stratification. It is necessary, however, to indicate briefly some of the main difficulties encountered in the use of such terms as class, estate and social status and to define the meaning I shall give to them.

Much of the controversy about class analysis revolves around two distinct problems which are related one to the other but which should not be confused: the notion of 'class' and the relevance of such a concept to particular social realities.

Class is sometimes used to refer to the economic or market situation of an individual or group and sometimes to the honour or prestige afforded to (or held by) individuals or groups. The first usage is that shared by both Marx and Weber: Weber's definition of class is 'any group of people (who have the same) typical chance for a supply of goods, external living conditions and personal life experiences, insofar as this chance is determined by the...power...to

[1] Though I am not primarily concerned with the Socialist-Revolutionaries, secondary sources indicate that this party was relatively weaker. 'At the height of its development' it had 50,000 members. 'Deeply fissured though it was...the Marxian party was much stronger than its Narodnik rival, even in point of numbers, not to speak of discipline or solidarity of organisation', O. H. Radkey, *The Agrarian Foes of Bolshevism* (N. Y. 1958), p. 63.

[2] See p. 6.

dispose of goods or skills for the sake of income in a given economic order... 'Class situation' is, in this sense, ultimately 'market situation'.'[1] Marx clearly states that class is determined by the relationship to the means of production: 'The owners merely of labour-power, owners of capital and landowners, whose respective sources of income are wages, profit and ground-rent, in other words wage-labourers, capitalists and landowners, constitute then three big classes of modern society based upon the capitalist mode of production'[2]. Marx and Weber hold similar though not identical views on class[3].

The second usage relates to social status, which has been defined as '...every typical component of the life fate of men that is determined by specific, positive or negative, social estimation of honor... (Status is) above all else a specific *style of life*...'[4] Both Marx and Weber considered the main classes in modern society to be the working class – which sells its labour power on the market, and the bourgeoisie – which owns the factors of production. Status groups (for Weber) are communities based on occupation, education or the consumption of particular goods or services. Though Marx[5] and Engels allow for social status, they give it little weight, believing that economic position determines social position and that (due to the laws of capitalist development) class position and social position tend to converge. Class consciousness, for Marx, was the psychological awareness by the members of a class of their shared experiences, life chances and common political interest. Weber, on the other hand, sees classes as communities existing only under certain conditions and he considers status positions as relatively autonomous: 'both propertied and propertyless can belong to the same status groups and frequently do with very tangible consequences'[6].

In modern sociology and social history the classical concept of class has largely been ignored and the layman's category of class, which includes status as defined above, has been used in research[7].

---

[1] R. Bendix, *Max Weber: An Intellectual Portrait* (1960), p. 105.

[2] 'Classes', *Capital* (Vol. 3) (M. 1959), p. 862. Marx also defines the main classes as bourgeoisie and proletariat, 'Bourgeois and Proletarians', in *Selected Works* (Vol. 1) (M. 1958), pp. 34-35.

[3] See J. Rex, *Key Problems of Sociological Theory* (1961), pp. 136-56.

[4] M. Weber, 'Class, Status, Party', in R. Bendix, S. M. Lipset (et al.), *Class, Status and Power* (1954), pp. 68-69.

[5] See *Capital*, Vol. 3, p. 862.

[6] Weber, 'Class, Status, Party', p. 69.

[7] For example, S. M. Lipset and H. L. Zetterberg, define class 'as used by American sociologists (to mean) roles of intimate association with others. Essentially social classes in this sense denote strata of society composed of individuals who accept each other as equals and qualified for intimate association.' S. M. Lipset and H. L. Zetterberg, 'A Theory of Social Mobility', in

To avoid ambiguity I shall use the term 'class' to refer to economic (or market) position, and 'status' to describe the honour or deference given to a person (or group of persons).

The relevance of these concepts to particular societies has caused many disputes. One of the main reasons for confusion is that it is not clearly realized that the validity of the concepts depends on the problem(s) with which one is concerned. Weber recognized this and pointed out that stratification by status is more likely to occur in societies where the acquisition and distribution of goods are relatively stable and that 'naked class situation is of predominant significance... (in) periods of technical and economic transformations'[1]. The historical records of a society coupled with the research interest of the writer give some indication of the relevant tools for research.

Weber's statement above should not be interpreted to mean that status is irrelevant even in periods of 'technical and economic transformations'. If one is concerned with establishing the social structure of a work-shop over a long period of time, the social division of labour, small differences of skill and earnings and gradations of status are important; but in the course of a strike or uprising such social status may be irrelevant and the class solidarity of the workers may be more significant. Obviously, two such studies – one based on status and the other on class – which would tell different things about the social position of the factory worker, do not mean that either concept or piece of research is wrong.

Professor Cobban, considering the social history of revolution, has called for an estimation of social position which is not '...based on a single criterion, legal, political or economic, as it often has been in the past, but on a plurality of tests – actual wealth and its nature, sources of income, social status and prestige, origin and direction of social movement of the individual and his family, legal order, political orientation, contemporary esteem, economic function, personal aspirations and grievances and so on'[2]. While such an analysis is certainly relevant to the study of social mobility, it does not preclude the usefulness of wider class groupings which may overshadow status and be more relevant in periods of revolutionary upheaval. Class consciousness, or the realisation of a common interest based on market position, is not a static concept. It may exist, in a given society, in extreme forms for only short periods of time during

---

Transactions of the Third World Congress of Sociology, Vol. III (1956), pp. 158-9. A. Cobban uses social status, in the Weberian sense, throughout and does not distinguish this concept from that of class, *The Social Interpretation of the French Revolution* (1964), pp. 19-24.
1 'Class, Status, Power', p. 73.
2 Alfred Cobban, *The Social Interpretation of the French Revolution* (Cambridge 1964) p. 22.

crises, while during other periods it may not be very apparent. In empirical work one must be careful to distinguish between the time span, the particular event and the level of generalisation that one has in mind; for the significance to each of class or status cohesion may be quite different.

The population of Russia, at the time under consideration, was officially divided on the basis of 'estate': nobility or gentry, 'townsmen' (*meshchane*), peasantry and the clergy. The notion of 'estate' has the following connotations: a community is legally divided into separate groups of families according to work, ownership and status; heredity plays an important part in determining an individual's estate, inherited traits being an important determinant of character and capability; membership of an estate, though not static, is fixed at birth; the relations between the estates are hierarchical but not antagonistic, each estate is considered to serve the others in a complementary manner. In Russia the gentry not only included the hereditary owners of large estates, but also senior government officials and officers of state thereby making it a broader group than in western European countries[1]. The bourgeoisie was composed of men living in the town: tradesmen, traders, shopkeepers and men employed on their own account. (Many handicraftsmen, of course, were employed by master craftsmen though they were still 'townsmen', and considered themselves to be craftsmen, not employees). The peasantry[2] consisted of men who worked the soil including those with small private plots. Legally all persons coming under the jurisdiction of a village court were 'peasants', even men not domiciled in the village but living and working in the town. The clergy administered the word of God and held office in the Russian Orthodox Church (this last estate was small and is of no interest to this study). In fact, these divisions of the population were losing much of their relevance by 1900, due to social mobility; nevertheless, the 'estates' did mark off social origin, even if not occupation[3]. 'Class' and 'estate' are closely associated notions: both are based on ownership and the division of labour and both assume these relations to be

---

[1] The term 'gentry' rather than nobility is used to translate *dvoryanstvo* to show its wider social scope.

[2] Marx regarded the almost self-sufficient peasantry as a class by their economic position and by their sharing of common cultural values; on the other hand, he says that because the 'identity of their interests begets no community... they do not form a class'. K. Marx, 'The Eighteenth Brumaire of Louis Bonaparte', Marx and Engels *Selected Works* (M. 1958), Vol. 1, p. 334. As an economic category the self-sufficient peasantry is a class.

[3] See Part Two, chapter IV, pp. 114-5.

closely associated with status; the main social difference between them is the mutual antagonism between classes which is absent from the notion of estate. Membership of an estate has given certain legal rights which have never been associated with membership of a class[1].

Officially the 'estate' of all inhabitants of Russia was recorded by the civil service and these are the main records we have. But the 'estate' on its own is not a precise indication of social position. The gentry was stratified into fourteen ranks, each having a different status. The main formal divisions were between the hereditary nobility (*potomst-vennoe dvoryanstvo*) and the personal gentry (*lichnoe dvoryanstvo*). In terms of occupation a *dvoryanin* may have been a wealthy and idle landowner or a poor and industrious civil servant. Similarly, a *krest'yanin* (peasant) may have been an agricultural labourer or a factory owner. The classifications however, should not be prematurely discarded, for if we consider the estates as groups a high proportion of the *dvoryane* had some material means derived from sources other than their own labour and proportionally more *meshchane* (townsmen) were small shopkeepers and petty businessmen than agricultural labourers.

Social class, as I have defined it, is a simple concept but is difficult to make operational because of the overlapping membership of different classes and the blurred edges between them. The two main classes for Marx and Weber, under the conditions of industrial capitalism, are the proletariat composed exclusively of wage-earners and salaried workers, and the bourgeoisie deriving their income from property. Between these two classes are other layers of workers-cum-capitalists (*petty-bourgeoisie*) owning a business (or farming a plot) but employing no hired labour and being dependent on selling services (independent professional strata should be included here) or produce on the market. In a feudal society, the gentry deriving its income from landowning is a separate class, as is the subject peasantry. Russia at the beginning of the twentieth century could be said to include all these social classes: gentry, bourgeoisie, proletariat and peasantry. In fact, of course, there was overlap between them, especially between the first two and between the last two classes.

Social status is usually based on a combination of many factors as cited by Cobban, though social esteem or honour is among the most important. Empirically, however, one cannot accurately determine from written records such subjective attitudes as 'contemporary esteem' or 'personal aspirations and grievances'.

[1] Sometimes, estate is defined in legal terms as by Bergel: 'a legally defined segment of the population of a society which has distinctive rights and duties established by law'. Egon Bergel, *Social Stratification*. (N. Y. 1962) p. 68.

3. Social Composition: General Features of the Movement

The data to be presented in this chapter are based on the available party statistics and a systematic analysis of the biographies of Social-Democrats. As biographies are not conveniently available, but scattered in many sources which could not be consulted concurrently and to avoid using the same material twice, a cluster sampling technique has been adopted. All the data about Social-Democrats with surnames beginning with the letters A and B and known to be active in the party between 1898 and 1907 were collected on punch cards. The main sources consulted were biographical dictionaries, encyclopedias and the name indexes in party congress reports[1]. As many entries did not show factional affiliation, the records of surnames beginning with the letters V and G were again searched for biographies of men who were defined as Bolsheviks and Mensheviks. Much of the social information collected was sparse and all cards which gave less than one piece of information both about party activity and social background were excluded from further analysis. Many of the entries – especially for the 'rank and file' category – contain only two, three, or four pieces of information. Nevertheless, the grouped data of 986 Social-Democrats show up fairly clearly the general composition of the movement and some of the main differences between the factions.

The data were collected to test the generalisations made by Lipset and Bendix and others mentioned earlier:[2] to discover to what extent leaders and members of the RSDLP constituted particular status or generation groups or were members of a particular class and to measure how far differences of class, estate or nationality help explain why the party split into two factions.

The basic data are collected on Table 1 (pp. 22-23), which represents the social backgrounds of the Social-Democrats as a whole. Along the top, Social-Democratic activists are shown by faction[3]: Bolshevik, Menshevik and unknown faction. Each group is divided by estate: peasant, townsman, gentry (for the Bolsheviks, columns B1,

---

[1] Main Sources: Vilenski-Sibiryakov (ed.), *Deyateli revolyutsionnogo dvizheniya v Rossii*, Vol. V, parts I, II (M. 1931); V. Nevski, *Materialy dlya biograficheskogo slovarya sotsial-demokratov*, part I (M.P. 1923). Biographies in – *Bol'shaya Sovetskaya Entsiklopediya:* 1st edition (1926-1948); 2nd edition (1950-1960). Name indexes in – *Protokoly RSDRP: Vtoroy s'ezd* (M. 1959), *Treti s'ezd* (M. 1959), *Chetverty s'ezd* (M. 1959), *Pyaty s'ezd* (M. 1963).

[2] See pp. 9. 4-6.

[3] In 1903 the Russian Social-Democratic Labour Party (RSDLP) split into two factions or a left and right wing. The leftists, or Bolsheviks were led by Lenin and his opponents, the Mensheviks, by Martov.

B2 and B3; for the Mensheviks E1, E2 and E3; the unknown faction
H1, H2 and H3). Those falling into a 'not known' category as far as
estate is concerned, have been further divided by the occupation of
parents: middle/upper and lower/working status groups (e.g. for
the Bolsheviks, columns C1 and C2). The social data have been
grouped according to occupation (rows 9-18), education (rows 20-24)
and age (rows 26-31).

We see that the Social Democrats as a whole were drawn dis-
proportionately from the higher estates. The gentry was well
represented, much more than in the population as a whole: about a
fifth of the known Social-Democrats (Bolsheviks 22% and Mensheviks
19%) were of the gentry, compared to only 1.7% of the total
population[1]. Fifty-five per cent of the known Mensheviks came from
the townsman estate, compared to 39.8% of the Bolsheviks and
10.7% of the population[2]. More Bolshevik activists came from the
peasantry than Menshevik – 38% compared to 26% – evidence of
Bolshevik support among lower strata and newcomers to town life.

The large numbers (about two-thirds of the total) in the 'unknown'
faction category (see column G) require comment. Probably the
majority were truly 'non-factional'. It is likely that some here had
been Mensheviks, but were later concealing the fact. The townsman
estate contains the largest number (269) – almost twice as many as
the peasants, (143). On the basis of our examination of total party
membership we know that both factions were more equal in size
than suggested by the results of the sample. Therefore, it is a
reasonable inference that many of the townsman of unknown faction
were in fact Mensheviks. A high proportion of them were handicraftsmen (15 × H2), who had been born in the southern and western
provinces and were active predominantly in the south and southwest.
I shall show below that these strata and areas tended to be Menshevik.

As far as class analysis is concerned, few of the Social-Democrats
were not 'workers'. Row 12 of Table 1 shows that only four of the
total admitted to be (or to have been) either traders or landlords.
(Of the seven on the table, three were clergy). If we include the
'unknown' factional allegiance, we may conclude that the RSDLP was
predominantly a 'working-class' party. This finding is of some
importance, for it refutes the commonly held view that the RSDLP
was composed 'mostly of middle-class intellectuals'. By looking
closely at the estate and occupation of the members, further deductions
may be made about class position.

[1] Pervaya perepis' naseleniya 1897g. (Spb. 1905), Vol. 1, p.XIII.
[2] Pervaya perepis'..., vol. 1, p. XII, vol. 1 prilozhenie, p. 66.

Table 1. The Social Composition of the Russian Social-Democratic Movement By Faction, Estate, Occupation, Education and Age

In each faction group, the "Estate" columns are Peasant, Townsman, Gentry; the "Unknown Estate — Parents' occupation" columns are Upper/Middle and Lower/Working; followed by "Not known."

Row	SOCIAL CHARACTERISTICS	BOLSHEVIKS Peasant	Townsman	Gentry	Upper/Middle	Lower/Working	Not known	TOTALS Bols.	Mens.	MENSHEVIKS Peasant	Townsman	Gentry	Upper/Middle	Lower/Working	Not known	Total	UNKNOWN FACTION Peasant	Townsman	Gentry	Upper/Middle	Lower/Working	Not known	Row
1	**ESTATE** Peasant	43						43	20	20						143	143						1
2	Townsman		45					45	43		43					269		269					2
3	Gentry			25				25	15			15				26			26				3
4																							4
5	Not known						55	119	63						31	175						104	5
6	(Parents middle/upper)				47								25			60				60			6
7	(Parents lower/working)					17								7		11					11		7
8	*Total*	43	45	25	47	17	55	232	141	20	43	15	25	7	31	613	143	269	26	60	11	104	8
9	**OCCUPATION** Middle/Upper Profes. and intelligentsia	4	4	7	11	0	8	34	28	1	6	3	6	1	11	28	4	8	4	7	0	5	9
10	Teacher	5	0	1	2	1	0	9	1	0	0	0	0	0	1	15	1	2	4	4	0	4	10
11	'Sluzhashchie'	2	3	0	4	2	4	15	6	1	4	1	0	0	0	30	5	16	1	3	1	4	11
12	Traders, landlords, clergymen	0	0	0	0	0	1	1	1	0	0	1	1	0	0	5	0	1	0	3	0	1	12
	Column A	B1	B2	B3	C1	C2	C3	D1	D2	E1	E2	E3	F1	F2	F3	G	H1	H2	H3	J1	J2	J3	

Column A	B1	B2	B3	C1	C2	C3	D1	D2	E1	E2	E3	F1	F2	F3	G	H1	H2	H3	J1	J2	J3
Lower/Working																					
13 'Worker'	5	0	0	0	2	8	15	2	0	2	0	0	0	0	61	33	16	1	0	0	11
14 Factory/mill worker	11	13	0	3	6	9	42	23	7	2	1	2	4	7	133	56	37	5	2	5	28
15 Handicraftsman	5	9	1	2	2	6	25	6	0	4	0	1	0	1	79	18	49	0	1	1	10
16 Printing, railway worker	2	4	1	2	2	2	13	11	3	3	1	0	0	4	21	2	12	0	0	1	6
17 Lower medical, others	0	0	0	1	0	0	1	6	0	2	2	0	2	0	26	2	13	0	2	2	7
18 Not known	9	12	15	22	2	17	77	57	5	20	7	14	1	10	215	22	115	11	37	2	28
19 *Total*	43	45	25	47	17	55	232	141	20	43	15	25	7	31	613	143	269	26	60	11	104
EDUCATION																					
20 Higher abroad	3	1	1	4	0	3	12	10	0	3	2	5	0	0	11	0	4	0	6	0	1
21 Higher All-Russia	5	8	17	25	1	11	67	41	4	9	10	8	0	10	90	6	24	13	27	3	17
22 Secondary	10	7	5	11	7	10	50	34	4	13	0	8	4	5	61	5	40	4	5	0	7
23 Primary	9	14	0	1	4	3	31	13	5	2	1	1	1	3	51	21	21	0	0	5	4
24 Not known	16	15	2	6	5	28	72	43	7	16	2	3	2	13	400	111	180	9	22	3	75
25 *Total*	43	45	25	47	17	55	232	141	20	43	15	25	7	31	613	143	269	26	60	11	104
AGE 1905																					
26 Over 45	1	0	1				3	3							12	4	2	2			4
27 30-44	8	11	9				46	43							166	41	71	13			41
28 25-29	10	9	8				54	42							141	37	66	8			30
29 20-24	14	17	7				71	29							168	35	87	2			44
30 10-19	5	6	0				26	3							23	5	16	0			2
31 Not known	5	2	0				32	21							103	21	27	1			54
Total	43	45	25	47	17	55	232	141	20	43	15	25	7	31	613	143	269	26			175

23

Examining the estate and occupation of the sample we see that of the townsman and gentry estate, many more have 'not known' occupations than that of the peasant. The relevant parts of Table 1 are as follows:

Table 2a. 'Not known' Occupation by Faction and Estate

	Bolsheviks			Mensheviks			Unknown		
	Total Col. 1	Not known Col. 2	Col. 2 / Col. 1 %	Total Col. 1	Not known Col. 2	Col. 2 / Col. 1 %	Total Col. 1	Not known Col. 2	Col. 2 / Col. 1 %
Townsman	45	12	26.7	43	20	46.5	269	115	42.8
Gentry	25	15	60.0	15	7	46.7	26	11	42.3
Peasant	43	9	20.9	20	5	25.0	143	22	15.4

No information is available on the occupation of from 42.3% to 60% of the gentry, 26.7% to 46.5% of the townsmen, and 15.4% to 25% of the peasants.

Table 2b. 'Not known' Occupation by Faction and Estate

Faction	Peasant Estate	Gentry	(Total)
Bolsheviks	9	15	24
Mensheviks	5	7	12
Unknown	22	11	33
Total	36	33	61

$\chi^2 = 5.42$ (Significant at .06 level)*

* The 'level of significance' is a statistical convention to show how likely the measured data are to be drawn from the same population (i.e. a population having the same characteristics). .06 means the chance of being drawn from an identical population is only six times in a hundred, .02 means only two times in a hundred. There is no one level which one must take as sufficient to show that the numbers are drawn from different populations. Usually anything less than .05 is accepted. The chief advantage of a statistical test is to show more precisely than rule of thumb methods the degree of association between two or more sets of numbers. The χ^2 test, of course, takes into account the magnitude of the numbers used. The danger of a small sample is that if we take too low a level of significance we may falsely reject a hypothesis. Therefore, I shall use a .08 level of significance and I shall also show in the tables all probabilities up to the .10 level.

Faction	Peasant Estate	Townsman Estate	(Total)
Bolsheviks	9	12	21
Mensheviks	5	20	25
Unknown	22	115	137
Total	36	147	183

$$\chi^2 = 8.44 \text{ (Significant at .02 level)}$$

The percentages show up the differences, but they do not tell us how significant the numbers are: did they occur by chance? Are the numbers large enough to warrant an explanation? By rearranging the data we may test statistically for randomness: we may determine whether the lack of information is associated with estate; whether the proportion of 'not known' varies considerably between the peasant and gentry classifications and between the peasant and townsman classifications.

The re-arranged data are shown on Table 2b, 2c from which we may infer that the absence of knowledge about occupation is related to the estate of the Social-Democrats. The most likely reasons for 'townsmen' and 'gentry' not stating their occupation are that many had no occupation, being maintained by their own private wealth, or that some (especially in the townsman classification) were of the petty-bourgeoisie. Various social and political factors probably account for them witholding this information. We may infer that a considerable number (about one-fifth) of Social-Democrats were by class position members of the gentry or petty-bourgeoisie. The data also show, again in contrast to what is often asserted, that the Menshevik rather than the Bolshevik faction had relatively more middle strata members.

In the absence of detailed studies of subjective attitudes, knowledge of the stratification pattern of early twentieth century Russia is limited. The variables which may be considered here are estate, occupation, and education: these factors separately and in combination may affect the social status of a person in a society. Membership of the gentry would obviously give greater prestige than peasant origin and higher education would give more honour than only primary education.

In terms of occupation, the membership was composed of many different groups. The results of the party census in 1922, in which information was given for the Bolshevik membership in 1905, show the following broad occupational division:

Table 3. *Bolshevik Membership in 1905*

	Workers	Peasants	White Collar (*sluzhashchie*)	Others	Total
Number	5,200	400	2,300	500	8,400
	61.9 %	4.8 %	27.4 %	5.9 %	100 %

Cited by E. Smitten, *Sostav vsesoyuznoy kommunisticheskoy partii (bol.)* (M.L. 1927), p. 21.

This information is based on the evaluation of the members, of whom more than half considered themselves to be 'workers'. The small number of 'peasants' here recorded is evidence that a 'peasant' estate classification referred to legal position at birth and not occupation: the bulk of the 'peasants' in the movement even in 1905 had already moved from the village to work in the factories.

The bulk of the known members, as stated, claimed to be factory/mill workers of one kind or another, but handicraftsmen, printers, office and shop workers and professional employees formed small distinct groups. Turning to the biographies in Table 1, we see that many, probably most, of the professional employees and intelligentsia came from the gentry or from a professional family background (row 9). Indeed, tracing the educational background of those from middle/upper families we see that half of those whose schooling was known had had a higher education (rows 20/21, columns C1, F1, J1). The striking fact about the educational background is the number of men with higher education who made up the largest single group both for Bolsheviks and Mensheviks, even if the 'not knowns' (row 24, column D1 and 24 × D2) are divided between primary and no formal education. The gentry, as far as the figures show, had not suffered downward social movement to any great extent: of the 66 in the sample, the occupation of 33 is unknown – probably most of these men had private means – only 6 were factory/mill workers. Nearly all of them had had higher education – 18 out of 25 Bolsheviks, 12 out of 15 Mensheviks and 13 out of the 26 unknown faction. Another seven of upper/middle social origin had fallen socially to the shop floor (row 14, columns C1, F1, J1) but are so few that we may reject the hypothesis that the downward socially mobile predominated in the party. I shall consider occupation and education in more detail below.

The discussion so far of the stratification of the RSDLP allows one to conclude that it was a party of many social strata; the wider notion of class provides a better common denominator for party members than does status. To this general conclusion, however, it might be objected that possible differences in social stratification between the factions have been ignored, and that certain status groups may have clustered in one faction rather than in the other thereby forming the social basis for a split in the party. Let us test this hypothesis. Below (Table 4) is abstracted the relevant data from Table 1.

Table 4a. All Members by Faction and Occupation

Occupation	Bolsheviks	Mensheviks	Total
Parents upper/middle	47	25	72
Parents lower/working	17	7	24
Occupation of activists			
Professional and intelligentsia	34	28	62
Teacher, *sluzhashchie*	24	7	31
'Worker' Factory/mill worker	57	25	82
Handicraftsman	25	6	31
Printing, railway worker, lower medical and other workers	14	17	31
Total	218	115	333

$\chi^2 = 14.79$ (Significant at 0.05 level)

Table 4b. All Members by Faction and Education

Education	Bolsheviks	Mensheviks	Total
Higher (abroad)	12	10	22
Higher (all-Russia)	67	41	108
Secondary	50	34	84
Primary	31	13	44
Total	160	98	258

$\chi^2 = 2.06$ (Not significant)

Considering the party as a whole, the evidence of Table 4a leads to the conclusion that there were significant differences between the occupational groups of the factions: the Mensheviks having more professional people and intelligentsia, the Bolsheviks more handi-craftsmen, but fewer railwaymen and printers. In terms of education, however, there is no overall difference between the two groups. This suggests that after receiving higher education, the Menshevik activists took work more in keeping with their higher qualifications, and that the Bolsheviks, on the other hand, were somewhat more downward socially mobile. Before rushing to conclusions from Table 4, the qualifications provided by Table 2 on the 'non-response' to occupation are necessary. On p. 25 we saw that many Menshevik townsmen withheld information about their occupation. This fact may explain the small number of handicraftsmen above. And the non-response may even tend to underestimate the number of Mens-heviks with higher education. The larger number of intellectuals and professionals and the relatively higher proportion of skilled workers (printers, railwaymen) among the Mensheviks are probably the main social differences between the factions. This is an empirical finding of some importance.

Let us now consider the stratification at the various organisational levels of the party: consideration of the party as a whole may have obfuscated significant differences at the lower levels. The social composition will be discussed at four levels of organisation: the top leadership, the local leadership, the activists and the rank and file membership.

The levels of an organisation may be defined in terms of the decisions which are taken in them. At the top, decisions affect the whole life of the movement: i.e. the general policy and the overall deployment of the movement. At the bottom, the range of policies is much narrower affecting the movement only within a limited geographical or functional area; the decisions taken here are circumscribed by the higher echelons. The organisational structure itself may be an important determinant of the decisions taken in the party. In defining the levels of organisation I shall comment on some aspects of the structure of the Bolshevik and Menshevik factions.

4. The 'Top Leadership'

The 'top leadership' of any organisation is difficult to pinpoint. This is more so in revolutionary organisations, in which formal power positions (say membership of a Central Committee) may not always coincide with the actual distribution of power. Lists of 'leaders' do not always agree with one another. To determine the composition of the party leadership, here five lists are considered, which cover formal positions of power and definitions of leaders by other specialists during the period between 1903 and 1907: firstly, the membership of the editorial board of *Iskra* ('hards' being pro-Lenin, 'softs' anti-Lenin)[1]; secondly, Leonard Schapiro's estimates[2]; thirdly, the estimates by the Soviet compilers of the Fifth Congress report[3]; fourthly, the members of the Bolshevik 'Bureau of the

Table 5. Leadership of Bolshevik and Menshevik Factions

Bolsheviks					Mensheviks				
Col. 1	Col. 2 Score (Possible 3)	Col. 3 Iskra Board 'hard'	Col. 4 Atten- dance II Congress	Col. 5 Wolfe	Col. 1	Col. 2 Score (Possible 3)	Col. 3 Iskra Board 'soft'	Col. 4 Atten- dance II Congress	Col. 5 Wolfe
nin	3	1	1	1	Aksel'rod	3	1	1	1
vinov	2				Martov	3	1	1	1
adov	3		1		Potresov	3	1	1	1
gdanov	2			1	Plekhanov	3	1 [a]	1 [a]	1
sev	2		1		Dan	3			1
mlyachka	2		1		Zasulich	2	1	1	
asikov	2		1		Martynov	2		1	1
	16	1	5	2 [b]		19	5	6	6

[a] Plekhanov then in Lenin's faction.
[b] Wolfe's list also includes Rykov, Krasin and Postalovski.

Committees of the Majority'[4], and fifthly, the identifiable members of the Menshevik Geneva Conference of 1905[5].

Men mentioned more than once in these five sources are shown below in Table 5 (columns 1), with their score in columns 2, 3 and

[1] 'Sostav organizatsii *Iskry* na s'ezde', *Leninski sbornik*, Vol. XI, p. 309. *Iskra* was a Social-Democratic journal founded in 1900 by Lenin, Martov and Potresov. It was the foremost Russian Social-Democratic journal of its time and campaigned to unite the various Marxist groups in Russia.
[2] L. Schapiro, *The Communist Party of the Soviet Union* (1960), pp. 59, 61, 102.
[3] *V S'ezd RSDRP: Protokoly* (1963), pp. XII-XIII.
[4] *III S'ezd RSDRP: Protokoly* (1959), p. VII.
[5] *Prilozhenie k No. 100 Iskry* (Geneva 1905), pp. 29-30.

4. In this table, membership of the *Iskra* editorial board is shown separately in columns 3 and the attendance of these men at the Second Congress is shown in columns 4. In columns 5, in addition, Bertram Wolfe's list of leaders is included in full for comparative purposes[1].

The higher score of the Mensheviks in all these columns (19:16, 5:1, 6:5 and 6:2) suggests that the Mensheviks had a firmer and larger central core to their faction. Wolfe's list shows $^6/_7$ agreement with my Menshevik list, but only $^2/_7$ agreement with my Bolshevik list, again suggesting that the Menshevik leaders were more clearly defined than the Bolshevik. This is confirmed by tracing the participation of all members of the II Congress at later congresses. Table 6 shows members at the II Congress in terms of (1) those who voted for Lenin's motion on Clause 1 of the Party rules; (2) those who voted against; (3) those who had no vote (or did not vote). The subsequent attendance of these delegates, by factional allegiance at the IV Congress (1906) and V Congress (1907) is also shown.

Table 6. *Continuity of Attendance at the II, IV, and V Congresses*

Attendance at II Congress		Attendance at IV Congress					Attendance at V Congress				
		Mensh.	Bolsh.	Unde-fined	Na-tional	Not present	Mensh.	Bolsh.	No faction	Na-tional	Not present
1. For Lenin	21	2[a]	3	1[b]	0	15	1[e]	3[d]	0	0	17
2. Against Lenin	22	4	0	0	1	17	6[f]	0	1[c]	4	11
3. Non-voters	14	2	1	0	2	9	4	0	0	1	9
Total	57	8	4	1	3	41	11	3	1	5	37

II S'ezd..., pp. 443-4.   *IV S'ezd RSDRP (Protokoly)*, 1959, pp. 537-42.   *V S'ezd...*, pp. 621-3

[a] Bekov and Plekhanov
[b] Dedov (L.M. Knipovich)
[c] Trotsky
[d] Lyadov, Lenin and Lange

[e] Plekhanov
[f] Includes L'vov from Vitebsk and Smolensk, possibly a different L'vov from the one at the II Congress.

Table 6 shows a great falling off in Bolshevik numbers: of the 21 supporters of Lenin at the Second Congress only four remained at the Fourth Congress and three at the Fifth Congress. The Mensheviks had a larger membership: of 22 at the Second Congress, eight

[1] B. Wolfe, *Three Who Made a Revolution* (1956), p. 314.

attended the Fourth, and eleven the Fifth. Those attending all three Congresses were, for the Bolsheviks, Lyadov and Lenin; for the Mensheviks, Zhordaniya, Aksel'rod, Martynov, Zagorski, Liber (of the Bund) and Plekhanov. The table clearly shows that there were few changes of side – three in all: Bekov and Plekhanov moved away from Lenin after the Second Congress; and Trotsky[1] assumed an undefined position at the Fifth – a possible Menshevik 'loss', but not a Bolshevik 'gain' at that time. The importance of Lenin as interpreter and source of policy is also immediately apparent. Full knowledge of previous decisions was accessible only to Lenin and Lyadov; the Mensheviks had many contenders. The emergence of Lenin as a leader is obvious and could be explained by the structure of the Bolshevik faction as well as by the psychological propensity to dominate so often attributed to him. The table helps explain the 'charismatic' leadership of Lenin in the Bolshevik faction and why no one 'leader' was accepted by the Mensheviks.

Table 6 shows that a large number of delegates did not attend subsequent congresses. Far from being a recurring clique of veterans, a study of the delegates to the congresses shows that a majority at any given congress were new to its work. The comparison of the Second and Fourth Congresses on Table 6 shows that only sixteen delegates out of a possible fifty-seven attended both. The table also shows that among the 'founders' of the party (that is, those at the Second Congress), the Mensheviks had greater continuity than the Bolsheviks. Of those attending the three congresses (in 1903, 1906 and 1907) the Bolshevik: Menshevik ratios were 21:23, 4:8, 3:11. Of the Bolsheviks, only Lenin and Lyadov attended all three Congresses. No Menshevik defected to the Bolsheviks but two went the other way.

A comparison of the delegates to the Fourth and Fifth Congresses shows that the same number of 'voting' delegates attended both congresses (14), although a higher proportion of Bolsheviks (14 out of a possible 46, compared with 14 out of a possible 66 for the Mensheviks). Taking observers and guests into account, each faction had the same percentage attending both congresses (26%). Both appear to have been equally successful in mobilising their supporters in Russia for attendance at congresses abroad. Considering that the Bolshevik delegates came further from the east of Russia than the Mensheviks, Bolshevik organisation could not have been much inferior. Whatever the differences which separated the factions, allegiance of members appears firm: at the level of congress delegates,

[1] Trotsky remained technically 'outside the factions'.

31

not one changed sides from the Fourth to the Fifth Congresses and only two from the Second to the Fifth. Despite the formal 'unification' of the party, both factions existed as separate organisations.

From the above, it seems that the Menshevik elite had greater continuity and stability than did the Bolshevik faction. Let us now consider how this was reflected in the social composition of the top leadership of the two factions. To the fourteen leaders defined on p. 43, here are added another four revolutionaries working in the Russian underground, who may have been underestimated by the methods used earlier: to the Bolsheviks, E. D. Stasova and L. B. Krasin, and to the Mensheviks, I. Ramishvili and N. Zhordaniya.

From incomplete biographical[1] information collected, it appears that there were again no major differences between the social status of the leaders of the Bolsheviks and Mensheviks: both factions being drawn from the upper social status groups. Of the nine Bolshevik leaders, two had fathers who were school inspectors, one a lawyer, one a petty official (*melki chinovnik*) and one an office worker (*sluzhashchi*). Of the Mensheviks, three had parents whose social positions were of the gentry and one father was an innkeeper. In terms of education, three Bolshevik leaders had attended University, two technical institutes and two secondary schools. Of the Menshevik leaders, two had attended University, one a mining academy and one a veterinary college (Warsaw). Between these leaders, however, there is one striking difference: the Bolsheviks were nearly all Great Russian by nationality whereas at least four of the nine Mensheviks were Jewish and another two were Georgian. Lenin himself, when commenting on the different factions on the *Iskra* editorial board distinguished between the 'hards': '3 plus 6 Russians' and the 'softs', '6 plus 1 Russian'. The non-Russians presumably being Jews[2].

Though the information is not always precise, the biographies provide more complete data on the early revolutionary experience of the leaders. The dates of entry into revolutionary organisations by the leaders defined above and the names of the first organisation are given below. In brackets are appended later affiliations to some of the first revolutionary groups.

---

[1] The biographies may be biased in the collection of facts. The chief sources used are the *Ukazateli imen* in the Congress Reports, the first (1926-48) and the second editions (1950-1960) of the *Bol'shaya Sovetskaya Entsiklopediya* and R. Pipes, *Social-Democracy and the St. Petersburg Labor Movement, 1885-97* (Cambridge, Mass. 1963), pp. 133-43.

[2] 'Sostav organizatsii *Iskry* na s'ezde', in L.S. XI, p. 309.

1. *Narodnik organisations*

(1886?) Student Narodnik group (Social-Democratic Committees
in Tver, Moscow, Tula)   [Bogdanov]

2. *Social-Democratic organisations*

1888	N. E. Fedoseev Social-Democratic group (*Stariki*, St. Petersburg S.-D.)	[Lenin]
1891	Brusnev group (Baku Social-Democracy)	[Krasin]
1892	Liberation of Labour (RSDLP, Siberia, Moscow, St. Petersburg)	[Krasikov]
1893	Social-Democracy (Moscow Workers' Union)	[Lyadov]
1896	Kiev Social-Democracy (*Iskra*, Odessa)	[Zemlyachka]
1896	Union of Struggle for the Liberation of the Working Class (Rostov S.-D. St. Petersburg, Odessa)	[Gusev]
1898	RSDLP in Chernigov (Kiev, S.-D. abroad)	[Litvinov]
1898	RSDLP (*Iskra*, Northern Bureau)	[Stasova]

1. *Narodnik organisations*

1873	Chaykovtsy (*Cherny peredel, Zemlya i volya*)	[Aksel'rod]
1875	Kiev Narodnik group (*Buntari, Cherny peredel, Iskra*)	[Zasulich]
1877	Narodnik (*Zemlya i volya, Cherny peredel*)	[Plekhanov]
1880	Narodnaya Volya (Union of Russian Social-Democracy)	[Martynov]

2. *Social-Democratic organisations*

1891	Students Group – St. Petersburg – Bund (*Stariki*)	[Martov]
1890	Union of Struggle for the Liberation of the Working Class	[Potresov]
1890	*Mesame-Dasi* Group (Georgian Social-Democracy)	[Zhordaniya]
1894	Union of Struggle for the Liberation of the Working Class (St. Petersburg)	[Dan]
?	? (Georgian Social-Democracy)	[Ramishvili]

There are two main differences between the Bolshevik and Menshevik lists. The Menshevik leaders began their revolutionary activity earlier: only two Bolsheviks were in revolutionary movements before 1890, compared with four Mensheviks, three of whom began as early as the seventies. Only two Mensheviks entered revolutionary activity after 1890, compared with eight Bolsheviks. The earlier revolutionary activity of the Menshevik leaders was much more closely connected with the Russian Populist movement than that of the Bolsheviks: half of the Menshevik leaders began as Populists, whereas only one Bolshevik did. Whilst ideological affinities over organisation may exist between some of the Populist theorists and

Lenin[1], there is no evidence to suggest that a significant number of Bolsheviks had been members of the Populist movement. Many writers, when discussing the ideological influence of the Populist movement on Russian Social-Democracy, point out that the roots of Menshevism lay with the *Cherny Peredel,* and those of Bolshevism with the *Narodnaya Volya*[2]. The first point is borne out by this research, but the revolutionary activity of the Bolshevik leaders would suggest that they began rather later than is usually asserted.

Chart 1. Delegates to Fifth Party Congress by Number of Years in Revolutionary Activity and by Faction

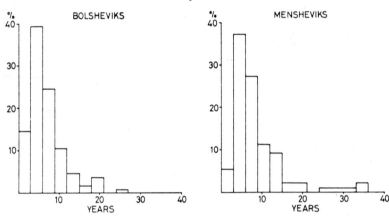

Many of the delegates to the Fifth Congress (1907) had also begun revolutionary activity in the late 1890's. The period of time they had taken part in revolutionary activity is shown on Chart 1. Clearly, the Bolsheviks had two and a half times as many delegates with less than two years revolutionary activity, while the Mensheviks had almost twice as many delegates who had begun revolutionary activity before 1895.

5. The Age Structure

Age structure itself may be as important a determinant of political

---

[1] As suggested by S. V. Utechin, 'Who Taught Lenin', *Twentieth Century* (1960), Vol. CLXVII, pp. 8-16 and R. Pipes, 'Russian Marxism and its Populist Background', *Russian Review* (October 1960), Vol. 19, No. 4, pp. 316-37.

[2] See, for example, S. V. Utechin, 'The 'Preparatory' Trend in the Russian Revolutionary Movement in the 1880's', *St. Antony's Papers*, No. 12 (1962), p. 21.

attitudes as status or class[1]. Youth in changing societies is more likely to be influenced by the new values of the school than by the old order transmitted by the family. Young people, especially if unmarried and geographically mobile, are likely to be socially less stable. Therefore many grounds exist for examining Russian social change in terms of age stratification. In fact, this has hardly ever been done: in the analysis of rural Russia, for example, the division of the peasantry into 'poor' and 'rich' by land ownership completely ignores intergenerational differences. Though L. Schapiro has pointed out that conflict existed between the older party intellectuals of the first circles of the 1880's and the younger strike leaders of the 90's,[2] this analysis has not been applied to later periods of party strife.

As far as the leaders are concerned, in 1907 the Mensheviks were much older than the Bolsheviks. Of the nine members defined above, the oldest Bolsheviks were Krasin, Lenin and Krasikov (all 37). The youngest were Litvinov and Zemlyachka (both 31). The average age of the nine Bolshevik leaders was 34. The Menshevik leaders had an average age of 44. This included four men over 50: Ramishvili (50), Plekhanov (51), Zasulich (58) and Aksel'rod (57). The youngest was Martov (34).

The leaders of both factions were older than the party's local leaders. The delegates to the Fifth Party Congress were on average 27.7 years old: the average Bolshevik was 27.1 and Menshevik 29.2.[3] The average age of the Menshevik leaders exceeded that of the Congress delegates by 15 years. The Bolshevik leaders were, on average, only seven years older. This information confirms the findings on the nature of earlier revolutionary activity; there would have been a greater chance of Menshevik participation in Populist groups than of Bolshevik. In terms of age, there can be no doubt that the Bolsheviks were a more homogeneous faction with possibly less consequent friction between leaders and led.

Let us now consider the local leadership of the party. This one may define as those men who either attended party congresses (or conferences) in Russia or abroad, or who were candidates in the Duma elections, or who held the post of party secretary, chairman, leading (otvetstvenny) propagandist or leading organiser, or who were

[1] For a discussion of age groups and social structure see S. E. Eisenstadt, *From Generation to Generation* (N.Y. 1956), p. 21 *et seq.* He points out the importance of youth in revolutionary movements and the lack of empirical research on this subject, (p. 311).

[2] L. Schapiro, *The Communist Party of the Soviet Union* (1960), pp. 30-31.

[3] *V S'ezd...*, p. 658. The other parts of the RSDLP (Bundists etc.) were also younger than the Mensheviks.

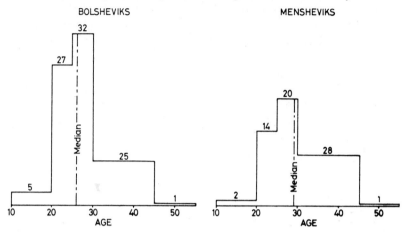

Chart 2. *Age Structure of Local Leaders of Russian Social-Democracy*

an executive committee member of a town Soviet. Of the total (986) in Table 1, 235 came within this category (Bolsheviks 99, Mensheviks 72 and unknown faction 64)[1]. The age structure of the local leaders is shown diagramatically on Chart 2. We see again that the Mensheviks tended to be older than the Bolsheviks. The median age for Bolsheviks was 26 and for Mensheviks 29.

At the lower levels of party organisation the difference is even more marked. Below is shown the age distribution of the 'activists' and the 'rank and file'. (For definitions, see below p. 46).

Table 7a. *Age Structure of 'Activists' by Faction*

Age	Bolsheviks	Mensheviks	Total
over 30	10	10	20
25-29	14	16	30
20-24	25	9	34
10-19	10	0	10
Total	59	35	94

$\chi^2 = 12.33$ (Significant at the 0.01 level)

[1] The full details of these men are shown as in Table 1 of this study in: D. S. Lane, *The Social Composition, Structure and Activity of Russian Social-Democratic Groups 1898-1907* (D. Phil. thesis, University of Oxford, 1966).

Table 7b. *Age Structure of 'Rank and File' by Faction*

Age	Bolsheviks	Mensheviks	Total
over 30	13	7	20
25-29	8	6	14
20-24	19	6	25
10-19	11	1	12
Total	51	20	71

$\chi^2 = 4.51$ (Not significant)

These two tables show that the Bolsheviks were younger than the Mensheviks at the lowest levels of party organisation and more so among the 'activists' than among the ordinary members. This suggests that the Bolshevik organisational structure allowed the young to advance to positions of responsibility more easily than did the Menshevik. It may also reflect the relative dearth of young members in the Menshevik faction. Particularly noteworthy is the fact that a sixth of the Bolshevik 'activists' were under 20, whereas none of the Mensheviks were (Table 7a); and of the rank-and-file the proportions were one-fifth for the Bolsheviks and only one-twentieth for their opponents (Table 7b). Possibly the more settled townsmen were more attracted to the Mensheviks and the younger men, together with the newcomers to town life who were cut off from their stable backgrounds, found the militancy of the Bolsheviks more to their liking. Politically, these young men may have provided more dynamic and vigorous leadership for the Bolshevik faction[1].

6. *Social and Educational Background of Local Leaders*

The social position of the delegates to four congresses has been given as follows:

Table 8. *The Social Position of Congress Delegates*

Congress	Workers	Peasants	Sluzhashchie and others	Unknown
II (1903)	3	0	40	8
III (1905)	1	0	28	1
IV (1906)	36	1	108	0
V (1907)	116	2	218	0

'VKP(b)', in *Bol'shaya sovetskaya entsiklopediya* (1930) Vol. XI, p. 538.

[1] Soloman M. Schwarz also recalls 'the greater appeal' of Bolshevism to young people. *The Russian Revolution of 1905* (Chicago 1967), p. 30.

The figures demonstrate the small number of working men present at the founding of the party and indicate the growing working class participation thereafter. These figures, however, do not give a very detailed picture and do not show differences between the factions. Probably the most representative congress was the Fifth in 1907, at which it was claimed that each delegate represented 500 local party members. The social composition of the Bolshevik and Menshevik delegates, by education and occupation (or former occupation), is shown on Tables 9a and 9b.

Table 9a. The Educational Background of Delegates to the Fifth Congress of the RSDLP (1907) by Faction

| Education | Bolsheviks | | Mensheviks | |
	N	%	N	%
Higher	21	20.0	13	13.4
Middle	34	32.3	46	47.5
Lower	39	37.1	35	36.1
Home	2	1.9	2	2.0
Self-taught	9	8.7	1	1.2
Total	105	100.0	97	100.2

$\chi^2 = 5.04$ (df = 2) (Significant at .07 level)

Table 9b. The Occupation (or Former Occupation) of the Members of the Fifth Congress of the RSDLP (1907) by Faction

| Occupation | Bolsheviks | | Mensheviks | |
	N	%	N	%
Manual workers	38	36.2	30	31.9
Office and shop workers (*sluzhashchie*)	12	11.4	5	5.1
'Liberal professions'	13	12.4	13	13.4
Professional revolutionaries	18	17.1	22	22.1
Writers	15	14.3	18	18.6
None	4	3.8	3	3.1
Students	5	4.8	5	5.2
Landowners	0	0	1	1.0
Total	105	100.0	97	100.4

$\chi^2 = 4.11$ (df = 4) (Not significant)

V S'ezd RSDRP..., pp. 656-9.

On the education table (9a) the percentages in each column indicate quite important differences. The Bolsheviks had a larger proportion in the higher education bracket, while the Mensheviks had a larger number of men with middle education. The Bolsheviks had many more who were self-taught, but this was a very small proportion of the total. To make statistically significant groups, the self-taught category has been added to the 'lower education' group and the 'home-educated' to the 'middle-education' group. The value of χ^2 is significant at the .07 level. The evidence suggests that the Bolsheviks had more of the very high and very low education groups. Both factions had a bigger proportion of men with middle and higher education than the population of European Russia[1].

The occupation table (No. 9b) shows a high degree of similarity between both factions. To make the expected frequencies large enough to be statistically significant, the 'students' have to be added to the 'writers', the one landowner and the 'none' category have to be ignored: statistically, the frequencies do not differ significantly. The only differences are in the clerical and manual workers' groups, of which more were Bolsheviks than Mensheviks, and in the professional revolutionaries' group where the Mensheviks had a slightly higher proportion than the Bolsheviks. This last item rebuts the commonly held assertion that the Bolsheviks were a faction of 'professional revolutionaries' in contrast to the Mensheviks. The similarity between the factions confirms the earlier analysis and conclusions.

7. Geographical Distribution of Membership

Let us now turn to discover from which areas the two factions were recruited. Lenin himself, even before the Second Congress, had drawn up his slate of anticipated supporters – 'hard' *Iskra*-ites and others ('soft' and 'anti' *Iskra*-ites). Lenin's forecast of the alignment may be summarised as follows[2]:

---

[1] In the 1897 census, of urban males between the ages of 20 and 29, 20.6 per thousand claimed to have received higher education; 72 per thousand claimed middle schooling; and 70 per cent claimed to be literate (presumably having had primary education.) C. Arnold Anderson, 'A Footnote to the Social History of Modern Russia...', *Genus*, (Rome), Vol. XII, No. 1-4 (1956), pp. 1-18.
[2] Based on notes in 'Sostav s'ezda', *Leninski sbornik* (M. 1924) vol. VI, pp. 80-83.

Table 10. Lenin's Estimates of Support at Second Party Congress

1. Abroad		Votes
Anti-*Iskra*		7
Hard *Iskra*		4
Others		4
	Total	15

2. Russian interior		
Anti-*Iskra*		1
Unknown views		15
Hard *Iskra*		13
Soft *Iskra*		7
	Total	36

Lenin's estimates show firstly, that he was unaware of the views of quite a large number of delegates from Russia, suggesting that not all the delegates had been selected with the connivance of *Iskra*'s agents. Secondly, that Lenin anticipated his main support to come from inside Russia.

One measuring stick of Bolshevik allegiance at the Second Congress was the voting on Clause 1 of the party's constitution in which the party divided over Martov's draft for a more 'open' form of party organisation compared to Lenin's. Voting on the motion was as follows:

Lenin's formulation of Clause 1,

'for', 23 votes (20 delegates);
'against', 28 votes (22 delegates).

From Russia were thirty-two delegates, nineteen for Lenin and thirteen against[1]. The votes are shown geographically on Map 1: Lenin's voters being shown by the light triangles, Martov's by the dark ones.

Lenin's pre-Congress estimates were not too far out. His support came from the Russian interior, only two votes came his way from the eleven delegates of Social-Democracy abroad. Those voting for the more 'open' form of the Menshevik party came from abroad and the south and south-east of Russia. Lenin's support came from the central provinces.

[1] *II S'ezd (Protokoly)*, pp. 278-280.

Map I. Voting on Clause One of Party Constitution (1903)

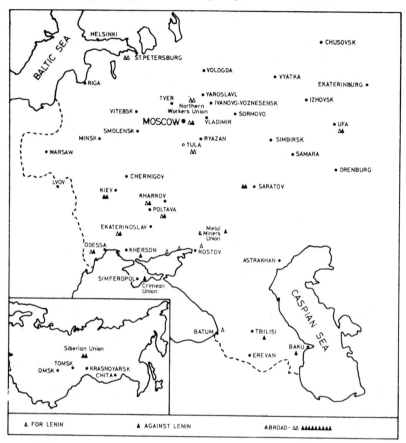

Let us now turn to Map II, which shows that by the Fifth Congress in 1907 these positions had become consolidated. The 'Bolshevik Committees' were in the Moscow area, Ivanovo-Voznesensk and the Urals. The Mensheviks obtained overwhelming support from the Caucasus, the Ukraine and the Western Provinces[1]. Some areas were mixed, particularly St. Petersburg and Siberia. There were, of course, significant minorities of Bolsheviks in Menshevik areas – in the Caucasus, Minsk, Kharkov and Odessa; and Mensheviks in Bolshevik areas – in Moscow and the Urals. But there seems little doubt as to where the support of each faction lay. By 1907, on a line from Astrakhan to St. Petersburg, to the west lay the Menshevik support and, with the possible exception of Siberia, to the east

[1] See *V S'ezd (Protokoly)*, p. XII.

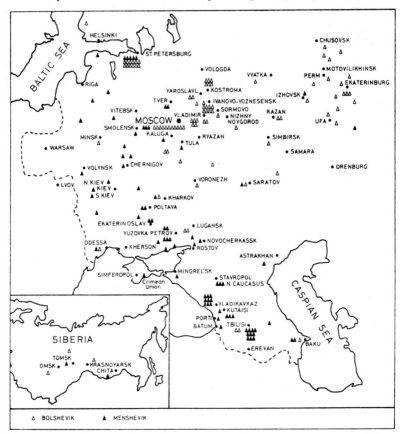

Bolshevik. This is also confirmed by the areas of operation of agents for the Bolshevik paper *Vpered*: of eleven agents, only one was working in south Russia[1]. The distribution of Social-Democratic support is quite different to that of the Socialist-Revolutionaries who, according to Radkey, had little support in the capitals, were centred on Saratov and had their chief strength in the black-earth and Volga regions[2].

[1] 'Otchet izdatel'stva *Vpered*', *Treti s'ezd RSDRP: Protokoly* (M. 1959), p. 524. Yu. Martov and J. Stalin have both commented on the geographical spread of factional strength: Yu. Martov 'Sotsialdemokratiya 1905-1907', *Obshchestvennoe dvizhenie v Rossii v nachale XX-go veka*, Vol. 3, (Spb. 1914), pp. 573-4. J. Stalin, 'The London Congress of the RSDLP (Notes of a Delegate)', *Works* (English edition 1954-), Vol. 2.

[2] O. H. Radkey, *The Agrarian Foes of Bolshevism* (N.Y. 1958), pp. 53-55. See also map showing the circles of the *Narodnaya Volya* in V. A. Tvardovskaya, 'Organizatsionnye osnovy Narodnoy Voli', *Istoricheskie zapiski*, No. 67 (1960).

The 986 Social-Democratic biographies described on Table 1 have been analysed again to show areas of operation between 1905 and 1907. To show activity geographically, the Russian Empire has been divided into nine regions: Moscow province, St. Petersburg province, the central region, west, south, Volga, Urals and north, Siberia and Central Asia, and the Caucasus; in addition an 'abroad' category is shown. It is true that the areas are not socially homogeneous: widely differing provinces such as Novgorod and Vladimir are both in the central area, as are Pskov and Estonia in the west; however, any classification is open to similar objections. The regional data on Table 11 record the location of the members during these years[1]. Due to a mobile membership, some men are counted more than once (if they operated in two or three areas, for example). The figures show the relative importance of the regions to both factions.

Table 11. Activity of Social-Democrats 1905-07 by Area and Faction

AREA	Bolsheviks	Mensheviks	Faction unknown
Moscow	43	21	17
St. Petersburg	39	31	22
Central region	33	10	26
West	14	5	8
South and south-west	48	48	66
Volga	21	4	17
Urals and north	11	3	4
Siberia and Central Asia	16	5	11
Caucasus	14	10	10
Abroad	11	9	2
Totals	250	146	183

The supremacy of the Bolsheviks in all areas, save the south, as shown in the table must be explained by a bias in the sources. The south and Caucasus were areas of Menshevik strength (note the large number in the residual column for the south (66), many here were probably Mensheviks). The table confirms the balance of the delegates to the congresses. As shown by Map 11, the Bolsheviks' strength

[1] Details of place of birth and area of operation are shown in: D. S. Lane, The Social Composition, Structure and Activity of Russian Social-Democratic Groups 1898-1907, (D. Phil. Oxford 1966).

lay in the central economic region and in the Urals. The numbers for the Caucasus are smaller than one might expect from the known totals of membership. This may have two explanations. First, 'membership' may have had a different connotation in the Caucasus than elsewhere (i.e. a larger number of passive supporters may be included in organisers' estimates). If so, then this would confirm that the Mensheviks in fact had a wider and looser notion of membership, with many of their members being more active in trade union affairs and being known as trade-unionists rather than as Social-Democrats (though of course they were both). Second, records may be less complete for this area and Georgian and Armenian language sources may not have been consulted as a basis for the biographies used.

Table 12. The Nationality of Delegates to the Fifth Congress of the RSDLP, 1907

| Nationality | Bolsheviks | | Mensheviks | |
	N	%	N	%
Russians	82	78.3	33	34.0
Jews	12	11.4	22	22.7
Poles	1	0.95	2	2.1
Letts	1	0.95	0	0
Georgians	3	2.7	28	28.9
Ukrainians	1	0.95	6	6.3
Armenians	2	1.9	1	1.0
Estonians	1	0.95	1	1.0
Germans	0	0	1	1.0
Finns	1	0.95	0	0
Tatars	1	0.95	0	0
Ossets	0	0	1	1.0
Greeks	0	0	1	1.0
Total	105	100	96	99.0

$\chi^2 = 40.66$ (df = 2). (Significant at .001 level)

V S'ezd RSDRP..., pp. 656-9.

Now let us consider the extent to which each faction was composed of different national groups. Unfortunately, biographies almost invariably omit nationality and the 'place of birth' may be misleading as an indication of it. The nationalities of the delegates to the Fifth Congress are shown on Table 12 which is probably the best source available on this question. It is obvious from the table that the Bolshevik faction was largely Russian by nationality, but with a

Map III. Great Russian Areas of Russia

PROVINCES WITH MORE THAN 60% OF POPULATION SPEAKING RUSSIAN

significant minority of Jews (about 10%). Of the Mensheviks, only a third were Russians, just less than a third were Georgians and about a fifth were Jews. The figures have been grouped into three to test for significance: Russians, Jews and other nationalities. There is a significant difference between the factions: this result could only be explained by chance far less than one time in a thousand.

The area of Bolshevik dominance coincided with the lines of a fairly homogeneous racial, linguistic and religious community. This is demonstrated on Map III[1] which shows shaded those provinces

[1] Based on tables in the 1897 census: *Pervaya perepis' naseleniya 1897g.* (Spb. 1905), Vol. I, pp. 82-87.

with over 60 per cent of the population speaking Russian alone (Russian language here excludes Ukrainian and Belorussian, which are sometimes included in statistics as 'Russian').

8. The Activists and the Rank and File.

Let us now turn to the lower reaches of the party to discover what kind of men were the active following of the RSDLP. These I have divided into two groups: activists, rank-and-file. 'Activists' are propagandists, public speakers, agitators or members of a local soviet or of an armed (Social-Democratic) detachment. The 'rank and file' contain men who were recorded in biographies either as 'Social-Democrats' or as 'taking part in' or 'being connected with' Social-Democracy. This may, of course, include some innocent victims of police zeal or inefficiency. Of the sample of biographies (Table 1), 240 came under the activist category and 511 were rank and file. Their allegiance to the factions is shown below. (Table 13).

Table 13. Activists and Rank-and-File by Faction

| Faction | Activists | | Rank and File | |
	N.	%	N.	%
Bolshevik	70	29.1	63	12.3
Menshevik	43	18.0	26	5.1
Unknown	127	52.9	422	82.6
Total	240	100	511	100

Table 13 brings out two facts: the decline in the number of Menshevik supporters at the lower levels and the large increase in the numbers in the unknown faction. The Mensheviks composed 18% of the activists compared to 5.1% of the rank and file whereas the Bolshevik proportions were 29.1% and 12.3%. Of the activists 127 were of unknown faction, which swelled to 422 of the rank and file. The second point is to be expected; the split was minimal at the lower reaches of the party. These men were 'Social-Democrats' rather than Bolsheviks or Mensheviks. The first point may have two explanations: at the lowest levels the Mensheviks may have had fewer activists, which would tally with what was said above about the lack of young men and may indicate that the faction was 'top-heavy'. This may explain the decline of the Mensheviks in Russia after 1905. Alternatively, it may be explained by the relative ease with which rank and file members could disown their Menshevik affiliation after the October Revolution. It is impossible to say which of these is true: perhaps the second is more likely, but the first may be borne in mind by researchers working on later periods of Russian history.

As one might expect, the better educated men with higher social status held the commanding positions in Russian Social-Democracy. Social position would seem to be important when the levels of party are examined. Let us consider comparatively the information available on education and level of organisation. Tables 14 show position in the faction held by members of various educational levels.

The table brings out interesting differences between the factions. The men with higher education were distributed at the higher levels of the party: the rank and file were composed much more of men with primary and unknown (probably low) educational backgrounds.

Table 14a. Local Leaders, Activists and Rank and File by Education: Bolsheviks

Education	Local Leaders		Activists		Rank and File		Total
	N	%	N	%	N	%	
Higher	43	44.3	26	37.1	10	15.9	79
Secondary	22	22.7	16	22.9	12	19.0	50
Primary	9	9.3	9	12.9	13	20.6	31
Not known	23	23.7	19	27.1	28	44.5	70
Total	97	100	70	100	63	100	230

$\chi^2 = 18.988$ (Significant at .01 level)

Table 14b. Mensheviks

Education	Local Leaders		Activists		Rank and File		Total
	N	%	N	%	N	%	
Higher	28	38.9	16	37.2	7	26.9	51
Secondary	17	23.6	11	25.6	6	23.1	34
Primary	7	9.7	5	11.6	1	3.8	13
Not known	20	27.8	11	25.6	12	46.2	43
Total·	72	100	43	100	26	100	141

$\chi^2 = 4.564$ (Not significant)

Table *14 c.* *Unknown Faction*

Education	Local Leaders		Activists		Rank and File		Total
	N	%	N	%	N	%	
Higher	15	23.4	23	18.1	63	14.9	101
Secondary	10	15.6	12	9.4	39	9.3	61
Primary	6	9.4	12	9.5	33	7.8	51
Not known	33	51.6	80	63.0	287	68.0	400
Total	64	100	127	100	422	100	613

$\chi^2 = 7.86$ (Not significant)

As little as 9.3% of the Bolshevik leaders had had only primary education compared to 20.6% of the rank and file, whereas 44.3% of local Bolshevik leaders were men of higher education compared to only 15.9% of the rank and file (Table 14a). This, it might be said, is hardly surprising, as it is probably true of all political parties. It is not true of the Mensheviks, however, whose membership in terms of social background was roughly the same at all levels of organisation. Among the Menshevik rank and file were few men with primary education – only 3.8% of the Menshevik rank and file, 11.6% of the Menshevik activists. As one reads horizontally across the Menshevik primary education row, the numbers fall from local leaders (7) to rank and file (1). It might be objected that the 'not known' education category might confound what I have concluded. The 'not known' category, however, contains very similar proportions for both Bolsheviks *and* Mensheviks (i.e. 44.5% of the rank and file Bolsheviks and 46.2% of the Menshevik rank and file). Dividing these figures between higher, secondary and primary would not refute my conclusions, though it might weaken them. The statistical tests show that only the Bolsheviks were drawn from *different* educational backgrounds at the various levels of organisation. Attention must also be drawn to the fact that both factions had among their local party leaders a considerable number of men with higher education: of the 'activists' above roughly a third came under this category. There can be little doubt that in the local groups, the intelligentsia led the Bolsheviks – 44.3% of their local leaders in my sample had certainly had higher education. In this respect, however, they were little different from the Mensheviks, indeed 26.9% of their rank and file were men of higher educational background, compared to only 15.9% of the Bolsheviks.

Let us now consider in more detail the social composition at the lower levels. The relevant data are shown on Table 15, the first section of which shows comparatively the activists and rank and file by occupational groups. The Bolsheviks are shown to have had relatively both more activists and rank and file members from the lower/working occupational groups. The second and third sections which show the rank and file by social origin and education confirm this. The numbers here, of course, are on the small side – totals of 64 and 49 respectively, and statistically do not fall within the limits set for the χ^2 test. However, the percentages do illustrate important differences. The second section shows that three times as many Bolshevik rank and file were of peasant and lower/working strata extraction in comparison with the Mensheviks. The third section of the table shows the predominance of men with a higher educational background among the Mensheviks (50%), whereas the largest Bolshevik group (37.1%) was that with primary education.

Table 15a. Activists and Rank and File, by Faction and by Occupational Groups

	\multicolumn{6}{c}{ACTIVISTS}	\multicolumn{6}{c}{RANK AND FILE}
Occupational Group	Bolsheviks		Mensheviks		Unknown Faction		Bolsheviks		Mensheviks		Unknown Faction	
	N.	%	N.	%	N.	%	N.	%	N.	%	N.	%
Middle/Upper	16	22.9	12	27.9	13	10.2	16	25.4	8	30.8	55	13.0
Lower/Working	30	42.9	17	39.5	64	50.4	30	47.6	11	42.3	223	52.9
Not known	24	34.2	14	32.6	50	39.4	17	27.0	7	26.9	144	34.1
Total	70	100	43	100	127	100	63	100	26	100	422	100

Table 15b. Rank and File by Social Origin and Faction

Social Origin	Bolsheviks		Mensheviks		Total	
	N.	%	N.	%	N.	%
Peasant	14	31.1	2	10.5	16	25.0
Townsman	12	26.7	8	42.1	20	31.2
Gentry	5	11.1	4	21.1	9	14.1
Parents: middle/upper	7	15.6	4	21.0	11	17.2
lower/working	7	15.5	1	5.3	8	12.5
Total	45	100	19	100	64	100

$\chi^2 = 5.666$ (Not significant)

Table 15c. Rank and File by Educational Background and Faction

Education	Bolsheviks N.	Bolsheviks %	Mensheviks N.	Mensheviks %	Total N.	Total %
Higher	10	28.6	7	50.0	17	34.7
Secondary	12	34.3	6	42.9	18	36.7
Primary	13	37.1	1	7.1	14	28.6
Total	35	100	14	100	49	100

$\chi^2 = 4.63$ (Significant at .10 level)

9. Summary

Let me recapitulate the main points I have made about the composition of Russian Social-Democracy. The RSDLP was socially a broadly-based party. The leadership was recruited mainly from the upper strata, at the top manual workers were very few. We can fairly safely say there were no significant social differences between the élites of the factions. Unlike other 'mass movements', the Russian Social-Democratic leadership contained a large element of the gentry. Any claim that movements such as Nazism and Bolshevism are based alike on the leadership of the 'middle class' (and especially the lower middle class) must be rejected. In terms of organization, the Mensheviks had a larger permanent core of personnel. The Bolsheviks had a great turnover and Lenin's involvement in, and experience of, directing revolutionary activity was much greater than that of others at the apex of the Bolshevik faction. He was in a position to exercise firm leadership, a necessary condition for the success of a revolutionary political party. At the lowest levels the data on social composition are sparse and a Bolshevik/Menshevik comparison is difficult with the sources available. It seems probable that the Mensheviks had comparatively more 'petty-bourgeois' members, and fewer working class supporters at the lower levels. The Bolsheviks attracted rather more men of peasant stock new to the towns, while the Mensheviks tended to recruit from the longer-settled townsmen. If judged by the bottom levels of the party and particularly by its popular support, it may be said that the Bolsheviks were a 'workers'' party. Middle strata or the 'petty-bourgeoisie' were important as supporters of the Mensheviks, but they are usually regarded as less antagonistic to liberal-democratic values than their Russian Social-Democratic competitors. The Bolsheviks were a slightly younger party and did not have a large difference in age between members and leaders as did the Mensheviks who seemed to be less able to recruit the very young age groups. The main and most significant difference between the factions lay in their national backgrounds. The Bolsheviks were far more homogeneous than the Mensheviks, they had a small minority of Jewish members but were overwhelmingly Great Russians; the Mensheviks were made up mostly of the national minorities – particularly Georgians and Jews. This research suggests that any explanation of the support of the two factions must take into account the bases of national sentiment and group cohesion.

So far we have studied party membership. Let us now turn to consider what popular support the party had. Supporters have been defined as people who agreed with the party's aims though did not perform any active work. It is impossible to measure very accurately who was 'sympathetic' to the RSDLP. One of the best indicators we have is given by the elections to the Second Duma.

Chapter two

THE SOCIAL SUPPORT
OF RUSSIAN SOCIAL-DEMOCRACY

1. The Duma Elections of 1907

The existence of an indirect electoral system and a stratified electorate in the Duma[1] elections of 1907 makes possible a comparative investigation of the popular support of the Social-Democrats. The Second Duma is chosen, being a more representative one than the First which was boycotted by the Bolsheviks. The standard English work on the Second Duma[2] has been concerned mainly with the Duma itself, here I shall consider the election as a measure of political support for the Social-Democrats. The returns to the Duma, together with the indirect curia system, make it possible to relate the parties to the social position of voters. Before discussing the results it is necessary to outline briefly the electoral system.

Chart 3 shows that the electoral system was divided into six streams[3]. The city electoral college, shown on the right of the diagram, was composed of twenty-six towns which separately elected their deputy at a city assembly composed of electors representing city districts. The other deputies were elected at separate provincial assemblies, which in their turn were composed of electors chosen from five curia – town, landowners', peasants', cossacks', workers'. In each of these curia the electors were chosen at preliminary district or village elections, with the one exception of the big landowners who voted directly in the landowners' curia.

The electoral specifications of the law of December 1905 allowed all persons owning land or real estate to vote in the preliminary curia, those owning estate worth more than 1,500 rubles were admitted to the curia direct. In the town and city curia, voters included property owners, those who paid a professional tax, rented premises, or received a pension for state service. Peasants holding

---

[1] The Duma was the Russian Parliament or Consultative Assembly, first elected in 1906.
[2] Alfred Levin, *The Second Duma* (Yale 1940).
[3] Levin, pp. 1-27.

52

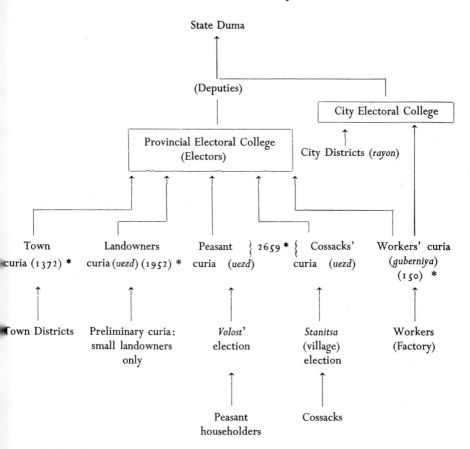

Chart 3. Second Duma Electoral System

State Duma

(Deputies)

City Electoral College

Provincial Electoral College
(Electors)

City Districts (*rayon*)

Town
curia (1372) *

Landowners
curia (*uezd*) (1952) *

Peasant
curia   (*uezd*)

} 2659 * {

Cossacks'
curia   (*uezd*)

Workers' curia
(*guberniya*)
(150) *

Town Districts

Preliminary curia:
small landowners
only

Volost'
election

Stanitsa
(village)
election

Workers
(Factory)

Peasant
householders

Cossacks

* Numbers of electors in curia.
F. Dan, 'Vtoraya Duma', in Martov, Maslov et al, *Obshchestvennoe dvizhenie v Rossii v nachale XX-go veka* (Spb. 1909-), vol. IV, ii.

commune land were to elect one representative for every ten house-holders to a *volost'* assembly, which elected two men to the *uezd* assembly. The regulations applying to cossacks were similar. Workers at enterprises employing fifty or more men had the right to elect a representative to the workers' curia. Factories employing more than 1,000 workers were to have an extra representative for each complete 1,000 men. Such representatives chose electors to city or provincial colleges. Small enterprises and agricultural la-bourers had no vote. On the other hand, multiple ownership or residence gave some more than one vote. Dan has estimated that the election system gave the landlords 31.8% of the seats, townsmen 22.4%, peasants 43.4% and workers 2.4%[1].

Not all voted as the regime used 'the resources of the bureaucracy, physical, legal and spiritual...in an attempt to create a Duma with a majority to the right of center, a Duma 'acceptable' to the administration'[2]. Many voters having legal qualifications were denied the vote, opposition parties were hampered in their campaigns[3]. The effect of these measures, which is what concerns us, was to reduce the numbers of anti-government voters. If any weighting must be given to the actual voting figures one should increase the numbers of votes to the anti-government parties, and among them the Social-Democrats.

The number of Social-Democratic candidates and 'electors' at the various stages of the election give an indication of their popular support. The election results are nowhere collected completely and accurately: the lower down the electoral system, the less reliable the newspaper sources tend to be[4].

The Social-Democratic members of the Duma show one level of support. The thirty-three Menshevik members, three Menshevik sympathisers, fifteen Bolsheviks and three Bolshevik sympathisers are shown by their electoral districts on Map IV[5]. The curia system of representation, involving blocs between Social-Democratic candidates and other left-wing parties may have influenced the areas in which Social-Democrats were successful, but it seems reasonable to assume that Social-Democrats were more likely to be elected where they were relatively stronger. Map IV confirms the regional support of the factions already shown by the delegates to the Fifth Congress: the Bolsheviks coming from the central economic area and the Mensheviks from the south. Let us now examine their curia.

The numbers of electors in the various curia are less likely to be affected by political alliances than the elected deputies. One drawback is that Social-Democrats, *Trudoviks* and Socialist-Revolutionaries

---

[1] F. Dan, 'Vtoraya Duma', in Martov, Maslov and Potresov, *Obshchestvennoe dvizhenie v Rossii v nachale XX-go veke*, Vol. IV, part II, p. 145.

[2] Levin, p. 60.

[3] Levin, pp. 62-3.

[4] The election supplement to *Rech'* (No. 30, 6 Feb. 1907) is extensively quoted in secondary sources but is incomplete, more detailed statistics are given in individual numbers of *Rus'*, but are less systematically collected.

[5] There is contradiction between sources on the numbers of Social-Democrats in the Duma. The definition of Menshevik and Bolshevik has been taken from the list of deputies appearing in *Pyaty s'ezd RSDRP: Protokoly* (M. 1963), pp. 660-2. The constituencies have been found by reference to numerous sources. Two members, Kozmodamianski and Saltykov, who appear in both Levin's and the Fifth Congress report's lists are neither to be found in newspaper reports nor in Vol. XVII of *Granat* in which biographies of members of the Duma are collected.

Map IV. Social-Democratic Deputies in Second Duma

are – with the exception of the workers' curia – lumped together in printed sources under the category of 'Leftists'. The 'left' electors are shown on Map VI. 'Leftists' in the peasant curia are shown in squares, from the landlords' in circles, from the town in triangles and the Social-Democrats in the workers' curia are shown in bold type. The numbers in hexagons refer to non Social-Democrats in the workers' curia. The Social-Democratic electors in towns with separate representation to the Duma are underlined[2].

[1] The original source is the election supplement to *Rech'* No. 30, which has also been summarized by A. Smirnov, *Kak proshli vybory* (Spb. 1907), pp. 234-39.

[2] These figures are conveniently collected in S. G. Tomsinski, *Bor'ba klassov i partiy vo vtoroy gosudarstvennoy dume* (M. 1924), p. 10.

Map V. Electors' Curia to Second Duma

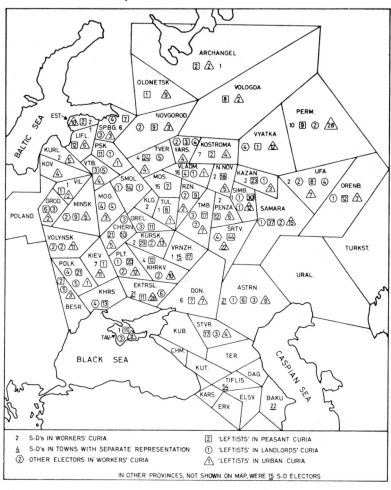

2	S-D's IN WORKERS' CURIA
4	S-D's IN TOWNS WITH SEPARATE REPRESENTATION
②	OTHER ELECTORS IN WORKERS' CURIA

2	'LEFTISTS' IN PEASANT CURIA
①	'LEFTISTS' IN LANDLORDS' CURIA
△	'LEFTISTS' IN URBAN CURIA

IN OTHER PROVINCES, NOT SHOWN ON MAP, WERE 15 S-D ELECTORS

To make the picture more complete one may consider the curia from which the Social-Democratic deputies were elected[1]. From the workers' curia came eleven Bolsheviks (including 'sympathisers') and twelve Mensheviks: all were elected with the agreement of other parties; from the town curia were fourteen Mensheviks and seven Bolsheviks: most of the Mensheviks from the Caucasus being elected without blocs with other parties; from the peasants' curia were seven Mensheviks and from the landowners', three Mensheviks.

[1] The votes for other parties are not discussed here; in fact, the combined 'left' vote outnumbered that of the Cadets and 'progressives' – 1862 against 1418.

2. Summary

Taking all the information available, some generalisations may be made about the support given to the Social-Democrats as shown by the election results. There can be no doubt that in the workers' curia the Social-Democrats were supreme, having ninety-eight out of a possible total of one hundred and forty-five electors. Bolshevik worker-voters were concentrated in the central economic region and the Urals, the Mensheviks in this curia were predominantly in the Ukraine and the Donbass. In the workers' curia the Bolsheviks received much greater numerical support than did the Mensheviks: witness the very large number of electors in Moscow (15), Vladimir (16), and Perm (10) (see Map v) – though the Mensheviks had some support in these places too. In the south the numbers of workers' electors were relatively lower – the largest being seven in Kiev. Generalisations which are sometimes made to the effect that 'the Mensheviks had a much wider base than the Bolsheviks among the Russian working class'[1] are inaccurate and misleading. Among the *Russian* working class the Bolsheviks were supreme, it was among the non-Russian that the Mensheviks had support. Other curia in the south gave much more support to the 'left' as a whole and a fair proportion of this must have gone to the Mensheviks. The Mensheviks had twice as many deputies from the town curia compared to the Bolsheviks; the Menshevik deputies elected from the peasants' and landowners' curia are evidence of much wider social support for them than for the Bolsheviks. Particularly in the Caucasus and Ukraine, the Mensheviks had support across class lines. Not only did the Mensheviks and Bolsheviks have different geographical areas of operation but the Duma elections suggest that the support varied by social composition. The Social-Democrats as a whole had the support of the majority of the working class, but the Bolsheviks were more exclusively centred on them than the Mensheviks; in this sense they were, therefore, more of a 'class party'[2].

Three objections may be made to the methods and evidence so far presented. First, that the data on the social background of the

---

[1] Barrington Moore, *Soviet Politics – the Dilemma of Power* (Harper Torchbook Ed. 1965) p. 177.
[2] Estimates had been made by the Tsarist administration of the loyalty of different areas. One of the main criteria of opposition was nationality. Sukhotin estimated on the basis of police arrests of insurgents (*buntari*) that only 5% of Russians were probably politically disloyal, compared to 65% of Jews. Areas 'against Russia' were Poland, the Caucasus, and fourteen 'doubtful' areas of west and south Russia. 'Pis'mo M. N. Sukhotina Gr. Ignat'evu', *Krasny arkhiv*, Vol. 32 (1929), pp. 229-30. (n.d. But probably written in 1905.)

activists are too general, that they do not bring out the clash of opposing factions in a given locality. Second, that the election results are not sufficient for assuming a strong identification of the masses with the party. Third, that what the party stood for, or what it did have been ignored. To meet these objections, therefore, I turn to describe seven local committee organisations of the RSDLP.

PART TWO

FOREWORD

While the general features of Russian Social-Democracy are known
to the specialist, a brief review of its development may be useful for
the general reader and will serve as a framework to the detailed description of party activity in the localities which follows. In 1898,
at the First Congress, an unsuccessful attempt had been made to
form a national all-Russian party and after this groups of Social-
Democrats styled themselves 'Committees of the Russian Social-
Democratic Labour Party'. But due to the arrest of most of the
participants, no permanent all-Russian organisation existed until the
Second Congress in 1903. The relatively late formation of the RSDLP
as compared with other western European socialist parties was largely
due to the peculiar difficulties of organisation under the autocracy.
It resulted in Social-Democracy being fragmented and formed prior
to national trade-unions whereas in England, particularly, the mass
Social-Democratic party developed from the trade-unions[1].

At the Second Congress, the party split into two groups: the
Bolsheviks, led by Lenin and the Mensheviks whose leader was
Martov. The members of both factions considered themselves
Social-Democrats and it was not until after the October Revolution
of 1917 that the Bolshevik wing called itself Communist. The party
was illegal in Russia until 1905 and was forced to operate in the
underground.

The chief revolutionary outburst we shall be concerned with was
the 1905 Revolution. This was a series of uprisings which occurred
throughout Russia between January and December 1905. It was
precipitated by the police and troops opening fire on peaceful
demonstrators in St. Petersburg in January: this event was known as

[1] This was not so in other countries in western Europe, see the discussion in *Bulletin for Labour
History*, no. 10 (Spring 1965), p. 12.

the 'Bloody Sunday' massacre. In May the first Soviet, or workers' strike committee was formed[1], which was paralleled later by similar groups in other towns. The best known is that in St. Petersburg[2] which was led by Trotsky and was constituted in the autumn. The Social-Democrats played an important part in the armed insurrection which took place in a number of areas and particularly in Moscow where a seizure of power occurred in December[3]. This was supressed by troops, thereby, in the main, ending the Revolution.

The response of the autocracy was to promise a number of liberal rights and participation in the government – these were published in the October Manifesto of 1905. Such promises gave the political parties and trade-unions a semi-legal character during the later part of 1905 and during 1906. The Duma, or Consultative Assembly, was formed in 1906. The chief effect of the Manifesto, as we shall see, was to weaken the liberal opposition to the autocracy in 1905.

The impossibility of describing all Russian Social-Democratic groups has already been pointed out and activity in seven areas only will be considered. I shall attempt to give a picture of the local Committees' structures and activity including their relations with neighbouring groups. The local studies have the following pattern: firstly, a brief introduction outlining the social structure of the area; secondly, the early history of Social-Democratic activity, up to the Second Congress; thirdly, the membership and structure of the RSDLP's local groups and the extent of a local Bolshevik/Menshevik split; fourthly, the activity and role of the Committee in the 1905 Revolution; and finally, a commentary on the main features of each chapter. Similar topics have been covered in each locality to enable comparisons to be made. Where necessary aspects of general party history are introduced in the local studies. To avoid burdening the text with too much repetition, some topics (such as finance and propaganda) are dealt with in detail where sources are fullest and only briefly mentioned in other places when nothing new may be said. Paucity of source material in other instances makes comparisons impossible. The material is marshalled under broad divisions, page references to more specific points are given on the contents pages and in the index.

---

[1] See chapter 5, section iv.
[2] See chapter 3, sections viii, and ix.
[3] See chapter 4, section x.

chapter three

THE STRUCTURE AND ACTIVITY
OF SOCIAL-DEMOCRACY IN ST. PETERSBURG

1. Economic and Social Background

At the beginning of the twentieth century St. Petersburg was the capital and largest city in Russia. In 1900 its population was 1,418,000 and rose to 1,635,100 in 1905[1]. Being the capital, 8.1% of its population was of gentry estate, merchants 1.4% 'townsmen' 19.1%, and peasants 63.1%[2].

Though there was a large number of diverse national groups, the population was overwhelmingly Great Russian by nationality and Orthodox by religian. In the 1897 census the largest other groups were Germans (50,700), Finns (21,000), Estonians (12,200), Letts (6,200) and White Russians (5,100)[3]. With the exception of the population of the Baltic provinces, the inhabitants of St. Petersburg were better educated than the remainder of the population – over 70% being literate[4].

By 1900, St. Petersburg was producing 9% of the industrial output of Russia (measured by value)[5], industrial[6] workers numbered 146,300. Though some of St. Petersburg's industry was founded before 1861, much development took place in the late 19th and early 20th century: its employed population rose by 44% between 1893 and 1900[7]. By the beginning of the twentieth century it was

[1] E. E. Kruze, and D. G. Kutsentov, 'Naselenie Peterburga' in *Ocherki istorii Leningrada*, vol. III (L.-M. 1956), p. 105.

[2] *ibid.*, p. 106. The figures (for 1900) ignore, of course, mobility after birth, many of the adult males coming under the peasant and townsman classifications were factory workers of one kind or another.

[3] *Pervaya vseobshchaya perepis' naseleniya*, vol. II (Spb. 1905), pp. 20-37.

[4] *Vseobshchaya perepis'* (*Prilozhenie*), vol. II, p. 42.

[5] E. E. Kruze, 'Promyshlennoe razvitie Peterburga v 1890-kh. – 1914 gg.', in *Ocherki istorii Leningrada*, vol. III, p. 12.

[6] 'Industrial workers' defined as those in units employing over 50 men.

[7] *ibid.*, p. 13.

one of the most important Russian centres of engineering and metal-
working and employed about half of St. Petersburg's industrial
workers[1]. In textiles were 30,436 workers, and from 1900 to 1908
production rose in value from 63.7 mill. rubles to 86.8 millions.
Shipbuilding, paper, food, tobacco and chemical industries accounted
for most of the remainder.

In addition to its government offices and industrial enterprises,
St. Petersburg was also an important centre of trade and finance.

It has been estimated that there were about 300,000 workers[2].
in the province of St. Petersburg between 1903 and 1906. Roughly
half of these came under the control of the factory inspectorate.
The others were employed in small workshops. Of those in the
province under the factory inspectorate in 1906, 36.5% (52,773)
were employed in factories of over 1,000 men, another 18% (25,997)
in factories from 501 to 1,000, and 31.3% in factories of from 101
to 500[3], thus over a third of the workers in the province were in
very large factories. This does not mean, as is sometimes supposed,
that they were strictly comparable to factories of a similar size in
western Europe or the USA, where productivity was higher.

Wages in St. Petersburg were higher than the Russian average: in
1905 the average annual income of 294 rubles was nearly twice that
of Moscow[4]. Though in that year more working days may have been
lost through disturbances in Moscow than in St. Petersburg. A more

Table 16. *Daily Wages in Building Trades: Moscow and St. Petersburg (Average 1900 to 1910)*

	Moscow	St. Petersburg
Bricklayer	1r. 19c.	1r. 36c.
Carpenter	1r. 28c.	1r. 47c.
Joiner	1r. 52c.	1r. 87c.
Painter	1r. 27c.	1r. 47c.
Plasterer	1r. 26c.	1r. 55c.
Labourer	0r. 90c.	0r. 96c.

K. A. Pazhitnov, *Polozhenie rabochego klassa v Rossii*, vol. III (M. 1925), p. 67.

[1] i.e. 64,513 in 1900, *ibid.*, p. 16.
[2] R. L. Moyzhes, *Politicheskoe vospitanie Peterburgskogo proletariata v kanun pervoy russkoy revolyutsii 1903-05 gg.* (Candidate's dissertation, Leningrad 1960), p. 163.
[3] 'Svod otchetov fabrichnykh inspektorov za 1906 g.' (Spb. 1908), pp. 44-5, cited in *Istoriya rabochego klassa Leningrada* (vol. II) (L. 1963), pp. 98-9.
[4] See table 19, p. 95 below.

permanent feature of St. Petersburg's economy were the engineering industries which paid higher wages, facilitated by the modern factories which were more capital intensive and could afford to pay higher rates. Even for similar trades, as shown by table 16, wages were higher in St. Petersburg than in Moscow.

2. The Early History of Social-Democratic Activity in St. Petersburg

As the history of the first Social-Democratic groups in St. Petersburg has been adequately covered by R. Pipes[1] and A. K. Wildman[2], and the general forms of the late nineteenth century workers' movement in St. Petersburg are fairly well known, I shall describe only their salient features.

Workers' circles for general education as well as for the discussion of politico-economic questions existed in the 1880's, particularly after 1885: in 1887 there were six workers' circles with members in many industrial establishments[3]. These early groups had the help of the radical intelligentsia, though according to Pipes, many of the workers' groups 'jealously guarded their organisational independence'[4] and were suspicious of, if not hostile to, the intelligentsia. Whilst Pipes's thesis of worker-intellectual antagonism is no doubt true in many instances, it is also true that many workers would respect the intelligentsia and welcome with open arms any opportunity for education which these groups provided. In 1891, for example, the Central Workers' Circle had organised at least twenty workers' groups in St. Petersburg[5]. Such circles held discussions on political economy, 'the workers' question', and the political structure of other western European states[6]. At this time Marxist ideas were known through brochures by Marx and Plekhanov[7].

By the middle nineties circle activities had broadened to include industrial action based on Martov's and Kremer's *Ob agitatsii*. The

[1] *Social Democracy and the St. Petersburg Labor Movement, 1885-1897* (N.Y. 1963).

[2] *The Proletarian Prometheans: the Young Social-Democrats and the Workers' Movement 1894-1901* (Ph.D. thesis, Chicago 1962), pp. 144-54.

[3] E. Korolchuk and E. Sokolova (eds.), *Khronika revolyutsionnogo rabochego dvizheniya v Peterburge*, Vol. I (Leningrad, 1940), p. 140, cited by Pipes, p. 9.

[4] Pipes, p. 10.

[5] V. Golubev, 'Stranichka iz istorii rabochego dvizheniya', in *Byloe*, No. 12 (1906), p. 115, cited by Pipes, p. 27.

[6] *ibid.*, p. 115.

[7] Yu. Martov, *Zapiski sotsialdemokrata*, I (Berlin, 1922), p. 90. E. L. Korol'chuk, '*Severny soyuz russkikh rabochikh' i revolyutsionnoe rabochee dvizhenie 70-kh godov XIX v. v Peterburge*, (L. 1946). chapters 1 and 2.

tactics advocated by this brochure were to prepare the working class for political power by successful 'agitation' on the basis of everyday economic needs[1]. In 1895, the Union of Struggle for the Emancipation of the Working Class was founded which stressed the 'economistic' struggle of the workers.

Until the 1890's the activity of both Marxist and Populist circles included 'propaganda' and 'agitation': the Marxists concentrating on long-term educative propaganda; the Populists on inciting the workers against the regime and advocating terrorist methods[2]. Discussions were held on political economy, the future of the Russian village, the *obshchina* (commune) and the development of Russian capitalism[3]. But later, in retrospect, Martov said that the Marxist activists regarded themselves as revolutionaries wanting to 'form a revolutionary party, linked with the workers and soldiers which at the right time (when the government would be in a state of confusion), would carry out a revolution in the capital to overthrow the autocracy and seize power'[4].

At the end of the nineteenth century, the Social-Democratic movement was at a low point. Mass arrests of activists severely depleted its ranks, due partly to the penetration of the movement by provocateurs facilitated by the open nature of the groups at this time[5]. The most important group was the Union of Struggle. Two kinds of groups were being formed: one led by intellectuals mainly based on 'economistic' principles and another which wanted to lead the workers in a wider more political struggle against the autocracy[6].

Against this background attempts were made to unite Russian Social-Democracy. Lenin's theory of party organisation and the aims of *Iskra* to quash the influence of 'economism' and to control and unify Social-Democratic activity in Russia are well known[7].

[1] See T. Dan, *The Origins of Bolshevism* (1964), pp. 215-217.

[2] Pipes, p. 14.

[3] Yu. Martov, *Zapiski sotsialdemokrata* (Berlin 1922), p. 88.

[4] Martov, p. 94.

[5] Wildman, pp. 145-7.

[6] Pipes, pp. 115-6.

[7] e.g. S.V. Utechin, *What is to be done?* (1963), J.L.H. Keep, *The Rise of Social-Democracy in Russia* (1963), pp. 84-106. Keep argues that 'the practical problems that faced any clandestine party in Russia' were 'something of a red herring' in the explanation of Lenin's views on party organisation, which he sees as a 'concept of a revolutionary *elite* as the custodian of proletarian consciousness' (Keep, p. 94). Keep here under-rates the relevance of *What is to be done?* to the practical problems of Russian Social-Democracy. Something like an *Iskra*-type organisation was necessary for the existence of a revolutionary political party in Russia during these times. Not only Lenin, but Ogarev and Tkachev before him had had similar views on organisational matters: S. V. Utechin, 'Who Taught Lenin', *Twentieth Century* (July 1960).

The main roles of *Iskra* were to take control of and to unite the existing Social-Democratic groups in Russia, and to set up groups where they were lacking. The period from 1901 to 1903 was primarily concerned with building up a network of correspondents, supporters and organisations which accepted *Iskra*'s leadership[1].

In 1901 the hegemony of *Iskra* over St. Petersburg Social-Democracy was opposed, and an open split took place between *Iskra* supporters and the members of Soyuz Bor'by. A separate *Iskra* group was formed in September 1901[2]. After much conflict between the protagonists of both sides an agreement was reached which gave the *Iskra* group the right to join the St. Petersburg Committee of the RSDLP as an autonomous body, having a representative on the executive committee, but having the right to secede from the Committee on organisational or tactical grounds[3]. At this time all Social-Democratic organisations were 'weak'[4]. Some factory circles existed but members were few due to the success of the police in rounding-up activists and sending them out of the capital[5].

Up to January 1903, when the leading members were arrested, the membership of the St. Petersburg Committee was composed of twenty-five factory and mill circles, a propaganda group of twenty-five men, a writers' group of five, and a students' group twenty-four strong[6]. It has been estimated that by May 1903, the size of the Committee including *Iskra* was between fifty and a hundred[7].

Iskra's leaflets exposed the *Zubatovshchina* (legal unions organised by the police chief Zubatov), decried legal trade-unionism and called for the freedom of the press and popular education[8]. Probably the most important activity at this time was the distribution of leaflets, many of which found their way into the factories where they were surreptitiously read[9]. Though the leaflets put political demands, the

<hr>

[1] A recent article by A. K. Wildman discusses the problems of the organisation of *Iskra* in much detail. A. K. Wildman, 'Lenin's Battle with *Kustarnichestvo*', *Slavic Review*, vol. XXIII, No. 3, Sep. 1964, pp. 479-503. See also the details of correspondence to *Iskra* based on archive materials in V.I.KPSS, No. 1 (1961), pp. 177-8.

[2] 'Doklad organizatsii *Iskry* II s'ezdu RSDRP V 1903 g.', in N. Angarski, *Doklady S.-D. Komitetov...* (M.L. 1930), pp. 32-33.

[3] N. K. Krupskaya, commentary to 'Doklad organizatsii *Iskry*...', Angarski, *Doklady...*, pp. 59-61.

[4] A. Il'in-Zhenevski, K.L. no. 4 (15) (1925), pp. 218, 227-8, 236.

[5] See reminiscences in, *O revolyutsionnom proshlom Peterburgskogo metallicheskogo zavoda 1886-1905* (*sbornik*) (L. 1926), pp. 15, 17.

[6] Letter Stasova-Krupskaya, cited in R. L. Moyzhes, *Politicheskoe vospitanie Peterburgskogo proletariata v kanun pervoy russkoy revolyutsii 1903-1905 gg.* Candidate's dissertation (Leningrad University 1960), p. 90.

[7] Moyzhes, p. 109.

[8] e.g. *Iskra*, no. 9, October 1901.

[9] Reminiscence of F. A. Bogdanov, *O revolyutsionnom proshlom...* (Leningrad 1926), p. 14.

economic ones were of most interest to the workers at this time[1]. Up to the Second Congress, public demonstrations were infrequent: even in 1903, the Social-Democrats did not call out the workers on May Day, probably due to the fear of arrest[2].

In July 1902, the St. Petersburg Committee issued a statement recognising *Iskra* and pledging solidarity to the paper[3], though the *Iskra* men who had joined the Committee had with it some 'differences over principles, organisation and tactics'[4]. The opposition to *Iskra*, which finally left the Committee in January 1903 on the organisational question, was the continuation of the earlier 'economistic' and 'democratic' trend in St. Petersburg Social-Democracy[5]. St. Petersburg was the only town represented by two rival groups at the Second Congress, showing the importance and intensity of the differences there[6].

3. After the Second Congress

The split between the party leaders which occurred at the 1903 Congress was not paralleled in St. Petersburg by two formal organisations of the RSDLP until the autumn of 1904 when the Menshevik 'Group' broke away from the Committee[7]. Until that time both factions existed in the Committee, the Bolsheviks being in the ascendancy: the Committee supported the Bolshevik 'Deklaratsiya 22-kh'[8].

The report of the St. Petersburg Committee to the III (Bolshevik) Congress said that in 1903 its work was badly organised: substantial disagreements existed on organisation and agitation. Five or six propagandists worked in different regions. The press printed leaflets agitating for the improvement of economic conditions, with few wider political demands[9]. The low level of activity is reflected

---

[1] Bogdanov, pp. 22-23.

[2] *Iskra*, No. 41, June 1903.

[3] *Iskra*, No. 26, 15 Oct. 1902.

[4] Letter of Nogin dated 1 Oct. 1901 in 'Kak *Iskra* zavoevala Peterburg', K.L. No. 4 (15) (1925), p. 227.

[5] See Martov's account in *Iskra* No. 30, Dec. 1902 claiming that the opposition to *Iskra* was largely under the influence of 'the bourgeois democratic intelligentsia', and 'Doklad Peterburgskogo komiteta RSDRP k III partiynomu s'ezdu' in *III s'ezd RSDRP (Protokoly)* (M. 1959), p. 538.

[6] 'St. Peterburgski raskol', in *II S'ezd (Protokoly)*, p. 639.

[7] *Iskra* (now a Menshevik paper), no. 84, Jan. 1905.

[8] *III s'ezd RSDRP: (dokumenty i materialy)* (M. 1955), p. 87.

[9] 'Doklad Peterburgskogo komiteta', *III s'ezd RSDRP: (protokoly)* (M. 1959), p. 540.

in the numbers of Bolshevik leaflets issued: fifty-five for the whole year and from July to December 1903 only nine (five in July)[1].

During the winter of 1903, the Committee attempted to set up sub-regions in the Neva, Town and Vyborg districts of the city. These groups were constantly disrupted by arrests and deportations: all their agitators were arrested in October and November 1903[2], and those of Vyborg and Town again in December and January 1904[3]. In December 1903, the Committee claimed factory circles at thirteen factories in six St. Petersburg districts[4].

By the end of December 1904 the Social-Democratic groups were still not developed in the factory regions. The St. Petersburg executive committee of the RSDLP included no workers and the rank and file were often hostile to it. A strike on 3 January 1905 at the Putilov works found the Committee with little support and its leaflets, distributed by its agitators, were destroyed by the strikers. Even a gift of 500 rubles from the Committee was 'received unwillingly'[5]. The Putilov works had a strong organisation of the 'Gapon Society' which opposed revolutionary change[6]. The workers were not inclined to support the wider Social-Democratic political demands for the abolition of the autocracy; immediate improvement of economic conditions by peaceful means was a more widely held object. Bogdanov, a worker in the Metal works, records that most of the workers thought their lives would be improved by the satisfaction of their 'economic' demands[7].

There can be little doubt about the importance of Gapon's Society: at the end of 1904, Gapon estimated that 6,000 men were members[8]. Many of the workers considered him to be 'a man seriously concerned with the question of improving the living conditions of the workers...'[9]. For the workers, Gapon's Society had

[1] Listovki Peterburgskikh bol'shevikov 1902-1917, vol. I (1902-1907) (L. 1939). This edition states that it lists only Bolshevik leaflets but it may include some of other groups.

[2] 'Doklad Peterburgskogo komiteta', p. 541.

[3] Ibid., p. 542.

[4] Ibid., pp. 541-550.

[5] Ibid., p. 545.

[6] A. M. Pankratova, Pervaya Russkaya revolyutsiya 1905-1907 (M. 1951), p. 57. Father Gapon was an Orthodox priest, a leading member of police-inspired workers' groups. See below.

[7] 'Vospominaniya F. A. Bogdanova', O revolyutsionnom proshlom Peterburgskogo metallicheskogo zavoda 1886-1905 (Sbornik) (L. 1926), pp. 22-23.

[8] Factory inspectors' report dated 28 Jan. 1905 in K.L. 2/13 (1925), p. 46. A. M. Pankratova says it had eleven sections (otdely) with more than 2,000 men, probably an underestimate, though she does point out that it had cells in the majority of the large factories, Pervaya Russkaya..., pp. 56-57.

[9] Memoir of a worker at the Bukh factory in Pervaya Russkaya revolyutsiya v Peterburge 1905 g., vol. II (sbornik), (L. 1925), p. 61.

the advantages of legal status, it revered the Tsar, provided social activities, and helped to improve conditions of labour. The Gapon sections put on concerts and dances in the factory canteens, and represented the cases of aggrieved workers to the management[1]. The factory groups with more militant attitudes had great difficulty in maintaining permanent associations due to police action[2]. A large proportion of the working class, though not unaffected by the revolutionaries' propaganda, regarded the Tsar as a protector of their interests[3]. This attitude may not be explained solely by emotional attachment to, or by the charismatic appeal of, the Tsar but out of fear of the consequences of revolutionary activity, and the belief that identification with the existing institutions might result

[1] On the Pechatkin paper works, see memoir of V. Aksenov, *O revolyutsionnom proshlom...*, p. 36.
[2] At the *Okhtenski* mill 40 trouble makers had been exiled in the early months of 1905. Memoirs of Sokolov, *Pervaya Russkaya...* II, p. 33.
[3] F. A. Bogdanov, p. 22.

Chart 4. *Organisational Scheme of the St. Petersburg Committee 1904*

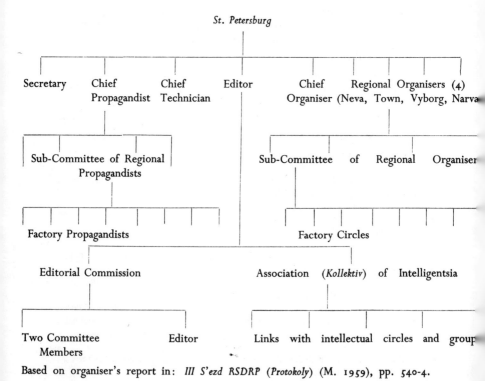

Based on organiser's report in: *III S'ezd RSDRP (Protokoly)* (M. 1959), pp. 540-4.

in some concessions. The sickness and hardship funds (*kassy*) set up under Gapon's influence began to be used late in 1904 for the payment of men on strike. Though the local leadership of the 'police unions' sometimes supported strikes, they were strictly illegal and it was quite improper for *kassy* to be used as strike pay; such illegal payments, therefore, are indications that the movement was getting out of police control[1].

The internal party conflicts did not help the growth of the St. Petersburg groups of the RSDLP, though many of the district cells even in 1904-05 were of a mixed Bolshevik/Menshevik composition, and many of the rank and file members were neither very conscious of the split nor of its significance[2]. In September 1904 the regional groups of Vyborg, Narva, Vasily Ostrov and Neva broke away from the Committee[3] presumably to form the Menshevik 'Group'.

In theory, the organisational scheme of the St. Petersburg Committee was as shown in Chart 4. The top echelon of the local organisation was the executive committee, on the second rung were regional organisations led by a committee-member organiser. A dual organisation of propagandists and organisers was arranged to maintain links with the factories: this was to ensure continuity if one or the other was arrested[4]. The intelligentsia, as shown, was linked to the Committee through the editor, probably because of their important role in preparing propaganda. The intelligentsia was divided organisationally into two sections (students and the rest). It is claimed that the Social-Democrats had branches in seventeen higher educational institutions[5]. In practice, the party organisation did not function smoothly due to the party split and the frequent police arrests of organisers[6].

4. Party Membership

The Bolsheviks carried out little activity in St. Petersburg in 1904. One edition of Bolshevik leaflets shows that in 1904 the Bolsheviks put out only eleven leaflets, compared with fifty-five in 1903 and a hundred and seventeen in 1905. From May to November 1904,

---

[1] A. Yakovlev, in *O revolyutsionnom proshlom...*, p. 53. The role of the *Zubatovshchina* is discussed further below, pp. 97-8.
[2] F. A. Bogdanov, *passim*.
[3] 'Doklad Peterburgskogo komiteta', p. 544.
[4] 'Doklad Peterburgskogo komiteta', p. 540.
[5] For details see, 'O postanovke raboty sredi intelligentsii', *Treti s'ezd RSDRP (Protokoly)*, p. 648.
[6] 'Doklad Peterburgskogo komiteta', p. 540.

only one leaflet was issued, in July[1]. The Menshevik *Iskra* for the autumn of 1904 contains little on the activity and strength of the Committee. Many of the members of the defecting regional groups mentioned above had joined the Mensheviks[2]. The Social-Democratic organisation in St. Petersburg prior to January 1905, by almost any criteria, was weak. In December 1903, the joint Social-Democratic organisation had about eighteen circles in the factories, and membership of circles was from seven to ten, which would give a total worker membership of not more than 180[3]. If the students and intelligentsia had about the same, as seems likely, total membership would have been 360. During the winter of 1904, the Committee's membership and activities declined[4], and the links with abroad were weak or non-existent[5]. The Bolshevik Committee was discredited by an unsuccessful demonstration on 28 November 1904 at which a student was killed. The Bolsheviks maintained that the Mensheviks had boycotted the meeting and were trying to undermine them[6]. The same correspondent says that the Mensheviks too were losing support: in one region where they had had fifteen to twenty circles, by December 1904 they had only four to five.

Up to the first week of January 1905 the Social-Democrats in St. Petersburg were characterised by internal division and dispute. Both factions had weak links with the working masses who sought less revolutionary social change and supported in large numbers the non-Social-Democratic organisations, particularly those of Gapon.

The shooting at the Gapon-led, icon-carrying petitioners of the Tsar on 9 January 1905 resulted in increased support for the Social-Democrats who had long opposed the Gapon movement and the associated 'Zubatovite' or police-inspired groups. The conditions of the underground make estimates of membership in factory circles difficult to collect with certainty. The report of the St. Petersburg Committee to the III Congress in 1905 claimed ninety-nine circles with a total of 737 members: seventeen cells in the factories of the Petersburg district, eighteen cells in the Vyborg district, twenty-nine in the Town district, twenty in the Neva district and fifteen circles among the handicraftsmen (see Map VI)[7]. These documents do not include the Vasily Ostrov and Narva districts, the latter including

[1] *Listovki Peterburgskikh bol'shevikov...*, passim.
[2] 'Doklad Peterburgskogo komiteta', p. 544.
[3] 'Doklad Peterburgskogo komiteta', pp. 541-550.
[4] *Ibid.*, pp. 544, 546.
[5] Letter of Gusev to Lenin, PR No. 3 (1921), p. 168.
[6] *Vpered* (Bolshevik paper), no. 1, Jan. 1905.
[7] *III S'ezd RSDRP (Protokoly)*, pp. 547-553.

Map VI. Bolshevik Groups in St. Petersburg, Spring 1905

PETERSBURG DISTRICT

Monetny dvor	c
Mekh. Zav. Langenzipena	c
Royal Fab. Shredera	c
Fab. Beka	c
Fab. tyulevoymanuf.	b
Stolyarnaya Mel'tsera	b
Mashinostroit. Zav. Semenova	b
Fab. Kirkhnera	c
Zav. Geyslera	b
Khimich lab.	b

17

128

VYBORG DISTRICT

Minny Zav. Parviayen		Zav. Feniks	(b)
Zavod Nobelya	(a)	Stary Arsenal	(a)
Fabrika Cheshera	(c)	Fab. Lebedeva	(a)
Spb. Metal. Zav.	(c)	Zav. Baranovskogo	(a)
Zav. Rozenkrantsa	(a)	Fab. Mal'tseva	(a)
Novy Arsenal	(c)	Fab. Shau	(a)
Mashinostroitel'ny Zav. Lessnera (stary)	(c)	Bol'she-Okhtenskaya Manuf	(b)
Novy	(a)	Remeslenniki	(b)
Vodokachka	(a)		

18

134

VASSILY-OSTROV DISTRICT

NEVA R.

TOWN DISTRICT (II)

Novaya Bumaga	5
Vestingauz	
Konfetnaya	
San-Galli	50
Bogdanova	

TOWN DISTRICT (III)

Shtiglits ▲▲
Al'bomny-Bekhli ▲
Ouf
Kazennoprobochny
Arsenal

75

8

TOWN DISTRICT (IV)

Remeslenniki (Handicraftsmen)

15 100

TOWN DISTRICT (I)

Rossiyskaya Bumaga ▲▲	Beyner
Ekateringofskaya Bumaga	Franko-Ruski
Voronina Bumaga	Kosteobzhigatel'ny
Rezinovaya Manufak.	Odner
Varshavskie zh.d.master ▲▲	
Galerny Ostrov	
'Trud'	
Svirski ▲▲	
Armaturny	

16 100

NEVA DISTRICT

20   .M 60

150

NARVA DISTRICT

5 50

△ NO. OF S-D CELLS IN DISTRICT

M MENSHEVIK CELLS

☐ NO. OF WORKERS IN S-D DISTRICT ORGANISATION

WORKERS EMPLOYED
0   1000

(a) FACTORY CELL 0-5 MEMBERS

(b) FACTORY CELL 6-10 MEMBERS

(c) FACTORY CELL 11+ MEMBERS

▲▲ MORE THAN ONE CELL

the important Putilov works – possibly because Mensheviks were stronger there. In the spring of 1905, the Putilov works was in a 'sorrowful state', in Narva there were about five propagandist groups with a total of fifty members. Activity consisted of haphazardly distributing leaflets: no real 'mass meetings' were held, but there were gatherings of about twenty men, organised by the Bolsheviks[1]. On the basis of this information, the Bolshevik groups in St. Petersburg were fairly widespread: they included cells among the handi-

[1] 'Doklad Narvskogo organizatora Pet. kom. RSDRP' (intercepted by police), republished in *Pervaya russkaya revolyutsiya v Peterburge 1905*, II (L. 1925), p. 96.

craft workers and in both small and large factories[1]. In January 1905, for the whole of St. Petersburg, the Bolsheviks claimed sixty agitators, more than half of whom were 'very young' and presumably new to revolutionary activity[2]. Nevertheless Gusev, secretary of the St. Petersburg Committee, considered the Bolsheviks to have a vast conspiratorial organisation in the city[3]. These local leaders seem to have been largely students. In the Town district, the fifteen agitators and ten propagandists claimed by the Bolsheviks were 'exclusively students'[4].

Of the school youth, 200 were members of the non-party Northern Students' Group[5] which split in 1905, the majority joining the Social-Democrats, but some others went over to the Socialist-Revolutionaries[6]. This information confirms the points made earlier about the prevalence of revolutionary ideas among youth.

The report to the III Congress mentions that the Mensheviks had sixty circles to the Bolsheviks' twenty in the Neva district[7]. *Iskra* claims in April 1905 that the Menshevik 'Group' had a membership of from 1,200 to 1,300[8]. It seems that in January the Mensheviks had been stronger. Gusev reported that the 'position of the Mensheviks is incomparably better'[9]. The financial means and the technical equipment (*tekhnika*) of the Mensheviks were also superior – the Bolsheviks had difficulty in getting paper and presses[10]. In the autumn of 1905, the Mensheviks were to play a leading role in the St. Petersburg Soviet of Workers' Deputies.

Membership figures, however, even if accurately collected do not measure quality of members and may not reflect influence, activity or power. One of the Menshevik activists complained to *Iskra* that they had the 'youngest and least influential element among

---

[1] One should be wary of making sweeping generalisations about the kind of enterprise which supported the different factions. The correlation coefficient between size of plant (in terms of men employed) and Bolshevik cell membership is $+.18$ overall. Separate correlations for each district show a highly positive relationship ($+.65$) in the large-scale factory area of Vyborg and a negative relationship ($-.33$) in the smaller works of the Petersburg district, suggesting that the Bolsheviks had proportionally more supporters in the very large and very small works, but fewer in the medium sized.

[2] Gusev to Lenin, PR, No. 3 (1921), p. 171.

[3] *Ibid.*

[4] 'Otchet o gorodskom rayone', p. 552.

[5] See estimates of members in individual schools, S. Dianin, *Revolyutsionnaya molodezh' v Peterburge* (L. 1926), p. 28.

[6] Dianin, p. 56 and chart p. 231.

[7] Nevski rayon, *III S'ezd RSDRP (Protokoly)*, p. 550.

[8] *Iskra* (now a Menshevik paper), no. 97, April 1905.

[9] Gusev to Lenin, pp. 167, 171.

[10] R. L. Moyzhes, p. 285.

the workers in their ranks'[1]. Many of the more experienced workers were in the non-Social-Democratic 'rabochie soyuzy'[2]. The wide support of these groups is confirmed by the voting for the Shidlovski Commission[3] on 29 January 1905. One hundred and fifty thousand workers voted: 20% or 30,000 for the Social-Democrats, 40% for 'leftish inclined' workers, and 35% for the workers with only 'economistic' demands, leaving a residual of 5%[4].

The Bolsheviks regarded this as an indication of the growth of revolutionary consciousness among the masses. The Mensheviks were more pessimistic: '...Social-Democracy in St. Petersburg has failed when it has independently called the proletariat to revolutionary action'[5]. *Iskra* argued for a movement more closely related to the trade unions. The Mensheviks, consistent with their theories and resolutions on the unions, played a prominent part in their development in St. Petersburg during the spring and summer of 1905[6]. At the Fourth Congress of the RSDLP the Mensheviks had advocated the formation of trade unions and even co-operation in the formation of non-party unions[7]. On the spot, Kol'tsov, writing in *Nachalo*, regarded the unions and workers' clubs as important parts of the party[8]. Not all of the St. Petersburg Mensheviks agreed with this policy: at one meeting, 'among those present an insignificant number had a negative attitude to the unions'[9].

There can be no doubt that the number of Social-Democratic cells increased in St. Petersburg in 1905. Though I have been unable to search party archives for precise information, reports in the local party press show that the number of members increased. In November, the Mensheviks claimed 150 members in the town district[10], on Vassily-Ostrov were 200[11], in Narva were 70, in the Vyborg district were 120, in the Petersburg district 200[12] – a total of 740 members for five districts. A search of the St. Petersburg Bolshevik *Novaya*

[1] *Iskra*, no. 100, May 1905.
[2] Workers' unions. *Ibid.*
[3] A government Commission set up to investigate the workers' grievances and strikes of January 1905.
[4] 1905 v Peterburge, p. vii. No further definition of these categories is given.
[5] *Iskra*, no. 100, May 1905.
[6] J. Martov, *Geschichte der Russischen Sozialdemokratie* (Berlin, 1926), pp. 109-110.
[7] *IV S'ezd RSDRP (Protokoly)*, (M. 1956), pp. 570-1.
[8] *Nachalo*, no. 8, Nov. 1905.
[9] *Nachalo*, no. 11, Nov. 1905.
[10] *Nachalo*, no. 4, Nov. 1905 and No. 10, Nov. 1905.
[11] *Nachalo*, No. 5, Nov. 1905.
[12] *Nachalo*, No. 10, Nov. 1905.

Zhizn' from 27 October to 8 December proved fruitless as far as statistics on party membership were concerned. Martov maintains that in October 1905 the strength of the two St. Petersburg factions was about equal – slightly underestimating the Mensheviks[1]. We have seen in Part One, that by the Fifth Party Congress, the Bolsheviks had mustered more men than the Mensheviks to vote in the internal party elections to the Congress. In St. Petersburg, in January 1907, they claimed 2,105 members to the Mensheviks' 2,156[2]. Some of these figures were contested by the Mensheviks and must be taken with some caution; even so, in the undisputed districts the Bolshevik membership was growing faster than the Menshevik.

The two wings of Social-Democracy were not the only political groups among the workers. At the Rechkin wagon-works, for example, several other parties had supporters – Cadets, Anarchists, and Black Hundreds[3]. Some Social-Democratic groups developed independently outside the two factions[4]: Trotsky, no doubt, was a member of one of them but no other information is available.

The relative strength of the Social-Democrats and Socialist-Revolutionaries has already been commented on in Part One. The Social-Democratic circles were much stronger in St. Petersburg than the Socialist-Revolutionaries', who had not even formed an organisation there until 1902[5]. In the Second Duma elections in St. Petersburg the Social-Democrats had more than half of the workers' electors (147 out of 272)[6]. Sources rarely show voting performance at the factory level, though in St. Petersburg we have the results for the Neva district factory elections in the workers' curia. Here seventeen Social-Democrats (plus one Social-Democratic sympathiser) were elected as against fourteen Socialist-Revolutionaries. Rather surprisingly, perhaps, the Socialist-Revolutionaries were most successful at the very large factories – nine of their worker 'electors' came from two giant factories (the *Semyanikovski zavod* and the

[1] Yu. Martov, 'Sotsialdemokratiya 1905-07', *Obshchestvennoe dvizhenie v Rossii v nachale XX-go veka*, vol. 3 (Spb. 1914), p. 572.

[2] V. I. Lenin, 'Reorganizatsiya i likvidatsiya raskola v Peterburge', *Soch.* (4th Ed.), vol. XII, p. 360.

[3] E. A. Rizgolet, *Pervaya russkaya revolyutsiya*, p. 88. The majority of the workers, according to this writer, were Mensheviks or followers of the Black Hundreds. The Mensheviks were in the workshops, foundry, carpenters' shop, wagon shop and the Black Hundreds were mostly wood-workers and blacksmiths.

[4] Moyzhes, p. 305.

[5] O. H. Radkey, *The Agrarian Foes of Bolshevism* (N.Y. 1958), p. 54.

[6] V. I. Lenin, 'Itogi vyborov po rabochey kurii v Peterburge', *Soch.* (IV Ed.), vol. XII, p. 70.

Obukhovski zavod)[1]. The Social-Democrats of both factions were mainly from the medium-sized factories (i.e. 50-100 employees). Lenin has compared the performance of Bolshevik and Menshevik candidates separately with that of the Socialist-Revolutionaries and has concluded that the Bolshevik performance was relatively better: the Socialist-Revolutionaries gaining two out of fourteen 'electors' when pitted only against the Bolsheviks, but fourteen out of thirty-two when fighting against the Mensheviks[2]. Obviously, these results may not be typical for other areas, or even for St. Petersburg as a whole, and the relative success of the Bolsheviks may be fortuitous or correlated with other factors. The figures suggest that the Socialist-Revolutionaries had much grass-root support in certain factories. Probably the largest factories contained higher proportions of unskilled workers who would have been among the more recent arrivals from the villages.

5. Party Activity in the Summer of 1905

But in 1905 political allegiance was not yet always clear cut. 'Revolutionary cells' were set up in many factories. They often contained workers supporting Gapon, the Social-Democrats, and workers of no organised faction. Social-Democratic cells, where they existed, sought to influence these groups. The links between such factory cells and the Social-Democrats were loose. The strikes early in 1905 were led by 'all-party' factory committees, with the encouragement of the Bolshevik and Menshevik agitators[3] and with the aid of Social-Democratic leaflets[4]. Many Social-Democrats could see no reason for the split and demands were made by some of the local members to end dissension. Bolsheviks and Mensheviks worked together on a local level in the Neva and Petersburg districts[5]. Both factions agitated for unity, the Bolsheviks for unification at a party congress, the Mensheviks for joint committees at local levels.

In 1905 the Social-Democratic factions moved from 'agitational'

[1] 'Otchet Semyannikovskogo podrayonnogo soyuza Nevskogo rayona', cited by V. I. Lenin, 'Bor'ba S.D. i S.R. na vyborakh v rabochey kurii v St. Peterburge', *Soch.* (IV Ed.), vol. XII, pp. 52-53.

[2] Lenin, *ibid.*

[3] *Vpered*, No. 10, March 1905, and *Iskra*, No. 97, April 1905.

[4] 'Otchet tekhniki Peterburgskogo komiteta', *Treti s'ezd RSDRP* (M. 1959), pp. 553-554. From November 1904 to March 1905, 91 leaflets were printed by the Committee: a total of 231,330 sheets.

[5] 'Doklad o polozhenii del v Vyborgskom i Peterburgskom rayonakh', *Treti s'ezd RSDRP* (*Protokoly*), p. 549.

activities to preparations for armed self-defence and uprising. This can be illustrated by the expenditure of the local groups. In February, the general income of the Bolshevik Committee was 2,400 rubles (£240), of which 265 r. were spent on the press and 375 r. on organisation. A separate weapons' fund had an income of 1,295 r. of which 850 r. were spent. The strike fund had an income of 981 r. of which about half was spent during February[1]. At an exchange rate of 10 r. to the £, this represents a total income of £468 in one month alone. In the first fortnight of July, expenditure by the Bolsheviks had risen to 800 r. on arms, 540 r. on organisation and 150 r. on literature[2].

The Mensheviks' income from 15 February to 15 March 1905 was larger than that of the Bolsheviks, being 4,039 r. (2,000 of which came from one contributor): of this sum 1,250 r. were spent on arms, 'organisation' in various regions came to 1,126 r. and 630 r. were spent on the printing press. On 15 February, in the strike fund reserves were an additional 2,506 r. and income totalled 247 r. (of which 200 r. were from a sympathiser)[3]. This made a total income of £679 in one month, and showed little difference in priorities of expenditure from the Bolsheviks.

Up to the summer of 1905 we have the following picture of Social-Democracy in St. Petersburg. The factions were not organised enough to give a real lead to the workers, though their influence was growing. Both factions had around a thousand members each. Significant groups of the working class, probably the majority, were unorganised, others were in non-party 'workers' unions'[4]. After the 'Gapon Massacre' the attitudes of the workers had become more militant. Gapon's prestige had fallen and the workers turned to the Social-Democratic organisations. Bolsheviks and Mensheviks co-operated in many of the factories, and in the lowest ranks of the party the significance of the split was minimal. In the summer of 1905 Social-Democracy in St. Petersburg expanded its work: on the one hand, wider forms of workers' associations (*rabochie kluby*) and Social-Democratic trade unions were formed and, on the other hand, the collection of arms for self-defence and for insurrection was begun. Before considering the activities of the St. Petersburg Social-Democrats in the autumn, it is necessary to summarise the views of

[1] *Proletari*, no. 11, July 1905.
[2] *Proletari*, no. 14, August 1905.
[3] *Iskra*, no. 96, April 1905.
[4] *Vpered*, no. 12, March 1905.

the leadership of the two factions about the impending revolutio.. ...
Russia and the role to be played in it by the Social-Democrats.

6. *Menshevik and Bolshevik Policy on the 'Bourgeois-Democratic' Revolution*

Both Mensheviks and Bolsheviks thought of the coming revolution
as, in Marxist terminology, 'bourgeois-democratic' – the power of
the autocracy would give way to the dominance of the capitalist class.
About the role and tactics of the Social-Democrats, the two factions
differed[1].

Lenin's lead on theory is unquestionable in the Bolshevik faction.
He argued that the proletariat should play a leading role in the
revolution, as a part of the bourgeoisie was treacherous and might
join forces with the autocracy against the proletariat before the
revolution had gone its full course. He distinguished between this
part of the bourgeoisie (the big capitalists and part of the intelligentsia) and the petty-bourgeoisie (owners of small enterprises and
particularly the small-holding peasantry), whom he regarded as more
revolutionary, more antagonistic to the feudal order: with this
group, Lenin argued, the proletariat (organised by the Social-Democratic party) should unite to abolish the autocracy. He recognised
that the petty-bourgeoisie would not carry out a socialist revolution.
In the revolution the Social-Democrats should aim to fulfil their
minimum programme – freedom of the person, speech, press,
association, the right to form political parties, a republican form of
government and certain minimum economic standards (including
the eight-hour day). To prevent a coalition between the bourgeoisie
and the autocracy or a counter-revolution before the minimum programme of Russian Social-Democracy had been achieved, Lenin advocated participation in a revolutionary government to secure the
class interests of the proletariat.

The Mensheviks[2] expected the bourgeoisie to play the decisive
role in the revolution. As no political reforms could be achieved
without the sanction of the bourgeoisie, the role of the proletariat

[1] These aspects of Social-Democracy have already been exhaustively studied, the best discussions are in: O. Anweiler, *Die Rätebewegung in Russland 1905-1921* (Leiden, 1958), pp.
80-93; J. Keep, *The Rise of Social-Democracy in Russia* (1963), pp. 191-202; B. Wolfe, *Three
Who Made a Revolution* (1956), pp. 289-293. V. I. Lenin's own views are best shown in, 'Dve
taktiki sotsial-demokratii v demokraticheskoy revolyutsii', in *Soch.* Vol. 9 (IV Ed.), pp. 1-119.
The best Menshevik source is J. Martow, *Geschichte der Russischen Sozialdemokratie* (Berlin 1926),
pp. 112-119.
[2] I shall exclude Trotsky's and Parvus's theories which differed considerably.

was to bring pressure on it from below and to form as wide a front as possible against the autocracy. The party was to widen its base and strengthen the power of the proletariat for the struggle with capitalism which was to follow the victory of the bourgeoisie. It would then be in a position to defend a socialist revolution in Russia following socialist revolutions in western Europe. The party in Russia, however, should still prepare for an uprising – though it should not lead it – and it should, where local conditions sufficed, take part in local revolutionary seizures of power, which would disrupt the Tsarist order. The party should not participate in a revolutionary provisional government which would identify it with the bourgeoisie; the policy of the Mensheviks should be that of extreme opposition to the bourgeoisie.

In theory the local Bolsheviks were called to prepare for and, when the time came, to lead the revolutionary forces: a seizure of power might be necessary to defend the workers' rights. The local Mensheviks, on the other hand, were advised to prepare for a revolution and to take part in local seizures of power – not to rule, but to disrupt the autocracy. The Mensheviks were to concentrate on more long-term goals: strengthening the party by spreading into the trade unions and thereby being in a stronger position to struggle with the bourgeoisie. The Mensheviks, therefore, were to take a less aggressive attitude than the Bolsheviks. The bourgeoisie was considered to be politically homogeneous by the Mensheviks, whereas the Bolsheviks distinguished between the position of the petty-bourgeoisie, particularly the peasantry, and that of the rest.

But how were these ideas and recommendations for action transmitted to the masses, and how far were such differences manifested in the propaganda of the factions? A report from St. Petersburg published in *Iskra* said that the Menshevik leaders there did not consider a successful 'coming-out' to be very likely: 'A triumphant national uprising cannot grow out of the passive and silent masses. The masses listen to us sympathetically... but they do not go with us at our call'[1]. Let us now turn to consider the propaganda contained in the leaflets circulated by the Social-Democrats.

7. Party Propaganda in St. Petersburg – a Content Analysis

To attempt to collect and measure all the messages conveyed by Social-Democratic propaganda would require very large resources.

[1] *Iskra*, No. 100, May 1905.

Martov has given figures for twenty-nine different Committees for various months in 1905 which show that approximately 631 leaflets were locally published – a total of two million sheets. These figures are very incomplete and only serve to illustrate the size of the Social-Democrats' propaganda effort[1].

Here I shall concentrate only on the slogans of the St. Petersburg Committee which summed up Social-Democratic policy – its goals and the means to achieve them. The slogans convey the crucial messages of the leaders of organised political parties to the masses, they illustrate in the most succinct and dramatic way party policy. Slogans stir up emotions and evoke enthusiasm for the cause; they exploit existing beliefs to bind individuals to the movement; they enable participants to give vent to their social and political convictions and thereby develop group consciousness and solidarity. These general functions are open to more intuitive interpretation. I shall be concerned with the ideological content of the slogans.

In Table 17, the slogans are analysed into categories – positive objectives and the means to achieve them; negative attitudes – the enemies of the party; reference groups – the social strata to which the party appealed in its propaganda. These categories are broken down into symbols, separate words or phrases. Under I (Positive symbols: 'endorse change') are collected the words which make a positive appeal to action (long live!)[2] revolution, uprising, arms (armaments), strike, struggle. Under II (Objectives) are grouped words which indicate the explicit objectives of the revolutionaries: Constituent Assembly, democratic republic, revolutionary provisional government, republic, people's government; socialism (and Social-Democracy), freedom, the eight-hour day, wage increase. Under III (Negative appeals) are listed the enemies of the party: the Tsar, autocracy, 'the government' (State Duma, police, army, war, militarism – grouped together), 'the capitalists' (capitalist, capitalism, the boss, bourgeoisie, liberals). In the last section (IV) the addressees are defined: these are the social groups mentioned at the *beginning* of leaflets, and are not part of the slogans.

In the analysis of slogans care has been taken to collect words used in the sense implied by the categorisation. For example 'war' is counted under section III, when used deprecatingly – 'Down with the *war*!' It is not counted when used against the enemies of the

---

[1] Yu. Martov, 'Sotsialdemokratiya 1905-07', *Obshchestvennoe dvizhenie v Rossii v nachale XX veka* (Spb. 1914), vol. 3, pp. 567-8.

[2] Neither 'long live', nor 'down with' are strictly symbols: they have been included to show the relative number of positive and negative appeals.

Table 17. Content Analysis of Slogans of St. Petersburg Social-Democracy 1905

I. Positive symbols: 'endorse change'.

	Bolsheviks N.	Bolsheviks %	Mensheviks N	Mensheviks %	Total
(long live)	(111)	–	(44)	–	(155)
struggle	2	4.4	5	27.8	7
revolution	17	37.8	5	27.8	22
strike	10	22.2	1	5.6	11
uprising	8	17.8	3	16.6	11
arms (armaments)	8	17.8	4	22.2	12
Total	45	100	18	100	63

II. Objectives.

	Bolsheviks N	Bolsheviks %	Mensheviks N	Mensheviks %	Total
socialism	20	17.5	6	8.1	26
specific rights	33	29.0	19	25.7	52
Constituent Assembly	20	17.6	15	20.3	35
freedom	12	10.5	8	10.8	20
specific freedoms	9	7.9	5	6.8	14
republic (democratic government)	8	7.0	14	18.9	22
democracy	8	7.0	4	5.4	12
economic demands	4	3.5	3	4.0	7
Total	114	100	74	100	188

III. Negative appeals: 'enemies of the party'.

	Bolsheviks N	Bolsheviks %	Mensheviks N	Mensheviks %	Total
(down with)	(74)	–	(35)	–	(109)
government	3	4.8	4	10.3	7
capitalists	1	1.6	1	2.6	2
autocracy	32	51.6	18	46.1	50
Tsar	19	30.7	10	25.6	29
war	7	11.3	6	15.4	13
Total	62	100	39	100	101

IV. *Addressees.*

	Bolsheviks		Mensheviks		Total
	N	%	N	%	
comrades	32	44.5	13	44.8	45
workers	26	36.1	11	37.9	37
citizens	6	8.3	2	6.9	8
soldiers	6	8.3	3	10.4	9
peasants	2	2.8	0	–	2
Total	72	100	29	100	101

	Bolsheviks	Mensheviks
Total number of leaflets:	75	47

1905 v Peterburge (L.M. 1925), *passim.*

revolutionaries – 'Long live the *war* of the people against the Tsarist government'. 'Tsar' and its derivatives are counted (in section III) when it means the enemy of the party ('Down with the *Tsar*'), but not when endorsed by it ('Long live the Kingdom (*Tsarstvo*) of the people'). In the second of the examples, 'Tsar' and 'government' would be counted in the group of opponents of the revolutionaries and 'war' would not be shown on the table.

The classification applies to all the slogans which appeared at the end of Social-Democratic leaflets in the sources cited. In cases in which a high proportion of the leaflets contain slogan-type statements, the last six lines only are considered.

With the exception of section I ('Endorse change'), Table 17 shows few differences between the intended images of the Bolshevik and Menshevik factions. Both factions saw their immediate enemy in the Tsarist autocracy (III Negative appeals), capitalists, as such, were rarely mentioned; both advocated specific freedoms of the individual (freedom of speech, press, the person) and a Constituent Assembly (II Objectives); and both factions addressed their appeals mostly to the workers (IV Addressees). The kind of change proposed, however, does illustrate some differences between the factions: calls for 'revolution' and 'strike' were made much more by the Bolsheviks (I). The Mensheviks, on the other hand, stressed the creation of a republic or democratic government (II)[1]. Looking more

[1] A comparison with eight Socialist-Revolutionary leaflets shows few differences. The Socialist-Revolutionaries opposed the autocracy; appealed to the workers, soldiers and peasants; wanted 'freedom, equality and justice', 'socialism' and the eight hour day. The main differences were the calls for the creation of the *Zemski sobor*, universal peace and brotherhood and – as one would expect – land for all the peasants. 'Socialist revolutionary brochures 1902-05', Box A – 117 – A (Helsinki University Library).

closely at the calls for 'revolution' in the original sources, one finds that the Mensheviks did not mention the word at all in their slogans from March to October, whereas the Bolsheviks did so. The content analysis of slogans confirms that the local Menshevik leaders in St. Petersburg were not so extreme as their Bolshevik rivals. We may now consider the effectiveness of the Social-Democrats by studying their performance in the Soviet of Workers' Deputies in the autumn of 1905.

8. The St. Petersburg Soviet of Workers' Deputies: Composition

The Soviet was an amalgamation of different loosely organised groups of workers, the history of which is obscure. We know that mutual aid associations had existed among the handicraftsmen from as early as 1862[1]. Such associations were organised mainly on a 'trade' basis, but some strike funds had even existed on a factory base in St. Petersburg in 1896[2].

These were the precursors of the trade unions, some of which were led by the Social-Democrats, formed in 1905. Reports in the Menshevik *Nachalo* for the autumn of 1905 show that trade unions under Menshevik control developed in many factories, some being 250-300 strong. An organiser reported that 'the workers have already turned to the Social-Democratic organisations to help them form trade unions'[3]. Such unions had subscriptions of about 25 copecks per month[4].

In theory, at least, members of the workers' clubs were required to recognise the leadership of the RSDLP over political and economistic matters. Their activities included the provision of libraries and talks on political topics[5]. The Bolsheviks feared that these clubs might become mere social organisations, with little political awareness[6]. At local levels a few unions were joint Bolshevik/Menshevik

---

[1] V. Grinevich, *Professional'noe dvizhenie rabochikh v Rossii* (Spb. 1908), p. 10 and S. Prokopovich, *Soyuzy rabochikh i ikh zadachi* (Spb. 1905), p. 3.
[2] M. Gordon, *Professional'noe dvizhenie v epokhu pervoy russkoy revolyutsii 1905-07 gg.* (L. 1926), p. 9.
[3] *Nachalo*, No. 1, Nov. 1905.
[4] Memoir of K. Bondarev, in *Pervaya russkaya revolyutsiya*, pp. 20-21.
[5] In the Moscow district the Social-Democratic clubs organised lectures on the meaning of capitalism, socialism, a democratic republic, the agrarian question and on the Socialist-Revolutionaries. (See account in *Nachalo*, No. 14, Nov. 1905).
[6] In this respect the development of the British Workingmen's clubs, affiliated to the Labour Party would seem to bear out the Bolsheviks' fears.

'carrying out the federative principle'[1], and the Bolshevik *Novaya Zhizn'* called all Social-Democrats to take an active part in forming workers' clubs[2].

Some of these unions had their own trades councils or 'soviets' of deputies of a particular trade on a town basis well before the autumn of 1905. The printers claim to have been the first union in the open, on 24 April 1905[3]. On 6 July a council of clerks was elected. By 8 September the shop assistants had formed a trade union with 2,000 members[4]. And by December 1905, there were more than 50 trade unions in St. Petersburg with 25,000 members[5]. From such groups and the Social-Democrats the town Soviet was formed.

The electoral curia set up for the Shidlovski Commission were later the basis for the election to the October Soviet[6]. Khrustalev-Nosar' has noted 'that many of the electors (proxies) to the Commission were (also) deputies to the Soviet'[7]. The voting statistics already given (p. 123), would be some evidence that the Social-Democrats were not in the majority in the Soviet. This is confirmed by another participant: 'The organisational links of the Social-Democratic parties with the masses were... very weak: the number of organised workers in relation to the whole mass was always insignificant'[8]. Even so, we must bear in mind that the numbers of 'organised' men from other parties were also small and that the Social-Democrats were probably relatively stronger. The membership of the Soviet was worked out on the basis of factory and trade union representation. In the middle of November 1905, one hundred and forty-seven factories and mills and thirty-four workshops were represented by five hundred and eight deputies, and sixteen trade unions by fifty-four deputies. Of the unions, the Telephone, Post and Telegraph Union had voice but not vote[9]. An executive committee of thirty-one deputies was elected at the fourth session (17 October): two each from seven town factory regions; two each from four trade unions; and nine party representatives, with voice but not vote – three each from the Bolsheviks, Mensheviks and the Socialist-Revolutionaries. The police estimated that the Soviet con-

[1] *Nachalo*, No. 6, Nov. 1905.

[2] *Novaya Zhizn'*, No. 17, 19 Nov. 1905.

[3] *Istoriya Leningradskogo soyuza rab. poligraf. proizvodstva*, Vol. I (1925), p. 145.

[4] M. Gordon, p. 17.

[5] *Vtoraya konf. prof. soyuzov* (St. Petersburg, 1906), cited by Grinevich, p. 42.

[6] Martow, (Berlin, 1926), p. 109.

[7] Khrustalev-Nosar', 'Istoriya soveta rabochikh deputatov', in N. Trotsky, A. Kuzovlev, T. Khrustalev-Nosar', *Istoriya soveta rabochikh deputatov St. Peterburga* (Spb. 1906), p. 48.

[8] A. Kozovlev, *Kak vosnik sovet*, in Trotsky et al, p. 31.

[9] S. N. Belousov, *Khrestomatiya po istorii pervoy russkoy revolyutsii 1905 g.* (Moscow, n.d.), p.223.

tained fifty Social-Democrats and twenty-five Socialist-Révolution-aries[1]. Khrustalev-Nosar' asserts that the Social-Democrats were represented by 'many delegates', of whom four were from the printers' trade union delegation of fifteen, five from eleven of the salesmen and two watchmakers[2] and others came from the factory workers.

The social background of all the Social-Democratic delegates would provide a useful comparison and check on Part One of this thesis. Unfortunately, a breakdown of the delegates by faction is not available. But on Table 18, I have collated the information on the social backgrounds of 155 of the 223 deputies arrested by the police, not all of whom of course were Social-Democrats.

The 'peasants' were obviously men who had been born in the countryside and had moved to work in St. Petersburg factories. Many of the 'professional' category were probably *dvoryane* (gentry) by estate. The social composition of the Soviet showed a similar ranking of social groups as St. Petersburg as a whole (see p. 63); peasants, townsmen and gentry – in that order. Turning to the second part of the above table, to the social composition of the executive committee, we see fewer men of peasant extraction (27% compared with 60%) and the 'professional' group has risen from 11% to 18%. Considering the two parts of the table we may say that in terms of the 'present occupation' of the deputies, the majority were engaged in factory or mill work. Even in the executive committee the proportion of workers is high[3]. Two other facts are brought out. First, that a higher proportion of the deputies came from middle and upper social strata than the population at large: 23% were from the lower middle strata and 11% from the professional strata compared to (at most) 10% of the population in both of these groups; and 3% from the nobility – twice the proportion in the population. Second, that in the executive committee, the proportion coming from higher social strata was greater than in the Soviet. Those with 'lower middle' backgrounds accounted for 45% of the members, professionals 18%, the peasantry which accounted for 60% of the members of the Soviet amounted only to 27% of the members of the executive committee. These conclusions bear out what I have said in Part One about the social composition of Russian

---

[1] Polkovnik Gerasimov, 'Zapiska okhrannogo otdeleniya 4 Noyab. 1905 g.', in *1905 v Peterburge*, Vol. 2 (Leningrad, 1925), p. 120.

[2] Khrustalev-Nosar'', 'Istoriya soveta...', p. 72.

[3] This differs from Rudé's finding that the leaders of the French Revolution were drawn from the commercial *bourgeoisie* and the crowd from the Parisian *sans-culottes*: *The Crowd in the French Revolution* (1959), p. 178.

Table 18. Social Origin (or Social Position) of Deputies of the St. Petersburg Soviet
Arrested in December 1905[1]

1. Members of the Soviet	No.	%
Gentry	5	3
Peasants	93	60
Meshchane (townsmen)	36	23
Professional[2]	17	11
Handicraftsmen	4	2.6
Total	155	99.6 %
No information	68	
Grand total	223	

2. Members of the Executive Committee		
a) Social position	No.	%
Peasants	6	27
Meshchane (townsmen)	10	45
Professional (*sovetnik*, doctor)	4	18
Handicraftsmen (including chemist's assistant)	2	9
	22	100 %
Refused information	2	
	24	
b) Present occupation	No.	%
Worker	8	47
Professional	4	23.5
Unemployed	5[3]	29.5
	17	100 %
No information	7	
	24	

'Spisok lits zaderzhannykh 3 dek. 1905 g. na zasedanii soveta rabochikh deputatov', in *1905 v Peterburge*, vol. II (Leningrad 1925), pp. 136-144.

[1] No basis for this classification is given, most of the information has probably been taken from the identity card which refers to legal status at birth.

[2] The 'professional' group may include men of any estate – though most probably they were gentry, or townsmen – the seventeen men recorded here were doctors, engineers, teachers, students, civil servants.

[3] Including persons recently arrived in the capital.

Social-Democracy though, of course, not all the members of the Soviet were Social-Democrats. We may now turn to consider the performance of the St. Petersburg Social-Democrats in the Soviet.

9. Activity of the Soviet

It is usually conceded that the Social-Democrats, or at least the Mensheviks, were the leaders on tactics. 'In all the activities of the (Petersburg) Soviet the Social-Democrats played a directing, leading role'[1]. 'The Soviet was created and led, in the first instance, by the Social-Democratic party (of both factions). The Socialist-Revolutionaries came later'[2].

The Bolsheviks in St. Petersburg were not agreed in their attitude to the Soviet. Nosar' recalls that the Bolsheviks insisted on the Soviet accepting the programme of Social-Democracy or being dissolved[3]. At a meeting of the Neva district executive committee on 29 October, one of the fifteen members opposed taking part in it at all because the 'elective principle could not guarantee its class consciousness and Social-Democratic character'. Four voted against taking part in the Soviet, if it did not accept a Social-Democratic programme[4]. The group among the *remeslenniki* (handicraftsmen) advocated forming a group in the Soviet but leaving if it had a non-Social-Democratic programme[5]. The Soviet was seen by some such Bolsheviks as an alternative to the party and revolutionary action. Lenin took the opposite view, holding that the tactics of the Bolsheviks should be to place in it as many members of the party as possible. The roles of party and Soviet were complementary: 'Both the Soviet and the party!'[6] In Lenin's view the task of the Soviet was to 'create a provisional revolutionary government'[7]. The Bolsheviks, apathetic at first, took part, though in St. Petersburg they were ineffective in the Soviet[8]. The Soviet was non-party. At

---

[1] A. I. Spiridovich, *Istoriya bol'shevizma v Rossii* (Paris 1922), p. 109.

[2] *Raboche-krest'yanskaya kalendar'* (Peterburg, 1922), cited in Belousov, p. 217. The role of the Socialist-Revolutionaries in the Soviet is obscure and may be underestimated by pro Social-Democratic writers. Further research might be attempted here, though there is little doubt in my mind that Spiridovich is correct.

[3] *Istoriya soveta...*, p. 150.

[4] Nine were for taking part and two did not vote. *Novaya Zhizn'*, No. 5, Nov. 1905.

[5] *Novaya Zhizn'*, No. 9, Nov. 1905.

[6] V. I. Lenin, 'Nashi zadachi i sovet rabochikh deputatov', *Soch.* (IV Ed.), Vol. X, p. 3.

[7] *Ibid.*, p. 5.

[8] The leadership is attributed to the Mensheviks by most Soviet writers. See G. S. Merkurov, 'Sovety v pervoy russkoy revolyutsii', in *Pervaya russkaya revolyutsiya 1905-07* (Moscow 1955), pp. 174-175, and A. M. Pankratova, *Pervaya russkaya...*, p. 153.

the ninth session of the Soviet the Bolsheviks raised the question of its political allegiance, and the Soviet was asked to accept the programme and leadership of the RSDLP. The proposal had little support and was defeated[1].

The political aims of the Soviet are summed up by its slogans: 'Overthrow the autocracy!' 'Long live the Constituent Assembly, the democratic republic and the eight hour day!'[2] It led three strikes, the October, the November and the Post-Telegraph, issued about half a million leaflets (many of these, however, were seized by the police), put into practice the freedom of the press and organised armed detachments for self-defence[3]. The aim of the Soviet was not primarily to organise an armed uprising. Nosar' recounts that armaments were only discussed once up to 29 October[4]. The Soviet 'was a local organisation ... it remained primarily the *Petersburg* council of workers' deputies'[5], fulfilling the Menshevik conception of 'a revolutionary self-government'. Trotsky, in keeping with his general theories of the spontaneous activity of the working class pointed out in his defence to the court that 'we did not prepare an uprising, we prepared for an uprising'[6]. In support of the Moscow strike on December 8, the St. Petersburg Soviet again called the workers to strike, but not to revolt[7]. Isaac Deutscher's conclusion that '... the tactics of the Soviet (were) to harass the enemy without engaging him in general battle...' is correct[8]. The circumstances of the arrest of the Soviet are generally known and need no repetition here.

The financial account of the Soviet defines rather more precisely its priorities[9]. Aid to workers who were unemployed or in need was the largest percentage of expenditure: it took 15,992 rubles out of a total of 34,315 (£3,432) – just under half. 'Special tasks' (presumably armaments) came to 3,473r.; 'expenses' 12,745 r. and printing 495 r. This shows clearly the priorities of the Soviet. The wide range of purposes to which the funds of the Soviet were put led the St. Petersburg Bolsheviks to argue that collections for armaments

[1] A. Geller and N. Rovenskaya, *Peterburgski i Moskovski sovet rabochikh deputatov 1905 g.* (M.L. 1925), p. 41.

[2] *Raboche-Krest'yanskaya kalendar'*, p. 218.

[3] S. N. Belousov, pp. 224-5.

[4] *Istoriya soveta...*, pp. 94-97.

[5] L. Trotsky, *The Soviet and the Revolution* (1908) (Ceylon 1954), p. 19 (his italics).

[6] Speech printed in *1905 god v Peterburge*, vol. II (L. 1925), p. 366.

[7] See proclamation of the St. Petersburg Soviet in *1905 god v Peterburge* (1925) I, p. 375.

[8] I. Deutscher, *The Prophet Armed* (1954), p. 135.

[9] 'Otchet kassy St. Peterburg soveta rabochikh deputatov' (*Golos Sotsialdemokrata* (1908), No. 5), printed in *1905 v Peterburge*, Part II (Leningrad 1925), p. 418.

should be channelled through them, as their only aim was an uprising[1].

Though the Social-Democrats took the lead on tactics this does not exclude individuals or groups having strong influence over decisions. Trotsky, for example, has declared that, '...all the decisions of the Soviet, with the exception perhaps of a few that were accidental or even unimportant, were shaped by me. I submitted them first to the executive committee, then in its name, I placed them before the Soviet'[2]. The attitudes of the parties, the executive and the Soviet were not always identical. The conflict of interests over the prolongation of the November strike, and the final success of the non-party elements show that they had ultimate sovereignty. At the thirteenth session on 4 November the executive committee passed a resolution by nine votes to three that the strike be ended[3]. The Federative Committee of the RSDLP was unanimously opposed to stopping the strike and argued against the motion in the executive committee. Presumably, the Social-Democrats were a minority among the voting members there. The general assembly of the Soviet, however, rejected the executive committee's recommendations by four hundred votes to four[4]. The Soviet's militancy was short-lived. On 5 November Trotsky, speaking to the Soviet on behalf of the executive committee, advised a return to work, believing that the revolutionary energy of the proletariat had been sapped[5]. At its meeting on 5 November, the Soviet reversed its previous decision[6]. Many of the workers had no enthusiasm for the strike and had begun to drift back to work. Indeed it was this that had prompted the non-party men in the executive committee to move for a return in the first place.

We do not know how the masses would have responded to more revolutionary leadership. Their subsequent meetings show that they were divided over the decision to go back to work. On 9 November, a meeting of the deputies of the Semyannikov factory decided to continue the strike and reaffirmed the need for the eight-hour day. The Kharlamov delegate at the meeting of the Soviet on 12 November said that they should not revoke the demand to work the eight-hour day. At the workers' meeting of the Obukhov factory, 1,906 men

---

[1] *Novaya Zhizn'*, No. 12, Nov. 1905.

[2] L. Trotsky, *My Life*, p. 158.

[3] The representatives of the parties had no vote here – Khrustalev-Nosar', p. 119. The *Izvestiya* of the Soviet reported that the voting was nine to six, 'Izvestiya soveta rabochikh deputatov', No. 7 (Spb.), printed in *1905 v Peterburge*, II, p. 41.

[4] *Ibid.*

[5] See account in I. Deutscher, *The Prophet Armed* (1954), p. 134.

[6] *Ibid.*

voted for working the nine-hour day, 2,630 for the eight-hour, but at the Arsenal and the Franco-Russian factory the workers did not favour supporting an eight-hour day[1]. At the Alexandrov factory voting for the eight-hour day was 1,452 against 105[2], the printing workers said that only the large factories could work the eight-hour day, the small ones not being strong enough[3]. Though these newspaper reports are not representative of the St. Petersburg proletariat as a whole, they show that some support existed to continue the struggle, though we cannot be sure how large this was. At the meeting of the Soviet on 12 November, it became clear that the executive committee and a large number of the delegates supported calling off the struggle with the capitalists, at least temporarily[4].

How far this condition was due to the influence of the Social-Democrats' propaganda before and during the autumn of 1905 is a matter of controversy. The content of the slogans shows that the local St. Petersburg leadership did not (as far as the masses were concerned) put much emphasis on an armed revolt or uprising. This is not surprising, for the Mensheviks, as I have pointed out, did not regard themselves as the leaders of the 'bourgeois-democratic' revolution. In *Nachalo*, Martynov made it clear that 'the slogan of 'the self government of the proletariat' could only exist under the flag of freedom, under the flag of liberal legalisation'[5].

Social-political relations in St. Petersburg in 1905 were not simply those of 'worker-boss' antagonism. The factory directorate, the higher management, the 'Third Element' (government employees), and the workers' strata had many things in common: between the time of the 'Gapon massacre' and the October Manifesto, many of them united against the autocracy. The Soviet's sources of income in October show the wide support it enjoyed. Total contributions amounted to 18,601 rubles[6] of which 6,000 came from the Union of Unions, 5,000 rubles came 'Ot III' – possibly the Third Element, 1,000 came from 'a friendly businessman' (*tov. khozyain*), numerous trade unions contributed 2,082, newspapers 770, all groups of the Social-Democrats 542, the Socialist Revolutionaries 200, other individuals (doctors, an 'unknown lady', pupils and workers) contributed small amounts[7]. The factory directorate had abetted the

---

[1] *Nachalo*, No. 1, Nov. 1905.
[2] *Nachalo*, No. 2, Nov. 1905.
[3] *Nachalo*, No. 1, Nov. 1905.
[4] See *Novaya Zhizn'*, No. 12, whose account of this meeting is reprinted in *1905 god v Peterburge*, vol. II, pp. 58-9.
[5] *Nachalo*, No. 2, Nov. 1905.
[6] Ten rubles were approximately equal to the pound.
[7] *Izvestiya soveta rabochikh deputatov*, No. 6 (St. Petersburg), Nov. 1905.

October strikes: workers were allowed to hold strike meetings in the factories, half wages were paid whilst on strike in October, and the management of the Putilov mill even paid full wages to any of its workers whilst in attendance at the meetings of the Soviet[1].

An insurrection against the autocracy would undoubtedly have had widespread support – whether it would have succeeded is another matter – but this was not the intention of the leaders of the Soviet in St. Petersburg. The October Manifesto was a concession by the Tsar but was scarcely satisfactory to the workers. At this stage, especially to achieve the objective of an eight-hour day, it was necessary for the working class to make a greater sacrifice. It was an issue, however, directed against the factory administrations and not against the autocracy. The administrations were willing to modify wage rates and improve conditions, but within limits. The eight-hour day was opposed by the factory management who, after its proclamation by the Soviet, locked out workers at seventy-two establishments[2]. The workers accepted the managements' terms. The emphasis placed by the Soviet and the leaders of the Social-Democrats on the eight-hour day, together with the promises of the October Manifesto turned much of the bourgeois support away from the working class to the side of the autocracy.

The Social-Democratic leaders were then opposed both by the autocracy and the bourgeoisie. A delegate from the Putilov works to the Soviet said that the workers were without bread and could not fight simultaneously on two fronts. He recommended that the autocracy be fought first to achieve political freedom, then the capitalists, to improve economic conditions[3]. The St. Petersburg leadership of the Soviet and the Mensheviks adopted this solution by calling off the struggle with the bourgeoisie. The October Manifesto satisfied many of the liberal strata and, now with less widespread support, the leaders of the Soviet, fearing a fiasco, did not call for an uprising. Elsewhere, it was to be a different story.

10. Summing-up

St. Petersburg had a relatively well-off working class before 1905. Its main political movement before the Gapon rally, when the Social-Democrats were very weak, was Zubatov's police union. Though

[1] Khrustalev-Nosar', p. 127.
[2] Khrustalev-Nosar', *ibid*.
[3] *Nachalo*, No. 1, Nov. 1905.

the Bolsheviks had members in both large and small factories, they were not dominant in St. Petersburg and they were poorly represented in the Soviet. In so far as the working class had leaders, they were the Mensheviks. But the existence of factory and craft-based workers' unions did not put the Mensheviks in a position of hegemony over the working class. The rapid growth of the Social-Democrats in organisation, personnel and their appearance at the head of workers' activity in the autumn shows that there was much latent support for Social-Democracy and revolutionary leadership. In theory, the Bolsheviks stood for a more aggressive policy: their propaganda emphasised revolution and strike action more than did the Mensheviks. But there was no uprising. This may be explained by the long period of revolutionary activity of the St. Petersburg working class resulting in its exhaustion in the autumn of 1905, and by the tactics of the Menshevik leadership of the Soviet which did not intend leading an insurrection. These factors interacted one with another and precluded a 'coming out' on a wide scale.

chapter four

THE STRUCTURE AND ACTIVITY OF
SOCIAL-DEMOCRACY IN MOSCOW

1. *Economic and Social Background*

The population of Moscow city[1] was growing at the beginning of the twentieth century. In 1897 its population was 1,038,000, by 1902 it had risen to 1,174,000 and in 1907 was 1,345,000[2]. The population of Moscow was recruited from the surrounding areas. In the 1880's and 1890's approximately two-thirds of the factory workers in Moscow province were recruited from the same province and one-third came from neighbouring ones (Kaluga, Ryazan, Tula, and Smolensk). Of Moscow city's population over ninety per cent came from Moscow and surrounding provinces[3].

Statistical sources showing the employment figures for Moscow city in 1905 vary between 300,000 and 350,000. Those subject to the factory inspectorate numbered 263,357 in 1901 and 279,048 in 1905[4]. One breakdown of the Moscow (city) proletariat at the beginning of the twentieth century is as follows:

Factory and mill workers	107,800
Railwaymen	39,000
Workers in handicraft industry (*remeslenniki*)	104,899
Workers in trade establishments	52,489
Casual workers (*podennye rabochie*)	8,918
Workers in 'cottage industries'	2,202
Apprentices	37,679

352,987[5]

[1] City refers to the administrative unit *gorod*, province to *guberniya*.

[2] 'Statisticheski ezhegodnik g. Moskvy...', Part 2 (Moscow 1927), pp. 9, 12, cited in *Istoriya Moskvy*, vol. V (M. 1955), p. 15.

[3] Yu. Polevoy, *Iz istorii Moskovskoy organizatsii VKP (b) (1894-1904 gg.)* (M. 1947), pp. 7-8.

[4] Cited by I. A. Shmeleva, *Bor'ba Moskovskikh rabochikh protiv Zubatovshchiny* (Candidate's dissertation, Moscow 1962), p. 26.

[5] 'Statisticheski atlas g. Moskvy' (1911), cited in Yu. Polevoy, *Iz istorii Moskovskoy...*, p. 7.

The Textile, metal working and food industries accounted for the majority of Moscow city's factory population. In 1900, of 195 textile mills employing 46,922 workers the eleven largest employed more than 50% of the textile labour force; in the metal working industry 19,980 were employed in 193 factories, 40% being in factories with over 500 employees; in the food processing industry were 13,316 men of whom in 1900 about half were employed in large factories (over 500)[1].

Though some of the machine-building, canning and textile factories were foreign-owned, most of Moscow's industry was Russian-owned and managed[2]. The employers in the Vladimir/Moscow/Kostroma triangle seem to have been much less 'progressive' in their industrial relations than their more western-based competitors elsewhere in Russia, some of whom believed in legal equality and even free trade unions[3]. Therefore, the factory management in the Moscow area was probably more hostile to the workers due not only to its 'Russianness' but also to the backwardness of the area in comparison with the new textile industry of Poland, and with the growing Donbass complex. Moscow had many of the features of a 'depressed area'.

It is general knowledge that the economic condition of the Moscow working class was low. From 1897 to 1903 the average wage per factory worker increased only by 13%, whereas the price of bread had risen 25%, and grain 36%[4]. Wages fell from 1903 to 1905, due

Table 19. Average Workers' Income Per Annum

Year	St. Petersburg (rubles)	Moscow (rubles)	European Russia (rubles)
1903	334	242	217
1904	366	204	213
1905	294	152	205
Average	331	199	211

'Svod otchet fabrichnykh inspektorov' 1903, p. 168, 'Svod...' 1904, p. 173, 'Svod...' 1905, p. 92. Cited by R. L. Moyzhes, *Politicheskoe vospitanie Peterburgskogo proletariata v kanun pervoy russkoy revolyutsii 1903-05 gg.* (Candidate's dissertation Leningrad 1960), p. 43.

[1] *Istoriya Moskvy*, vol. v, pp. 31-36.
[2] Shmeleva, p. 28.
[3] A. M. Pankratova, 'Tekstil'shchiki v revolyutsii 1905-1907 gg.', *Proletariat v revolyutsii 1905-1907 gg.* (M.L. 1930), p. 112.
[4] 'Doklad fabrichnykh inspektorov Moskovskoy gub. ....', cited in V. V. Simonenko and G. D. Kostomarov, *Iz istorii revolyutsii 1905 goda v Moskve* (M. 1931), pp. 180-1.

to short-time working and to the laying-off of workers during the disturbances in 1905. A comparative table has been constructed on the basis of factory inspectors' reports and is shown above. Obviously, to determine changes of income in particular trades and industries one would need more detailed statistics than I have cited here, but these will suffice to make two general points: in Moscow real wages were falling, and Moscow was relatively worse off than other areas.

To sum up the main points: between 1900 and 1905 the population of Moscow was industrial, slowly growing and nationally homogeneous. The working class was generally backward, many being employed as textile operatives. The factory administrations, probably due to growing competition from newer, more capital-intensive competitors, sought to keep wage costs down, and hostile industrial relations developed. For the factory worker real wages were falling and he was faced with considerable uncertainty about employment. Against this social-economic background Social-Democracy in Moscow evolved.

2. The Early History of Moscow Social-Democracy

In the eighties, Populist circles existed which were small in number, led by, and mainly composed of, the intelligentsia. The groups were isolated, had little continuity and few links with the working class[1]. As Radkey has pointed out, 'Narodnik groups in Moscow had exhibited neither strength nor stability...'[2].

In the early 1890's small Social-Democratic circles came into existence and were mainly composed of the intelligentsia. These groups tried to make contacts with the workers, to organise circles among them and to train organisers and propagandists. One of the first was the Moscow Workers' Union formed from students' circles and others in 1894-95. Its propaganda was directed to improving workers' conditions, by strike action if necessary. Besides discussion circles, strike and welfare funds (kassy) were also organised by this group. The formulas advocated in the brochure Ob agitatsii[3], and the forms of workers' organisation in western Russia had a big

[1] B. I. Nikolaevski, commentary on 'Doklad o Moskovskom sotsial-demokraticheskom dvizhenii na II s'ezde RSDRP', in N. Angarski (editor), Doklady sotsial-demokraticheskikh komitetov vtoromu s'ezdu RSDRP (M.L. 1930), p. 131: Yu. Polevoy, Iz istorii Moskovskoy organizatsii VKP (b) (1894-1904 gg.) (M. 1947), pp. 11-16.
[2] O. H. Radkey, The Agrarian Foes of Bolshevism (N.Y. 1958) pp. 53-54.
[3] See pp. 65-6 above.

influence on the Moscow proletariat at this time[1]. Some of the leaders had had experience in the western provinces. For example, L. S. Tseytlin (Veysman), the Moscow delegate to the Second Congress, had been born in Smolensk, studied in Vitebsk where he had taken part in illegal activities after which in the late 1890's he moved to Moscow[2].

These *rabochie soyuzy*, of which up to twenty may have existed, continued during the late nineties: they put out revolutionary literature in popular editions and sought to exploit workers' grievances[3]. The Moscow Workers' Union's links with other Social-Democratic groups in the factories were weak despite the attempts by its central committee to 'lead all activity in Moscow...and to conduct relations with other towns and abroad'[4]. Polevoy has argued that this Union had the allegiance of about 500 men in 1896, though during the late 1890's many separate revolutionary circles existed[5].

In Moscow, activities at the end of the 1890's included printing pamphlets and circulating the mimeographed paper 'Volna'[6]. Many of the workers seemed ready to receive propaganda. Shestakov has described the educational courses held for workers as follows: 'On the courses illegal political work was carried on amongst us... Some of the workers would quickly join the illegal Social-Democratic circles and take up revolutionary work.'[7] At the turn of the century, though Marxism was now gaining ground at the expense of Populism, workers' activities were based mainly on the need to improve wages and conditions of work: 'economism' had a wide influence. In the winter of 1898-99 the Moscow Committee of the RSDLP was founded. In 1900 it supported the 'economistic' struggles of the workers, putting out leaflets advocating the solidarity of the proletariat and calling, often unsuccessfully, for strike action[8].

A significant feature of Moscow's political life was the existence of a strong and active police force. In the late nineteenth century many *agents-provocateur* worked among the circles leading to the

[1] B. I. Nikolaevski, p. 133, S. I. Mitskevich, *Revolyutsionnaya Moskva* (M. 1940), pp. 180-81, and S. Polidorov (ed.), *Put' k oktyabryu* (M. 1923), pp. 12-13.

[2] 'Iz avtobiografii L. S. Tseytlina (Veysmana)', O. Pyatnitski (ed.), *Iskrovski period v Moskve* (M.L. 1928), pp. 46-49. After the Second Congress Tyetlin became a Menshevik.

[3] Nikolaevski, p. 133 and S. E. Mitskevich, pp. 256-8.

[4] 'Doklad o Moskovskom sotsial-demokraticheskom dvizhenii na II s'ezde RSDRP', *Vtoroy s'ezd RSDRP: Protokoly* (M. 1959), p. 624.

[5] Yu. Polevoy, *Iz istorii...*, pp. 43 *et seq.*

[6] A. Kuz'mich, *Moskovskaya organizatsiya na II S'ezde RSDRP* (M. 1963), p. 13.

[7] A. V. Shestakov, 'Prechistenskie rabochie kursy' (p. 196), cited in Kuz'mich, p. 14.

[8] 'Doklad o Moskovskom S.D. ...' (*Protokoly II S'ezda*), pp. 625, 632.

arrest of members[1]. The attempts of the police-chief Zubatov to contain the workers' revolutionary movement within the framework of the autocracy were more positive than arresting and banishing the revolutionary ringleaders. Zubatov regarded the absence of legal forms of organisation as being conducive to the spread of revolutionary ideas and the growth of secret societies. He wanted to set up a legal organisation and a Workers' Council (*Rabochi sovet*) which would 'guide the activity of the workers but would not give them power'[2]. The *Zubatovshchina* was strong and well-organised in Moscow. At the Trekhgorny mill, for example, a police union was started before a Social-Democratic group and it had recruited 'a very large part of the advanced workers'[3]. On the first of January 1903, at this factory alone, the union had 1,213 members[4]. According to a recent Soviet writer, the movement rested on a relatively narrow base of 'loyal and well-off' workers and this led to its failure later.[5] This is untrue for even if the leaders were relatively better off, there can be no doubt that support was more widely based. Besides, Zubatov did not have the support of all the factory owners. A large number, headed by Yuri Guzhon, opposed the Moscow authorities, and opposed even what the police regarded as 'just demands'.[6]

Much of the activity of the Moscow Committee was concerned with exposing the Zubatovites and warning the revolutionary workers of the danger of provocateurs[7]. There can be no doubt that police provocateurs successfully disrupted the organisations, and most probably quite a large number of workers were prepared to collaborate with the police. Teodorovich recalls that one of the main reasons for the success of the police during this time was the large percentage of workers just out of the village who had little class consciousness[8].

[1] For example, arrests of members of the Moscow Committee of the RSDLP took place in February, April, May, June, October and December 1899: 'Doklad o Moskovskom S.D. ...' (*Protokoly II S'ezda*), p. 632 and commentary in Angarski, p. 135.

[2] Police letter, dated 2 April 1902 in *Krasny arkhiv*, no. 1, 1922, p. 310.

[3] V. S. Morozov, 'Avtobiografiya', *Rabochie Trekhgornoy manufaktury v 1905g.* (M. 1930), p. 72.

[4] The subscriptions were a down payment of between 50 copecks and 2 rubles depending on earnings, and monthly payments of between 25 copecks and 1 ruble. During unemployment benefits ranged from 2 rubles 75 copecks to 11 rubles per month (Chaadaeva, in *Rabochie Trekhgornoy manufaktury*, p. 33).

[5] I. A. Shmeleva, *Bor'ba Moskovskikh rabochikh protiv Zubatovshchiny* (Candidate of Science dissertation, Moscow 1962), p. 63.

[6] K.A., No. 1, (1922), p. 311.

[7] See letters in *Iskra* No. 9, October 1901, and No. 14, January 1902. Warnings about the connexion of particular 'self-help' groups with the police also appeared in *Iskra* No. 20, May 1902, No. 22, July 1902 and No. 31, January 1903.

[8] 'Vospominaniya I. A. Teodorovicha', in *Iskrovski period v Moskve* (M.L. 1928), p. 61.

Probably to avoid the dire consequences of public meetings, the Social-Democrats from 1900 to 1902 concentrated their activities on spreading leaflets: Kuz'mich has estimated that in 1902 the Moscow Committee put out 10,000 copies of leaflets[1]. The Moscow Committee also called the workers to demonstrate on May Day and to carry out a struggle with the autocracy and the capitalists[2].

It is impossible to get accurate numbers of persons taking part in these early circles. Probably active Social-Democrats at any one time would not have been more than a hundred or so and many of these would be working alone and not connnected with the Moscow Committee of the RSDLP. In April 1902, Milyutin has recalled that the *Iskra* Social-Democratic group had seven factory groups making up a total of forty men[3]. Recollections about the 'Dinamo' factory, printed after the October Revolution include the biographies of the members of its Social-Democratic cell in 1902: of thirteen members, nine were mechanics or fitters (*slesary*), two draftsmen, one a metal-drawer, and one an armature winder; of five other active helpers, three were fitters, and two turners[4]. Though the number of organised men was small, one should not underestimate the extent to which literature circulated and the influence of socialist ideas on the masses. Teodorovich says that he received seven hundred copies of *Iskra* to distribute through his circles[5].

In May 1903, proclamations were circulated demanding an end to the autocracy and the introduction of an eight-hour day. For a short time after this the *Iskra* committee became more active, until in June arrests of members cut short its work[6]. Considering his membership of the Moscow Social-Democratic groups from 1895 to 1902, Teodorovich estimates that due to police intervention the average life of a Social-Democratic group was only three months[7].

Whilst the main Social-Democratic activity was in the town of Moscow, groups existed in 1902 and 1903 in the settlements outside. In Serpukhov, for example, there were circles of Social-Democrats among the intelligentsia, the grammar school youth and the workers[8].

[1] *Moskovskaya organizatsiya na II S'ezd RSDRP* (M. 1963), p. 34.

[2] Proclamation dated 30 April 1902 in K.A., No. 82 (1937), p. 183.

[3] N. Milyutin, 'V Moskovskoy S.D. organizatsii 1902 g.' in O. Pyatnitski, *Iskrovski period v Moskve* (M.L. 1928), p. 80.

[4] *Dynamo 25 let revolyutsionnoy bor'by* (M. 1923), p. 103.

[5] 'Vospominaniya I. A. Teodorovicha' in O. Pyatnitski et al, *Iskrovski period v Moskve* (M.L. 1928), pp. 68-9.

[6] 'Doklad Moskovskogo delegata Veysmana na II s'ezde', p. 59.

[7] 'Vospominaniya I. A. Teodorovicha', p. 60.

[8] A. A. Burdukov (reminiscence) in *Put' k oktyabryu* (M. 1923), pp. 68-87. This book contains dictated reports by participants in these circles.

Earlier, even as late as 1901, some of these groups had given their allegiance to the Socialist-Revolutionaries, and most probably in 1903 (and later) many of them had strong elements of Socialist-Revolutionary ideology[1]. Some of the members of these Social-Democratic factory groups were workers who had been sent home for their misdeeds from Moscow[2].

With the development of strikes (there were 77 in Moscow in 1903), the Social-Democrats put out leaflets of support. At the Bromley factory in June-July 1903, a group called *Trud* distributed *Iskra* leaflets decrying the absence of political liberty and advocating the freedom of strike and speech and the right to form trade unions[3]. Though the Moscow Committee of the RSDLP gave active encouragement and support to the strikers and on occasions led them, the strikes developed out of particular grievances (fines, arbitrary treatment by foremen) which the Social-Democrats exploited for their own political ends.

In addition to the internal conflicts between *Iskra*'s editorial board and the agents working in Russia[4], the attitude of the local Social-Democratic groups to the journal's leadership was often hostile. As in St. Petersburg, the 'recognition' given to *Iskra* was often preceded by conflict or accompanied by the refusal of a minority to give allegiance.

Iskra's agent in Moscow was N. E. Bauman who has claimed that the Moscow Committee went into association with it in October 1901. But this did not occur without internal division in the Committee. A dispute on the relationship of the group to *Iskra* lasted for two months: the opponents of the journal arguing that its supporters wanted to usurp power[5]. The other internal disagreement was over the 'closed' or 'open' nature of revolutionary activity[6]. By July 1902 the Moscow Committee was controlled by *Iskra*-ites, a note in the paper said that the Committee intended to contribute 20% of its income to the paper[7]. In practice the *Iskra* leaders were coopted: I. A. Teodorovich recalls that 'our organisation had obvious defects, there was no democracy, there was no elected committee. But this

---

[1] Ovsyanikov, in *Put' k oktyabryu*, p. 201.

[2] *Ibid.*, p. 202.

[3] 'Proklamatsiya sots-dem. kruzhka *Trud*' (July 1903) in K.A., No. 56 (1933), p. 140.

[4] See N. Krupskaya, commentary to 'Doklad organizatsii 'Iskry' II s'ezdu RSDRP', in Angarski, p. 64 and L.S. VIII, pp. 184, 204.

[5] 'Doklad o Moskovskom sotsial-demokraticheskom dvizhenii na II s'ezde RSDRP', *II S'ezd (Protokoly)*, p. 634.

[6] *Ibid.*, p. 636.

[7] *Iskra*, No. 22, July 1902.

was an epoch when any other kind of work was impossible'[1]. One method of forming cells in Moscow with allegiance to *Iskra* was to send in Social-Democratic working men from outside areas, such as Smolensk and Tula[2].

After the arrest of the Moscow Committee together with a representative of *Iskra*, in November 1902, the Committee was very weak: it had lost its leading personnel, files, and correspondence and it had very few funds. In 1903 new *Iskra* organisers came from outside and, with the help of school-pupil propagandists, links were made with the Brest railway repair-shops, and the Prokhorov, Bromley, Gonner, Mussa, and Borodin factories[3]. These groups, however, were not very tightly bound together, many of them still having 'separate aims'[4].

3. The Moscow Committee after the Second Congress

After the Second Congress both factions of the RSDLP tried to enlist support but a formal split did not take place in Moscow until May 1905. By the spring of 1904, the Mensheviks had members in the leading positions of the Moscow Committee: of a group of five, two were Bolsheviks and three Mensheviks[5]. In 1904, however, the Social-Democrats in Moscow had only a few cells[6]. 'During the summer and autumn of 1904 the RSDLP in Moscow appeared to be thoroughly routed. Its leaders were in jail and its activities had been brought to an almost complete halt'[7]. The leaflets of the Committee are an index of its activity: of 252 leaflets published in *Listovki Moskovskikh bol'shevikov v period pervoy russkoy revolyutsii* (M. 1955), only 16 were printed in 1904. In the Moscow Committee's organisations Bolsheviks and Mensheviks often worked together up to 1905, though a participant recalls that at factory cell meetings there were many heated discussions between them[8]. It is sometimes claimed

---

[1] 'Vospominaniya I. A. Teodorovicha', O. Pyatnitski, *Iskrovski period v Moskve* (M.L. 1928), p. 70.

[2] 'Vospominaniya I. A. Teodorovicha', p. 67.

[3] A. Kuz'mich, *Moskovskaya organizatsiya na II S'ezde RSDRP* (M. 1963), pp. 47, 51, 54.

[4] 'Doklad Moskovskogo delegata Veysmana na II s'ezde RSDRP' in O. Pyatnitski et al, *Iskrovski period v Moskve* (M.L. 1928), pp. 55-57.

[5] A. Kuz'mich, *Moskovskaya organizatsiya na II S'ezde* (M. 1963) p. 76.

[6] Kuz'mich, p. 71.

[7] R. M. Slusser, *The Moscow Soviet of Workers' Deputies of 1905* (Ph.D. Columbia, 1963), p. 13. See also letter of Zemlyachka describing St. Petersburg and the disorder in Moscow. Letter from Moscow dated 29 August 1904, K.A. No. 68 (1935), p. 29.

[8] 'Uchastnik-vospominaniya', in N. Morozov-Vorontsov, *Zamoskvorech'e v 1905 g.* (M. 1925), p. 35.

that the theoretical differences over the nature of party organisation were an important cause of dispute, but in practice the Mensheviks did not apply very different organisational principles from those of Lenin and the Bolsheviks: 'the organisation (of the Moscow Committee) was built from the top to the bottom on the principle of cooption'[1]. Garvi recalls that he was coopted directly onto the all-city committee of the Moscow Group and became the leading organiser of the Khamovnichesko-Presnya district.

At the end of 1904 the Mensheviks were weak in Moscow, their strength may be indicated by the voting for the calling of the Third Party Congress, which they opposed. On the Moscow executive committee, four were in favour of the Congress and one abstained from voting; of the Committee's organisers, eleven were in favour and two against; of the propagandists, eleven were in favour and five against[2]. In the summer of 1905, the Mensheviks had numerous district committees, an organisation among the students and a *voenny* (soldiers') group. They had some workers' circles, but their factory committees were not organised, their chief work centred on the trade-union and student groups.

In spring 1905, trade-unions of white-collar workers were formed in Moscow. The Social-Democrats as a whole took part in this movement and as individuals they joined the unions of teachers, lawyers, shopworkers, and doctors. Mitskevich recalls that they placed special significance on work in the teachers' union which was more left-wing than the others; many of the village teachers in fact had allegiance to the Socialist-Revolutionaries[3]. At the end of April, the Moscow Bolsheviks who were members of such unions were called upon by the party centre to leave, because they had a political platform inimical to the Social-Democrats. This decision led to some controversy among them, many thinking that such action would increase the influence of the liberals and Socialist-Revolutionaries[4]. The Mensheviks, in line with their general policy of encouraging trade-union activity played a large part in their formation in Moscow.

After the Third Party Congress in May 1905, the Mensheviks formed the separate Moscow Group of the RSDLP[5]. Garvi has recalled 'there can be no doubt that the organisational and political influence of the Bolshevik Committee in Moscow was greater than that of our

[1] Garvi, *Vospominaniya sotsialdemokrata* (N.Y. 1946), p. 520.
[2] *Vpered*, No. 9, Feb. 1905.
[3] S. I. Mitskevich, *Revolyutsionnaya Moskva* (M. 1940), pp. 341-3.
[4] Mitskevich, p. 350.
[5] Mitskevich, p. 353.

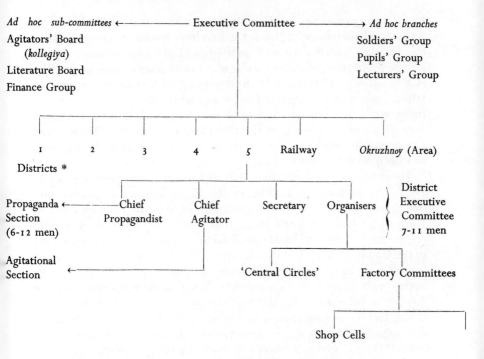

Chart 5. *Moscow Organisation of the RSDLP: Spring-Summer 1905*

Ad hoc sub-committees ←——————— Executive Committee ——————→ *Ad hoc branches*

Agitators' Board   Soldiers' Group

   (*kollegiya*)   Pupils' Group

Literature Board   Lecturers' Group

Finance Group

1   2   3   4   5   Railway   *Okruzhnoy* (Area)

Districts *

Propaganda ←———————Chief   Chief   Secretary   Organisers   District

Section   Propagandist   Agitator   Executive

(6-12 men)   Committee

                                                                         7-11 men

Agitational

Section   ←———————————————   'Central Circles'   Factory Committees

                                                                                 Shop Cells

'Otchet o deyatel'nosti Moskovskogo komiteta RSDRP vesnoy i letom 1905 g.',
Revolyutsionnoe dvizhenie v Rossii (*Apr-Sen. 1905*). Part I. (M. 1957), p. 367.

* Later in the summer 1905 there were nine districts in all: Presnya, Zamoskvorech'e, Rogozh,
Lefortov, Sokolniki, Butyr, Town, Railway, and the Okruzhnoy. (*Proletari*, No. 22, Oct. 1905).

Group'[1], though among the students and in the trade unions the
Mensheviks had as much, if not more, influence.

At the beginning of 1905, the joint Committee had five district
committees, the railwaymen's committee and a number of separate
groups (soldiers', pupils', lecturers'). In the summer, there were
nine Bolshevik districts, each led by an organiser who was a member
of the Moscow Party Committee. An organisational scheme is shown
on Chart 5. In March-April 1905, the Committee consisted of 9-10
men: a secretary, the chief propagandist and seven leading district
organisers[2].

[1] Garvi, p. 596.
[2] Mitskevich, pp. 351-2.

4. Party Strength

In the spring of 1905, in Moscow, it is claimed that there were over a thousand members and about a hundred worker-propagandists in the Moscow RSDLP with two underground printing presses[1]. Quite a large proportion of these local leaders were intellectuals or youths: at a Moscow conference held in May 1905, of 100 district representatives only 30 were reported to be workers[2]. By the summer 1905, there were five presses, and total membership had risen to 1,435 men of whom 400 were in the *Okruzhnoy* Committee. There were 123 propagandist circles – 28 in the *Okruzhnoy*[3]. Most of these groups had been formed only in 1905.

There can be no doubt that cells and membership grew rapidly in 1905. V. Savkov, an activist in the Zamoskvorech'e district says that it had the widest party organisation in Moscow, though early in 1905 there had not been more than three to four factory circles (at Bromley, List, and the Dobrov factories) and individual members at the Ganter factory and the electric station[4]. The Mensheviks were supreme among the printing workers in this district, the Bolsheviks having only individual supporters[5]. When Savkov returned to the district in July 1905, he 'did not recognize it' – there were ten to fifteen factory committees, a party district conference of 50-60 men, and agitation and propaganda sections[6]. In each circle there were from 20 to 25, giving a membership of 200 to 375 men[7].

There are few detailed figures of Bolshevik strength in the district organisations, but one may make some estimates of their importance from other known factors. Table 20 shows the numbers of leaflets sent to each district and the amount of money allocated to them by the Moscow Committee for the months of October, November and December, 1905. This table shows the large scale of the Committee's printing efforts (three quarters of a million copies of various publications in three months), and the distribution to each region. Ob-

[1] *Istoriya Moskvy*, Vol. V (M. 1955), p. 122.

[2] *Vpered*, No. 5, May 1905.

[3] A. M. Pankratova (ed.), *Revolyutsiya 1905-07 gg. v Rossii: dokumenty i materialy*, Apr.-Sep. 1905, Part I (M. 1957), p. 368, S. I. Mitskevich, *Revolyutsionnaya Moskva*, p. 372.

[4] V. Savkov, 'Zamoskvorech'e v 1905 g.' in N. Morozov-Vorontsov (ed.), *Zamoskvorech'e v 1905 g.* (M. 1925), p. 7. At the Mikhaylov textile factory in 1905 there was a Social-Democratic cell six strong (augmented by three from another factory) out of six hundred mainly female workers: S. Tsvetkova, *Na barrikadakh 1903 god po vospominaniyam rabotnitsy* (M.L. 1926), pp. 20, 23.

[5] *Ibid.*, p. 10.

[6] *Ibid.*

[7] *Ibid.*, pp. 11-13.

Table 20. Finance and Publications of Moscow District Organisations,
October, November, December 1905

District	Nos. of Publications					Finance (Rubles)				
	Oct.	Nov.	Dec.	Total 000's	Rank	Oct.	Nov.	Dec.	Total	Rank
ᶻamoskvorech'e	40,326	48,086	22,524	110.9	2	560	549	419	1,528	2
ᵀown I	30,156	9,074	3,355	42.5	8	224	150	—	374	9
ᴿogozh	25,511	35,785	23,094	84.4	3	324	1,321	544	2,189	1
ˢokol'niki	20,390	25,031	9,310	54.7	6	220	170	242	632	6
ᴮutyr	20,390	26,171	9,502	56.0	5	200	325	436	961	3
ᵀown II	652	26,713	13,135	40.5	9	—	100	210	310	10
ᴸefortov	—	—	—	—	—	50	391	441	8	
ᴿailway Union (or District)	30,265	28,032	11,475	69.7	4	145	193	187	525	7
ᴷhamovnichesko-Presnya	—	11,425	5,326	16.7	11	100	174	475	749	5
ᴼkruzhnaya	48,000	39,085	24,204	111.2	1	315	500	–	815	4
ᵀrade unions	—	5,882	8,682	14.5	12	–	–	–	–	–
ⱽoennaya	8,372	23,754	15,072	47.1	7	–	50	–	50	11
ᴵntelligentsia	18,621	11,355	276	30.2	10	–	–	–	–	–
Total*	268,588	307,044	145,943	721.5						

'Otchety...' in *1905*, Ed. M.N. Pokrovski (M.L. 1926), accounts for various months: pp. 324-333; 368-377; 398-404.

* Total issued: may exceed sums of columns as leaflets distributed at meetings and rallies are here excluded.

viously, the Zamoskvorech'e, Rogozh and *Okruzhnoy* were the most important, the low priority given to the trade unions, with the exception of that of the railwaymen, is clearly brought out. It is interesting to note the rather low priority given to the Khamovnichesko-Presnya district, which became the stronghold of the insurgents[1].

5. Finance

Turning to finance, the publication of most of the Moscow Committee's

[1] This may bear out Keep when he infers that the Bolshevik strength here has been exaggerated. *The Rise of Social-Democracy*, p. 255 n.

Table 21. Income by Monthly Account and Size of Contribution

0-10 rubles	11-25 rubles	26-50 rubles	51-100 rubles	101- rubles	Total rubles

FEBRUARY-MARCH ACCOUNT

| 7 | 8 | 5 | 3 | 5
 (2,876 r.) | 3,826
 (incl. b.f. 190) |

APRIL-MAY

| 6 | 7 | 10 | 5 | 9 | 8,389
 (incl. b.f. 1,013) |

JUNE

| 4 | 9 | 3 | 9 | 4 | 9,891
 (b.f. 1,013) |

OCTOBER

| 126 | 44 | 21 | 18 | 101-500
 24 (6,057 r.)

 501-1000
 3 (2,441 r.)

 1001-
 6 (21,586 r.) |

 35,310
 (b.f. 1,121) |

NOVEMBER

| 67 | 30 | 7 | 8 | 13
 (7,472 r.) | 27,886
 (b.f. 18,975) |

DECEMBER

| 72 | 37 | 15 | 22 | 17 | 15,536
 (b.f. 5,079) |

Table 22. Distribution of Expenditure

Month	Arms (+ Militia) rubles	'Tekhnika' (+ printing) rubles	Personnel (+ organisation) rubles	Districts rubles	Central Committee rubles	Total Expenditure rubles
Feb.-March	470	1,471	459	480	0	3,826
April-May	700	1,208	830	1,195	2,000	8,389
June	838	1,530	1,666	1,039	855	9,891
October	7,721	1,013	2,334	2,088	326	35,310
November	10,530	2,574	1,062	2,882	1,290	27,886
December	166	1,422	756	2,694 (420 on arms)	credit 500	15,536

Accounts published in, *1905*, Ed. M.N. Pokrovski (M.L. 1926).

Feb.-March,	pp. 110-111	October,	pp. 331-342
April-May,	pp. 148-149	November,	pp. 374-380
June,	pp. 203-204	December,	pp. 402-409

accounts for 1905 allows a fairly detailed study to be made. Up to May 1905, before the split in Moscow, one may assume that the accounts include the finance of both factions and only after May that of the Bolsheviks, though one cannot be absolutely sure of this. Martov's estimate of an average monthly income of 4,200 r. (£420) for the first six months of 1905 agrees with the figures shown on table 21[1]. The published accounts from February to December are summarised here in tabular form. In Table 21, the income is divided by size of contribution for each account: for example, in February-March, seven contributors gave less than 11 r., while five gave 101 r. or more; these five large contributors donated 2,876 r. – out of a total income of 3,826 r. On Table 22, the expenditure is shown: each account is divided to show payments on armaments, printing and presses, the maintenance of personnel, and on transfers to districts (which may include all three) and to the Central Committee.

The February-March account (Table 21) shows at first sight the important part played by a few large contributors: two of these sums, however, amounting to 975 r. probably represented grouped contributions. One of a thousand rubles ('From El'ves') is most prob-

---

[1] Martov does not divide the accounts by faction – as he does for St. Petersburg – again suggesting that finance was joint. 'Sotsialdemokratiya 1905-1907 gg.', *Obshchestvennoe dvizhenie v Rossii v nachale XX veka*, vol. III, (Spb. 1914), pp. 568-569.

ably one individual's donation. In the April-May account 7/8ths were large sums, of which about 2/7ths were joint contributions: 4,552 r. (over half) were explicitly donated 'by friends'. Other contributions came from women school teachers (22 r.), railway servants (22 r.), and the 'third element' (250 r.); 'members subscriptions' came to 316 r., though other subscriptions may be included under different headings (e.g. 'income from various establishments' – 1,537 r.).

The accounts of the Committee for June 1905 show that it had a total income of 9,891 r. (£989): 1,013 r. being brought forward (see Table 21,) and 554 r. collected in support for the Ivanovo-Voznesensk strike (not shown in the tables). The income included several very large sums, 4,000 r. from 'a friend', and one of 3,500 r. 'for arms'. It is known that there were many rich sympathisers with the Bolshevik cause, including A. M. Gorki and the son of a factory owner[1], but there is no evidence to show that they had any undue influence over the policies of the group. The other individual subscriptions amounted only to 1,378 r.

Considering the accounts only for June (Table 22), the largest outgoings were on 'organisation' including the regions (1,039 r.), 'tekhnika' (printing) (1,530 r.), the Central Committee (855 r.), armaments (838 r.), travel (477 r.[2]), and the support of the arrested (315 r.[2]). A balance of 3,184 r. was carried forward, of which 2,887 r. was intended for arms. This expenditure shows that the regions had considerable importance but that expenditure on arms was as yet relatively small.

The income for October (Table 21) shows a large increase in the number of contributors, especially in the lowest bracket. Many of the contributions were totals on collecting cards, and represent many more individuals than the numbers show. The 33 large contributions (over 100 r.) are broken into three sub-groups (101-500 r., 501-1,000 r., 1,001 —r.). The six donations over 1,000 r. represent nearly two-thirds of the income. Some of these large contributions were from rich sympathisers: two of 4,000 r. and 8,400 r. were from 'friends', others amounting to 6,888 r. were defined (unsatisfactorily) as 'general collections' and 2,295 r. came from the finance group. But the account shows as well a wide variety of social groups contributing to the Committee's funds: students, lawyers, factory workers, office workers, shopworkers, engineers, (army) officers and doctors. In October, arms expenditure was supreme

[1] Kuz'mich, p. 94.
[2] Not shown on Table 22.

and the Committee had set aside a further 9,352 r. for weapons which were unspent at the end of the month.

The November accounts (Table 21) show a falling-off in income. The proportion of large contributions was maintained (7,472 r. out of 8,911 r. 'new income'), though as much as five-sevenths of this (5,268 r.) probably represented group contributions. The named contributors still represented diverse social groups, a donation of 10 r. was received from a 'non Social-Democrat', presumably out of sympathy for the Social-Democrats' general revolutionary aims. Apart from one individual sum of 1,000 r. in this month, large individual donations did not play an important part in the finance of the Committee.

The December account (Table 21) shows a fall in the number of very large sums, only one being over 1,000 r. and this (of 2,616 r.) was a transfer (*perekhodnaya summa*) to the Soviet of Workers' Deputies. The other income consisted mainly of small contributions from individuals, and group collections. One difference from the earlier accounts is that 500 r. were donated by the Central Committee (Table 22). The outstanding item of expenditure (Table 22) in the October and November accounts was the large purchases of arms (over 18,000 r. – £1,800). By December this had fallen in total to 586 r. (420 r. in the districts).

In interpreting the accounts one must bear in mind that they may not be complete: some payments may have been excluded, and many of the entries are grouped ones. Considering the accounts as a whole, they show that the Bolsheviks had sympathisers among many groups of Moscow society. A few individuals contributed large amounts which are very important financially, more significant socially is the large number of small subscriptions and donations from 'middle class' groups. The expenditure shows that a relatively small part of the income went on maintaining functionaries. Printing was regular and absorbed a large proportion of funds: but arms, even at the beginning of 1905, were purchased and very large expenditures on weapons took place before the uprising of December. One of the most striking facts shown in the accounts is the size of them: an income equal to some £3,000 in October alone and a total income of about £10,000 in 1905.

The finances reflect the priorities and activity of the district Committees: here it is impossible to describe the activities of all of them. Before considering some of the Social-Democratic groups in the factory regions, I shall describe the Moscow Area (*okruzhnoy*) district Committee.

6. The Moscow Okruzhnoy District Committee

Social-Democratic groups in the Moscow province sprang up later than in the city; a mixed Socialist-Revolutionary/Social-Democratic group was formed in Podol'sk *uezd* in 1902. One of the first Social-Democratic groups was founded in Egor'evsk in May 1904, it not only discussed Marxist theory but also carried out propaganda in the factories. Other circles among the school pupils and intelligentsia were formed in August 1905[1]. By the beginning of 1905 many circles had been started in the factories, their work included collecting subscriptions, organising a welfare fund (*kassa*), studying political economy and the party programme, and carrying on agitation against the Japanese-Russian War[2]. Other groups existed in Pavlov, Bogorodsk, Kolomna, and Serpukhov[3].

In the summer of 1904 the Moscow Committee of the RSDLP attempted to establish contacts with these circles and late in 1904 a special district of the Moscow Committee was set up to organise the surrounding areas[4]. In August 1905, it formed itself into a separate Committee[5]. The *Okruzhnoy* (or Area) Committee[6] was to be autonomous for activities within its area and to have special responsibility for work among the peasantry but the Moscow Committee was to help it financially and with printing[7]. The *Okruzhnoy* Committee was Bolshevik controlled. But a weaker Menshevik organisation existed which was formed in January 1905. Later, probably during the autumn of 1905, the two factions joined[8].

The *Okruzhnoy* Committee carried out circle discussions, 'flying meetings' (*letuchki*), and some mass meetings. By the summer of 1905, there were Social-Democratic groups in the industrial settlements of Orekhovo-Zuevo, Bogorodsk, Egor'evsk, Kimry, Pushkin, Serpukhov, Podol'sk, Kolomna, Dmitrov, Sergiev Posad, and other places[9]. In July 1905, 100 men were active in the organisation, in-

[1] E. Popova, 'Pervye kruzhki', in *1905 v Moskovskoy gub.* (M.L. 1926), p. 30.
[2] E. Popova, 'Ot stikhiynoy k partiynoy organizatsii', in *1905...*, p. 58.
[3] 'Pervye kruzhki', pp. 30-38.
[4] 'Kratki ocherk deyatel'nosti okruzhnoy organizatsii Moskovskogo komiteta po iyul'', in *1905 v Moskovskoy gub.*, p. 169.
[5] E. Popova, 'Moskovskaya okruzhnaya organizatsiya', in *1905 v Moskovskoy gub.* (M.L. 1926), p. 158.
[6] *Okruzhnoy* is retained to avoid ambiguity with *rayonny* which is translated by district.
[7] 'Resolyutsiya o vydelenii Moskovskogo okruzhnogo komiteta v samostoyatel'nuyu edinitsu' in *1905 v Moskovskoy gub.*, p. 159.
[8] Reminiscence of Meshcheryakov in S. Polidorov (ed.), *Put' k oktyabryu* (M. 1923), pp. 179-80.
[9] *Proletary* No. 10, July 1905, S. I. Mitskevich, *Revolyutsionnaya Moskva* (M. 1940), p. 30 (for an account of Social-Democratic activity in Serpukhov, see I. Kokushkin, *Dve revolyutsii* (M.L. 1925)).

cluding all those taking part in *letuchki* or distributing leaflets, the number participating came to 500[1].

The information is too scanty to say very precisely how the Social-Democratic groups were organised or how strong they were in the *Okruzhnoy* organisation. A member of the factory circle at the Russian-French works in Pavlovsk recalls that at the beginning of 1905 there were 14-16 members of the party[2]. According to one of the *Okruzhnoy* organisers, by the autumn of 1905 the Serpukhov group 'had links with nearly all the factories'[3]. Other reminiscences give the impression of firm groups at many factories, having (before the summer of 1905) from six to twenty members. In Orekhovo-Zuevo, the Social-Democrats, it is claimed, were 500 strong at the beginning of 1906: the committee at this time being composed of two Mensheviks and nine Bolsheviks[4].

Moscow province contained many landless peasants: in Dmitrovsk *uezd* in 1900 31.6% of peasant families had abandoned their plots and became free labour, carrying out handicraft work or working in Moscow factories[5]. This linked the villages very closely with the towns and had important political repercussions. Factory inspectors, reporting on the causes of the January 1905 strikes, pointed out that 'the majority of the Moscow factory workers have preserved their links with the villages and, from their meagre earnings, they send home what they call 'the village drag' (*derevnya tyanet*) for their needs[6]. Such provision of material means would probably have given the town worker a high status in the village community.

The *Okruzhnoy* Committee set up a special section to extend its work in the villages. A report of one of its organisers recognised the importance of peasant support in general and that of the 'proletarianised' elements of the peasants in particular. To have the greatest influence on the peasant masses, he recommended that agitation be based on questions near to them – on 'the size of land holdings, conditions of work in the factories and the handicraft trades, and on the powers of the landlords and so on'. He recommended that agitation should be carried out at the village meetings; discussion circles should be organised, and money should be collected for the

[1] 'Kratki ocherk deyatel'nosti...', p. 171.
[2] Reminiscence of Zharov, in *Put' k oktyabryu* (M. 1923), p. 192.
[3] S. Polidorov, *Put' k oktyabryu* (M. 1923), p. 73.
[4] Kvasman (reminiscence), in *Put' k oktyabryu* (M. 1923), p. 117.
[5] 'O kharakternykh chertakh dvizheniya v Moskovskoy gub.', *1905 v Moskovskoy gub.* (M.L. 1926), p. 101.
[6] 'Doklad fabrichnykh inspektorov Moskovskoy gub. ...', in V. V. Simonenko and G. D. Kostomarov, *Iz istorii revolyutsii 1905 g. v. Moskve* (M. 1931), p. 182.

party. Mass meetings and demonstrations against the autocracy should be called[1]. How far rural elements were susceptible to Social-Democratic propaganda is difficult to measure. But it is possible that many had turned away from a 'peasant way of life' and had some respect and sympathy for, if not very much commitment to, the Social-Democrats. Whilst direct efforts by Social-Democratic organisers were important for spreading Social-Democratic ideas, the indirect influence of the factory worker taking proclamations and 'the message' home with him, probably is more significant[2]. A police report states that in nearly all of the villages in the Mozhayski *uezd*, peasants working in the Moscow factories distributed revolutionary proclamations during the Easter holidays[3].

Many of these Social-Democratic leaflets were skilfully composed and showed acute awareness of the peasant and his problems. Written in the first person plural they played on the land hunger of most peasants and pointed out that the best land was in the hands of the landlords and Tsar. The peasants were called upon to create a 'people's society, a democratic republic' which would 'give freedom to all – freedom of assembly, speech, writing, the freedom to strike and to form unions, the freedom to travel without passports'. In order that the Constituent Assembly know the will of the people, the peasantry was called upon to form 'peasant committees'. However, it was necessary that these be under the RSDLP in order 'to find out from the Social-Democrats about everything that is going on in Russia, about what the Tsar, the government, the gentry, the workers in the towns, peasants in other provinces, and the soldiers are doing'. The peasants were called upon to go into a 'brotherly union' with the party of the working people, the RSDLP[4]. Another leaflet pointed out that 'the Tsar and his ministers say that it is impossible for the peasantry to get their land free, it must be bought through the state bank'; the Social-Democrats it continued rejected these policies, their slogans were, 'All land to the peasantry!' 'Land committees in the localities!' 'Long live the Constituent Assembly!'[5]

[1] 'K voprosu ob organizatsii derevenskikh komitetov', in *1905 v Moskovskoy gub.* (M.L. 1926), pp. 173-5.
[2] E. Morokhovets, 'Krest'yanskoe dvizhenie *1905-07 gg. i sotsial-demokratiya*', in P.R. no. 4 39 (1925), pp. 60-61.
[3] Cited in Popova, p. 104. See also S. I. Mitskevich, *Revolyutsionnaya Moskva* (M. 1940), p. 380. Of course, neither propagandists nor their literature were exclusively Social-Democratic.
[4] Proclamation – 'Kak otobrat' zemlyu u pomeshchikov i udelov', (signed) Okruzhnaya organizatsiya MK, Sep. 1904, in *Iz istorii revolyutsii 1905 g. v Moskve i Moskovskoy gub.* (*Materialy i dokumenty*), eds. V. V. Simonenko and G. D. Kostomarov (M. 1931), pp. 47-51.
[5] 'Krest'yane, trebuyte vsey zemli i zemel'nykh komitetov!', *ibid.*, pp. 51-52.

The success of the Social-Democrats in terms of membership and influence is difficult to gauge. The chief forms of activity by individual Social-Democrats among the peasants were spreading the word orally, sometimes at open air meetings but usually in the village pub or teashop, and the distribution of leaflets and proclamations[1]. As has been pointed out, membership in the countryside was small, but influence may have been greater[2]. Shestakov says that the Social-Democratic circles in the villages had some influence on the village or *volost'* meetings of the peasants, where they sometimes had their resolutions carried[3].

7. Factory Circles

While Social-Democratic attempts to influence the semi-proletariat in the villages in Moscow province had modest results, one must consider what support they had in the towns. Obviously, one must distinguish between different strata of workers. The general regional characteristics of the Russian working class – the more highly skilled western provinces and St. Petersburg, the concentration of handicraftsmen and modern heavy industry in the south – are relatively well-known. Much less is known about the structure of the working class in particular factories and the way trade or industry influenced allegiance to Social-Democracy. Ideally, one would like detailed breakdowns of the composition of the working class and its membership of the different political groups. The existing sources do not permit this: in the area studies I can only indicate the factories in which the Social-Democrats had support.

On Moscow, the best source available is a work on the *Trekhgorny* textile mill[4]. This shows that statements about 'the very high rate of labour turnover'[5] which would tend to work against, but not prevent, the formation of strong social-political bonds based on place of work, are rather misleading. An examination of the pay records of 7,812 workers shows that 27.66% were on the books for five years or more (1905/06 compared with 1900/01), and that they were dis-

---

[1] S. I. Mitskevich, *Revolyutsionnaya Moskva*, p. 380.
[2] This sometimes had unexpected results. In one village in Moscow province a police report records that two Social-Democratic propagandists collected a crowd of about a hundred young men who persuaded the agitators to go to the local priest's house to ask him to preach a sermon on the struggle for freedom ('Protokol doznaniya o revolyutsionnom dvizhenii sredi krest'yan', in V. V. Simonenko and G. D. Kostomarov, *Iz istorii...*, pp. 268-71).
[3] A. Shestakov, *Krest'yanskaya revolyutsiya 1905-07 gg. v Rossii* (M.L. 1926), p. 75.
[4] *Rabochie Trekhgornoy manufaktury v 1905 g.* (M. 1930), cited hereafter as *RTm*.
[5] J. Keep, *The Rise of Social Democracy in Russia* (1963), p. 5.

tributed very unevenly throughout the firm; of the shops with a high proportion of skilled workers (*gravery, rezchiki, naboyshchiki* and *raklisty*), two-thirds were five-year men, among the workers of the 'mechanical shops' the proportion fell to one-third, among the unskilled of the cotton shop, less than a fifth had more than four years continuous service[1].

The social composition, too, shows very marked differences when separate workshops are considered. Of 7,136 workers (based on pay accounts, a few hundred short-service workers being excluded) the majority belonged to the peasant estate – 93.65%; 5.6% to the townsmen; and to other estates (gentry and clergy), 0.63%[2]. In certain shops different social strata were concentrated: in the shops with the most skilled workers a large proportion were *meshchane*, – in the *sittsepechatnoe*, 41.08%; in the *reznoe*, 31.58%; in the *gravernoe*, 25%. The correlation coefficient between the numbers of townsmen and the numbers of workers with five years or more continuous service is +.924. There can be no doubt that the better qualified workmen and those with continuous service at this factory came from an earlier generation of townsmen. Semenov writing of the St. Petersburg metal workers confirms that those of peasant origin were mainly unskilled workers[3]. This does not preclude, of course, some others falling socially to the lowest occupational levels. One quarter of the total number of *meshchane* (i.e. 105) were working in the weaving shop, and about 20% worked in the *sittsevoe*.[4] Most of these were women (we have no sex breakdowns here), probably members of large families who had seen better days and were unable to perform more skilled factory work because of occupational barriers based on sex. The influence of these women on their fellow workers may have been politically decisive, and such declassé women may account for many of the women who took up the revolutionary cause. I shall touch upon this again, but the detailed study of women in the Social-Democratic movement awaits an investigator.

We must now consider to what extent the majority of 'peasant estate' workers were connected with the land. Obviously, the 'peasant' passport entry is misleading concerning their present social

---

[1] *RTm*, p. 12. In St. Petersburg, in 1906, 8.8% of the workers in one factory had ten or more years continuous service: A. I. Davidenko, 'K voprosu o chislennosti i sostave proletariata Peterburga v nachale xx veka', *Istoriya rabochego klassa Leningrada*, vol. II (L. 1963), p. 104.
[2] At the *Baltiyski zavod* in St. Petersburg in 1901 the comparative figures were: 80.6%; 16.7%; and 2.7%. A. I. Davidenko, *ibid*.
[3] F. Semenov, 'Metallisty v revolyutsii 1905-07 gg.', *Proletariat v revolyutsii 1905-07 gg.* (M. 1930), p. 50.
[4] i.e. cotton shop.

position (neither their residence nor work was completely in the village) though it does tell us about their social origin.

Table 23 below, shows the numbers of employees absent for different months of the year from 1901/2 to 1905/6.

Table 23. *Workers Absent by Months of the Year in the Cotton Shop* (Trekhgorny Mill)

	WORKERS ABSENT			
Month	1901/2	1903/4	1904/5	1905/6
May	41	94	70	34
June	118	196	89	224
July	186	180	166	88
August	130	130	137	62
September	148	81	115	60
October	106	134	112	90
November	99	64	61	81
December	62	52	69	464
January	64	95	47	188
February	74	89	41	55
March	56	2	817	51

(Source: *RTm*, p. 14. Based on wage accounts 1901/06.)

In 1901/02 and 1903/04 there was not a mass exit, but it was much larger in summer than in the winter months, from which one may infer that the workers were returning to the village for the summer. But of the total employed in the shop (2,500) it was not a very large percentage. It may underestimate the links with the village: work contracts ran from Easter to Easter and workers might fear legal sanctions for absence; work was more busy during the summer and they may not have been re-engaged in the autumn. Thus, it was quite possible for a worker to travel home at weekends or holidays and still be a regular employee in the factory. The figures of absentees during the 1905 Revolution confirm this hypothesis: 817 left in March 1905, 464 in December 1905 and 188 in January 1906. Those leaving in fear of repression would most probably be linked to the land. One may conclude that while a proportion (say 1/5 at the most) of the Moscow factory workers had some direct contact with the villages, and the majority shifted their jobs frequently, about a quarter could be described as a settled working class. But how did this affect their political allegiance?

The Bolsheviks seem to have been successful in making contact with groups of factory workers; in the Rogozh district, for example, there were links with twenty-five factories, and six factory committees had been formed[1]. At the end of the summer of 1905, the Bolsheviks in Moscow claimed forty factory cells[2]. A local organiser wrote that the workers were 'heterogeneous' (*raznorodny*) and therefore not class-conscious. The textile workers had 'patriarchial' attitudes, the metal workers were the most sympathetic but lost in the masses of other workers[3]. In some factories, such as *Guzhon*, Social-Democratic circles existed but were cut off from the party leadership, partly due to the arrest of their leaders[4]. At others, fairly regular lectures and discussions were organised by the Social-Democrats[5]. At the Trekhgorny mill, the Socialist-Revolutionaries had members from 1903, and one of them (I. M. Kuklev) was a delegate to the Moscow Soviet in 1905. The Social-Democrats had their supporters (fewer in number) among the more skilled workers – the *raklisty* and *gravery*. G. A. Kaleev was a *raklist* elected to the Soviet and he, like many other Social-Democrats at *Trekhgorny*, was Menshevik[6].

At the early stages of the formation of the political factions their adherents had hazy ideas about policies: 'We were workers, not theoreticians and simple *praktiki-revolyutsionery*. If we were told that a strike was useful, that it would improve the lot of the working class, then we agreed with it. There was no difference who said it – Socialist-Revolutionaries or Social-Democrats.'[7] Morozov had been a Social-Democrat then became a Socialist-Revolutionary[8]. V.I. Ivanov, a *graver*, recalls that he had not heard of the differences between Mensheviks and Bolsheviks up to 1905, he had only heard of Social-Democracy[9]. The rank and file membership of the revolutionary groups might for many purposes be regarded as one group, the members having 'revolution' as the common goal and showing little awareness of the details of policies. Those who subsequently

---

[1] *Proletari*, No. 21, Oct. 1905.

[2] *Proletari*, No. 22, Oct. 1905.

[3] *Revolyutsiya 1905-07 gg. v Rossii (Apr.-Sep.* 1905), Pt. I, p. 368.

[4] P. D. Puchkov, 'Vospominaniya', in *Rabochie Serp i Molot (b. Guzhon) (Sbornik)* (M. 1931), pp. 179-80.

[5] In the Butyrsk district it is claimed that as many as 150 men attended lectures. *Bor'ba*, No. 8, Dec. 1905.

[6] See his autobiography, *RTm.*, pp. 132-142, and that of a fellow Menshevik, S. G. Mazur, pp. 181-186, P. A. Garvi's memoirs also bear this out, *Vospominaniya sotsialdemokrata* (N.Y. 1946), pp. 597, 599.

[7] V. S. Morozov, 'Avtobiografiya', *RTm.*, p. 69.

[8] *Ibid.*, pp. 70-71.

[9] 'Avtobiografiya', in *RTm.*, p. 89.

claimed to be members of the Social-Democrats would probably have had only a vague political affinity and many in Moscow were more accurately Social-Democrat/Socialist-Revolutionary in ideology. A local articulate worker or orator, or the existence of a revolutionary circle, might recruit members regardless of his own factional association. In this way existing groups might reinforce themselves, having something of a snowball effect. As Benney, Gray and Pear have pointed out for quite another context: 'Families and groups of friends who agreed politically enjoyed the sense of sharing a common cause and helped to reinforce each other's convictions'[1].

In so far as there was a conscious choice of party, the Social-Democrats tended to be supported by the more skilled workers, the Socialist-Revolutionaries by the less skilled. But apathy was probably the most common of political attitudes. One worker in the *sittsevoe* has recalled: 'I read no books or papers as I was illiterate. I was not interested in world affairs. I sometimes listened when they read the Bible, but as to the revolutionary leaflets and proclamations, I did not hear (them). During the fighting in 1905 I sat in my room... I neither saw the barricades nor heard the gun-fire or about the arrests'[2]. At the Trekhgorny, as elsewhere, many of the workers were under the spell of 'monarchism, tradition and religion'[3].

The reverence for the Tsar led many Bolshevik agitators to fear speaking of him in derogatory terms. Vasil'ev Yuzhin, one of the Bolshevik leaders in Moscow in 1905, says that agitators often were beaten for crying, 'Down with the Tsar'[4]! Another worker in the *Guzhon* factory says that the shooting of the Gapon petitioners in St. Petersburg in January 1905 cleared away all doubts that he had of the good intentions of the Tsar; but many workers, of course, still regarded him as their protector[5].

The workers' clubs, which I have described for St. Petersburg, were to attract workers of the latter category to the party. Though the Bolshevik newspapers for Moscow do not mention much about the formation of such clubs, a few had been started, as at Butyrsk in November[6] and in Sokolniki[7]. In Moscow, the Bolsheviks put more

[1] M. Benney et al, *How People Vote*, (1956), p. 184.
[2] P. V. Lukachev, *RTm*., p. 22.
[3] O. Chaadaeva, 'Rabochie Trekhgornoy manufaktury v revolyutsii 1905 g.', *Rabochie Trekhgornoy manufaktury v 1905 g.*, (*RTm*). (M. 1930), p. 31.
[4] M. Vasil'ev Yuzhin, 'Iz vospominaniy o Moskovskom vostanii 1905 g.', PR No. 5 (1922), p. 185.
[5] 'Vospominaniya F. S. Andreeva', *Serp i Molot* (*b. Guzhon*) (M. 1931), pp. 65-6.
[6] *Bor'ba*, No. 6, Dec. 1905.
[7] *Vpered* (Moscow), No. 2, Dec. 1905.

effort into organising fighting units, and into preparations for an uprising. Many of the Moscow workers who had previously been apathetic were probably swept into revolutionary activity. This would confirm the general proposition that political conformity and interest in politics are *not* related and, that when participation in politics by the politically apathetic takes place, it follows the lines of those involved[1].

An examination of the background of twenty-one *Trekhgorny* workers who took part in the 1905 Revolution shows that only three were women. Not surprisingly the average age was low, nearly half were under 25[2]. Just over half of the fathers of these revolutionaries were also factory workers: seven were permanent factory workers, three part-time factory workers, one was a railway signalman, another a landless soldier, the remaining nine were peasants living in the village. Though first generation working class, the majority of these activists had been born in the village and lived there as children, many of their fathers living or moving later with them to the town: only four of this sample were born in a town.

On the basis of the *Trekhgorny* study one may conclude that the Mensheviks tended to recruit supporters from the more settled and skilled workers, many being the second or third generation of 'townsmen'. This is not only true of the *Trekhgorny*, but is also the case with the political allegiance of printers who were among the staunchest Moscow Mensheviks. At *Trekhgorny*, the newcomers to town life were Socialist-Revolutionaries. The Bolsheviks, no doubt, also had some supporters among both these strata. It is tempting to conclude that many of the less settled and partly-skilled workers, born in the village, having lived in the town for most of their lives, provided the membership of the Bolshevik cells at their lowest levels. One can only tentatively infer this from the materials so far examined, but the hypothesis would fit with other studies of the anomic state of individuals having moved rapidly from rural society to the diffuse and differentiated urban way life. To such men the vision of a socialist society and revolutionary action may have had greater appeal. But, of course, I do not suggest that the Bolsheviks were the only groups with revolutionary aims in 1905, though in Moscow they were among the most militant.

---

[1] Benney et al, p. 185.
[2] Age in 1905; 35-39: 3; 30-34: 2; 25-29: 5; 20-24: 8; 15-19: 2; not known: 1; total: 21.

8. Social-Democratic Activity: Summer 1905

We have seen that in 1904 and at the beginning of 1905, the Social-Democrats in Moscow were comparatively weak in numbers and were not very active. From the spring of 1905 this began to change. On the eve of May Day the troops in Moscow were put on alert. On May Day, mass meetings were held at which revolutionary agitators harangued the crowds, which often dispersed singing revolutionary songs[1]. The period from May to September was one of relative calm: strikes occurred at some factories but there was no general strike as in other places.

At the June conference of Moscow Bolshevik party workers, attended by 80 delegates, it was decided to organise a general strike and to go over to an armed revolt[2]. From then on money was collected to buy weapons and to train small detachments of armed workers[3]. They called for an 'armed struggle' with the Tsarist government[4]. Later in the summer it was resolved to carry out propaganda for a general strike and to bring out the workers on strike wherever possible[5]. We cannot know exactly the mood of the Moscow population in the summer of 1905. It was not a compact political group. Keep has pointed out that, 'as late as July 1905 workers at one large textile mill had refused to listen to agitators advocating an eight-hour day, let alone hear their political views...'[6] On the other hand, an organiser, writing in *Proletari*, reported that even the men with little Social-Democratic 'consciousness' at mass meetings had said: 'You talk about the necessity for an armed uprising and about a provisional revolutionary government. We are agreed on this, it cannot be otherwise! But give us arms, organise us'![7]

In October, Bolshevik propaganda called for an insurrection: 'With weapons in our hands we shall conquer, with weapons we shall gain a democratic republic, the eight-hour working day, a human life, freedom for our future struggle for socialism... Arm yourselves, comrades! In the factories and mills, organise armed detachments! Arm every person with weapons...'![8] Though it is impossible to know precisely how 'typical' these conflicting attitudes

[1] *Proletari*, No. 3, May 1905.
[2] *Istoriya Moskvy*, Vol. V (M. 1955), p. 125.
[3] R. M. Slusser, *The Moscow Soviet of Workers' Deputies of 1905* (Ph. D. Columbia, 1963), p. 17.
[4] *Revolyutsiya 1905-07 gg. v Rossii Apr.-Sep. 1905*, Pt. 1 (M. 1957), p. 337.
[5] *Revolyutsiya 1905-07 gg. v Rossii...*, Pt. I, p. 371.
[6] J. Keep, *The Rise of Social-Democracy in Russia* (1963), p. 218.
[7] *Proletari*, No. 22, Oct. 1905.
[8] *Listovki...* (M. 1955), pp. 325-6.

were among the Moscow working class, a detailed analysis of the slogans of the Social-Democrats enables one to say what was emphasised in their propaganda. As no Menshevik materials are available for Moscow, I am not able to repeat the St. Petersburg Menshevik/ Bolshevik comparison of slogans. It is only possible to show the emphasis of the Moscow Bolsheviks' propaganda. In Table 24 are analysed, in the same way as previously (see Table 17, p. 82), 131 leaflets covering the months from January to December 1905[1].

As would be expected, the main differences compared with the leaflets of the St. Petersburg Bolsheviks was the greater emphasis on calls for strike and uprising (I opposite). Another difference was the relatively higher proportion of the Moscow Bolsheviks' leaflets addressed to the troops (iv). The table shows that the emphasis in the Moscow Bolsheviks' propaganda was very similar to that of the Bolsheviks in St. Petersburg. Calls for strike action, revolution and uprising were the most important slogans (Table 17, p. 82). Opposition to the 'capitalists' was also mentioned more often in Moscow than by either Bolsheviks or Mensheviks in St. Petersburg[2].

There are two aspects to revolutionary propaganda: condemnation of the existing regime, and the advocacy of the new. The Moscow Bolsheviks' stress on the more 'positive' alternative is shown by the much larger numbers of positive symbols (254) compared to St. Petersburg (155 for both factions, see Table 17). We may fairly confidently say that the propaganda in Moscow sought to inculcate a more active attitude to political change.

The extent of revolutionary consciousness as opposed to revolutionary propaganda cannot be accurately gauged. In the summer of 1905, one can say with certainty that a sizeable minority, led by the Bolsheviks, was ready for action, by force of arms if necessary. In Moscow, unlike in St. Petersburg, the moderating influences of Mensheviks and non-party trade union groups (the *kassy* or *rabochie soyuzy*) had less effect[3].

Already in the summer a strike committee was set up which was a forerunner of the Soviet in November, but it differed in many aspects. Though we only have reminiscences to go by, the summer strike committee, in which the Union of Unions had some influence, contained a majority of 'radical intelligentsia, hostile to the Social-

---

[1] *Listovki Moskovskikh bol'shevikov v period pervoy russkoy revolyutsii* (M. 1955), *passim.*

[2] 10.5% in Moscow, compared to 1.6-2.6% in St. Petersburg, *ibid.*

[3] The attitudes and activities of the Socialist-Revolutionaries were probably an important determinant, possibly they were stronger in Moscow than in St. Petersburg. This aspect needs further research.

Table 24. Content Analysis of Slogans of Moscow Bolsheviks 1905

I. *Positive symbols* (occurring more than 5 times)

	N.	%
(long live)	(254)	–
strike (general strike)	29	25.4
struggle	22	19.3
revolution (revolutionary provisional government)	23	20.2
uprising	22	19.3
arms (armaments)	18	15.8
	114	100

II. *Objectives*

	N.	%
Constituent Assembly	40	22.3
democratic republic	47	26.1
socialism (Social-Democracy)	46	25.6
freedom	24	13.3
specific freedoms	15 (62)*	8.3
people's government	8	4.4
	180	100

III. *Enemies of the party* (mentioned more than five times)

	N.	%
(down with)	75	–
autocracy	54	62.8
Tsar (ism)	16	18.6
capitalist	9	10.5
war	7	8.1
	86	100

IV. *Addressees*

	N.	%
comrades	70	45.7
workers	52	34.0
soldiers	20	13.1
citizens	9	5.9
(peasants)	2	1.3
	153	100

Total numbers of leaflets: 131

Listovki Moskovskikh bol'shevikov v period pervoy russkoy revolyutsii (M. 1955).

* 15 groups – freedom of speech, press, etc. – 62 mentions.

Democrats, and especially to the Bolsheviks'[1]. It is quite inaccurate to say, as suggested by Trotsky[2], that the Soviet developed out of this body, which was opposed by both Mensheviks and Bolsheviks: indeed, the Soviet was formed to combat its influence[3].

In September 1905, the Moscow Bolsheviks called all workers to strike: 'Organise yourselves, comrades, unite into a closely-linked and firm brotherly organisation, not only under the cover of the legal trade unions, but...under the red flag of the RSDLP (join) in the life and death struggle for the bright future of the workers of all the world – for a socialist order, under which there will be neither poor nor rich, neither employers nor employed'[4].

On 19 September a printers' strike began, which by the 24th encompassed most of the printing industry and had spread to other industries. It had been called by the Menshevik 'Moscow Union of Typographical Workers for the Improvement of the Conditions of Labour'[5]. On 25 September a printers' soviet was formed of 264 deputies from 110 printing establishments[6], each representing (officially) 20 workers.

The printers' strike was followed by other trades and became a Moscow general strike on 27-28 September. Economic demands were paramount during these strikes[7].

9. The Moscow Soviet

On 2 October a meeting of representatives from five groups (printers, carpenters, metal-workers, tobacco-workers and railwaymen) decided to appeal to all Moscow workers to form a general Soviet of Workers' Deputies[8]. According to Vasil'ev Yuzhin (a Bolshevik)

[1] M. I. Vasil'ev Yuzhin, *Moskovski sovet rabochikh deputatov v 1905 g.* (M. 1925), p. 12.
[2] L. Trotsky, *1905*, 3rd ed. (M. 1925), p. 120 n.
[3] M. Vasil'ev Yuzhin, 'Moskovski sovet rabochikh deputatov v 1905 g. ...', in P.R., No. 4 (39) (1925), p. 94.
[4] *Listovki Moskovskikh bol'shevikov v period pervoy russkoy revolyutsii* (M. 1955), p. 255.
[5] In July 1905 it formally became part of the RSDLP joining the Menshevik 'Group'. (P. A. Garvi, *Vospominaniya sotsial-demokrata* (N.Y. 1946), p. 539).
[6] V. V. Sher, 'Moskovskie pechatniki v revolyutsii 1905 g.' in A. Borshchevsky et al, *Moskovskie pechatniki v 1905 g.* (M. 1925), p. 53, cited by Keep, p. 220.
[7] See, for example, the twenty-three points for improvement of pay, working hours and conditions by the *Gustav List* factory workers and the fifteen demands by V. Ya. Gonner's strikers, in *Revolyutsiya 1905-07 gg. v Rossii: (Vse. Pol. Stachka v Okt.)*, Part I, pp. 65-66.
[8] Whether this body was under Menshevik or Bolshevik control is a matter of controversy. See R. M. Slusser, 'The Forged Bolshevik Signature: A Problem of Soviet Historiography', in *Slavic Review*, vol. XXIII, no. 2, (June 1964), p. 303.

this was to bring groups of non-party workers under party control[1]. Before 1905 the management had often met representatives of the workers who had sometimes been called 'deputies' and who had stated the workers' grievances[2]. The trade unions, at least in the textile factories grew out of the *institut* of factory deputies which carried out discussions with the management as well as leading strikes[3]. These deputies in all probability were non-party, though they may have had some Social-Democrats or Social-Democratic supporters among them. Given the Mensheviks' greater interest in these non-party elements, it is most likely that they would have tried to organise them into town soviets. But the political origins of the Soviet in Moscow are a matter of controversy, all the details of which need not occupy one here. The Mensheviks were probably responsible for initially calling the Soviet, though this does not mean that the Bolsheviks were hostile to it. Their attitude at first was not to give such bodies very much priority[4]. It is also probably true, as Slusser has suggested elsewhere, that during its early days the Soviet was largely under Menshevik influence[5]. Later, however, there can be no doubt, as I shall show below, that its policies were determined by the Bolsheviks.

There is disagreement between various sources on the numbers attending the first meeting of the Soviet on 21 November. The most detailed source claims that 145 representatives from 72 factories and political parties attended. They were elected from eight districts in two stages – one representative being elected by 50 workers and one delegate to the Soviet being elected by each ten workers' representatives[6]. Later at the end of November, from 134 factories were directly elected 204 deputies, representing about 100,000 workers[7]. To the executive committee were elected two representatives with full voting rights from each of the political parties – Bolsheviks,

---

[1] M. Vasil'ev Yuzhin, Moskovsky sovet rabochikh deputatov v 1905 g.', P. R. no. 4 (39) (1925), p. 96.

[2] 'Doklad fabrichnykh inspektorov Moskovskoy gub. ...' in V. V. Simonenko i Kostomarov, *Iz istorii revolyutsii 1905 g. Moskovskoy gubernii* (M. 1931), p. 184.

[3] S. Spektor, *Moskovskie tekstil'shchiki v gody pervoy revolyutsii (1905-07 gg.)* (1929), pp. 3, 70.

[4] See R. M. Slusser, 'The Forged Bolshevik Signature: A Problem in Soviet Historiography', in *Slavic Review*, vol. XXIII, no. 2 (June 1964), pp. 294-308; V. A. Kondrat'ev, 'Iz istorii izdaniya dokumentov o deyatel'nosti sovetov rabochikh deputatov 1905 g.', in M. N. Tikhomerov (ed.), *Arkheograficheski ezhegodnik za 1957 g.* (M. 1958), pp. 189-209.

[5] R. M. Slusser, *The Moscow Soviet of Workers Deputies*, pp. 1, 94-5.

[6] *Materialy po professional'nomu dvizheniyu rabochikh* (Vyp. 1, M. 1906), p. 45, cited by V. A. Kondrat'ev, 'Iz istorii izdaniya dokumentov o deyatel'nosti sovetov rabochikh deputatov 1905 g.' in *Arkheograficheski ezhegodnik za 1957 g.*, p. 194. See also Vasil'ev-Yuzhin, *Moskovski sovet rabochikh deputatov v 1905 g.* (M. 1925), p. 33.

[7] *Izvestiya Moskovskogo soveta rabochikh deputatov*, No. 1, Dec. 1905.

Mensheviks and Socialist-Revolutionaries – and eight district representatives, who have also been claimed as Social-Democrats[1]. According to Vasil'ev-Yuzhin, there was no permanent chairman, the governing body was a Presidium to which the six party representatives alone belonged[2]. The majority of the delegates considered themselves to be 'non-party'. Vasil'ev-Yuzhin recalls that the Socialist-Revolutionaries had few representatives and the leadership of the Soviet was in Bolshevik hands[3]. A Bolshevik, for example, was elected to accompany the delegate of the St. Petersburg Soviet to other towns. On the other hand, the chairman of the Soviet, according to Garvi, was the Menshevik printing worker, N. Chistov[4]. At the second meeting on 27 November, it was resolved that members of the Soviet be elected on the basis of one deputy for every 500 men at large factories, workers in small factories were to form electoral colleges, one elector representing every 50 men – ten of whom were to elect one deputy, trade unions with more than 500 members were to have one representative, those with less than 500 were to be considered specially[5]. The Bolsheviks were suspicious of Menshevik influence in the unions, and this method of representation probably reduced their influence.

While the Mensheviks may have had supporters in the Soviet and had representatives at its apex, this does not mean that they had much say on policy. It is true, as Slusser has pointed out, that little mention is made in Bolshevik sources of the Menshevik chairman, but it is doubtful if he had much influence on policy *per se*. In the first place, there were many administrative organs: the plenum of the Soviet, its executive committee (elected from the district Soviets and two representatives each from the Bolsheviks, Mensheviks and the Socialist-Revolutionaries), the information bureau (including the representatives of the Bolsheviks, Mensheviks and Socialist-Revolutionaries), the federative council (Social-Democratic factions only), and finally, the party committees themselves[6]. There can be no doubt that the decisive forces in the Soviet were the Social-Democrats, and of the two factions the Bolsheviks were supreme. In the party federative council[7], Yuzhin recalls that by presenting a united front,

[1] Maksakov, 'V dekabr'skie dni', in *Dekabr'skoe vosstanie v Moskve 1905 g.* (M. 1919), p. 217.

[2] Vasil'ev-Yuzhin, *Moskovski sovet rabochikh deputatov v 1905 g.* (M. 1925), p. 35.

[3] Vasil'ev-Yuzhin, p. 35.

[4] P. A. Garvi, *Vospominaniya sotsialdemokrata*, p. 605.

[5] *Bor'ba*. No. 5, Dec. 1905.

[6] Garvi, p. 606.

[7] Composed of Shanster and Vasil'ev-Yuzhin for the Bolsheviks, and Isuf and Zaretskaya (later replaced by Isakovich) for the Mensheviks (Vasil'ev-Yuzhin, *Moskovski sovet...* (M. 1925), p. 20.

the Bolsheviks usually managed to get their way[1]. There is general agreement that the Bolsheviks were in control here[2]. In the second place, and probably more important, was the regional structure of the Moscow Soviet. In the Khamovnichesko-Presnya district, Garvi says that the regional Soviet was strong, elected from the bottom to the top: it considered all aspects of workers' activity[3]. During the uprising, which will be considered next, the regional Soviets were '...the leaders of activity in their disticts'[4], thereby reducing the importance of the all-city Soviet.

The significance of the district Soviets, it has been argued, was to make the Moscow Soviet less responsive to pressure from below and more amenable to external (Bolshevik) control than was the case in St. Petersburg[5]. On the other hand, one could argue that the more centralised an organisation, the greater the opportunities for a Bolshevik-type organisation to seize control. It is doubtful whether either of these interpretations had much relevance to the situation. More important was the existence in St. Petersburg of relatively strong non-party groups and weak Bolshevik support, whereas in Moscow the non-party groups were weakly organised and the Bolsheviks were strong.

10. The Moscow Uprising

The greatest political difference between Moscow and St. Petersburg was the armed uprising which took place in Moscow in December 1905. It would not be surprising if the greater strength of the Bolsheviks there may account for it. As is generally known, the Bolsheviks at the Third Party Congress (May 1905) had decided to prepare propaganda and to agitate for an uprising, to form fighting groups and to work out a general plan for revolt[6]. As I have shown, Bolshevik propaganda in Moscow in the summer already contained phrases inciting uprising. Though the Mensheviks were not 'counter-revolutionary'[7], as some have argued, their emphasis lay in widening the party, forming a widely-based Soviet and in leaving more revo-

---

[1] Vasil'ev-Yuzhin, p. 21.
[2] Keep, p. 244.
[3] Garvi, p. 602.
[4] Maksakov, p. 225.
[5] Keep, p. 245.
[6] O. Anweiler, Die Rätebewegung in Russland 1905-1921 (Leiden, 1958), p. 91.
[7] Keep, p. 249.

lutionary activity to the bourgeoisie, whereas the stress of the Bolsheviks lay in fomenting armed action.

The initiative for the local uprising in Moscow came from the local party leadership, which was not unanimous about calling it. Whether Lenin was aware of the decision before or immediately after it had been taken is not known[1]. Probably he was not. On the 4 December, after discussing the matter with I. A. Sammer who had brought the news of the arrest of the St. Petersburg Soviet, the Moscow Bolsheviks proposed to call a general strike and uprising. A Moscow Conference of party workers was called for 5 December. At the 400-strong Bolshevik all-Moscow conference, Novov has recalled that the workers' representatives were enthusiastically for the uprising, and it was said that the workers would come out themselves even if the Committee did not advise it. The troops, it was thought, would not fire on the people[2]. Despite a gloomy forecast by the leader of the workers' militia[3], when it was put to the vote not one of the delegates voted against the strike or the decision to turn it into an uprising[4].

The Mensheviks, on the other hand, were more restrained. Though there is no doubt that they endorsed the general strike, they 'were categorically opposed to calling a simultaneous uprising'[5]. Keep has argued that the only difference between the Mensheviks and Bolsheviks on the issue of the armed uprising was a 'semantic one'[6]. He does point out, however, that the Mensheviks felt 'an overt summons...was likely to misfire. They recommended calling for 'a general political strike which should transform itself into an armed uprising'.'[7] But there is a great difference between letting a general strike 'transform' into an uprising and calling explicitly for an uprising. The decision to call an armed uprising in itself is one of the most crucial in revolutionary strategy, and though the Bolsheviks in the federative council of the Soviet agreed to the wording above, they clearly intended to start an uprising simultaneously. The Mensheviks were hesitant rather than counter-revolutionary and later, on 7 December, endorsed the call not only for the general

[1] Yuzhin, *Moskovski sovet...* (M. 1925), p. 72.

[2] N. Novov, 'Pyaty god', in *Dekabr'skoe vosstanie v Moskve 1905 g.* (M. 1919), p. 18. See also Vasil'ev-Yuzhin, *Moskovski sovet rabochikh deputatov v 1905 g.* (M. 1925), p. 80.

[3] Mitskevich, *Revolyutsionnaya Moskva*, p. 446.

[4] Mitskevich, p. 447.

[5] P. A. Garvi, *Vospominaniya sotsialdemokrata*, p. 609.

[6] Keep, p. 249.

[7] *Ibid.*, p. 249.

strike, but for the armed uprising as well[1]. Later in December the Mensheviks published at least one leaflet endorsing the Moscow armed uprising, believing that it heralded an all-Russian insurrection[2]. At the meeting of the Soviet on 6 December, the strike and uprising were (according to Vasil'ev-Yuzhin) enthusiastically backed by Bolsheviks, Mensheviks and Socialist-Revolutionaries[3].

Whether the decision to call an uprising was a good or bad thing does not concern us here, and neither does the detailed history of the course of the revolution. A brief summary will suffice. A general strike was called for midday 7 December[4]. By 10 December, the strike was general and barricades were set up, 'partisan' methods of combat were put into operation, detachments of two-three men were formed who opened fire from the rooftops[5]. The insurgents held parts of the Presnya district from 11 to 17 December and controlled the main railway lines until the revolt was put down by loyal troops sent from St. Petersburg. Many Muscovites found themselves swept up by the revolutionary events and it is probable that the insurgents had a great deal of sympathy, even if the active participants were not more than a few thousand[6].

The social background of persons arrested by the police during the December uprising gives some indication of the social groups which took part (see Table 25)[7]. Obviously, one must approach the data with caution: the criteria for arrest by the police were very wide – among the arrested were some not directly involved in the revolt. I have constructed Table 25 from the published records of people arrested for taking part in the Moscow uprising. The table shows that just over a third (38/93) were not manual workers (or if they were, had at one time not been so). The number of doctors (eleven) is high: some of them may not have taken part in the uprising. The largest group is that of the 'peasantry' (46), though

[1] See for example, the appeal addressed to 'all workers, soldiers and citizens', endorsed by the Moscow Soviet, the Bolsheviks, Mensheviks and Socialist-Revolutionaries, in M. N. Pokrovski (ed.), *1905* (M. L. 1926), pp. 387-9.

[2] Leaflet, 'Moskovskoe vosstanie', in Pokrovski, pp. 443-5.

[3] Vasil'ev-Yuzhin, *Moskovski...* (M. 1925), p. 85.

[4] *Izvestiya Moskovskogo soveta rabochikh deputatov*, No. 1, 1905.

[5] For details see P. V. Kokhmanski, *Moskva v dekabre 1905 g.* (M. 1906).

[6] A police report says that the Moscow revolt had wide support among the workers, 'Ezhedel'-naya zapiska po departamentu politsii za period vremeni s 8 po 15 Dekabrya', in K. A. 11-12 (1925), p. 164. Another report says that 10,000 to 12,000 men took part in the uprising and that after it, in addition to the execution of 63 leaders, cossacks killed 300 men. 'Ezhedel'naya zapiska ... 15 po 22 Dekabrya', K. A. 11-12 (1925), p. 172.

[7] G. Rudé, for example, has based much of his fruitful analysis of the participants in the French Revolution on police records – see *The Crowd in the French Revolution* (1959).

Gentry	1
'Citizens' (*Grazhdane*) (a)	4
Teachers (b)	5
Doctors (c)	11
Nurses	3
Students	5
Priest	1
Sundry 'lower-middle class' (d)	8
Workers (e)	8
'Militiamen' (*druzhinniki*)	3
Peasants (f)	46

93[1]

[1] (Two persons having two entries each).

Notes.

a Personal 1, hereditary 3.
b 2 Female. One male also included among the peasantry.
c Including one vet. and one dentist; two doctors being women.
d Including 2 '*meshchane*', a doctor's widow, a priest's daughter, a clerk, an auditor, the son of a college assessor (*assessor*), and the son of a college secretary.
e Including one also counted among the peasantry.
f Only one being a woman, and including one village elder (*sel'ski starosta*).

'Spisok lits, arestovannykh za uchastie v dekabr'skom vooruzhennom vosstanii 1905 g. v Moskovskoy gub.', *Vysshi pod'em rev. (Noya-Dek.* 1905), Part 1 (M. 1955), pp. 809-812.

all of this group were working (or had been working) in Moscow factories.

The records of casualties also provide an indication of the social composition of the participants. The figures shown in Table 26, unfortunately, contain a very big omnibus first category. Nevertheless, the seventy or so students and 'professional' workers, together with the rather small number of those with an unknown occupation, lead one to conclude that probably the insurgents included diverse social groups of the population and that the majority were not feckless layabouts or 'toughs' as sometimes asserted by historians of revolutionary movements.

But crucial to the success or failure of an uprising is the attitude of the government's armed forces to the insurgents as well as the strength of the latter's own armed detachments. Agitators and propagandists had attempted to indoctrinate the troops before 1905, mainly by spreading illegal literature, but in Moscow a *voennaya* fighting organisation under the Moscow Committee of the RSDLP was not formed until January 1905[1]. This work was carried out by both Mensheviks and Bolsheviks, though no one can hold that the troops were very seriously affected. Even the Moscow Social-Democratic *voennaya*, one of the strongest, had only 250 men 'taking part'[2].

At most the revolutionaries had sympathisers among the garrison. Many of the troops were disaffected, mainly because of conditions of service. A 'Soldiers' Committee' of twenty men was set up on 2 December in the Rostov regiment, which drew up a list of 56 demands, some of the more important being: no discrimination against strikers, immediate transfer to the reserve of those called up in 1901-1902, free use of leisure time, freedom of assembly to discuss soldiers' needs and requirements, the abolition of searches, the abolition of the censorship of papers and journals, an end to the practice of using soldiers for police duties[3].

On 3 December a mutiny broke out among the garrison, a committee was set up to formulate their demands and a list of grievances was submitted to the commanding officer. This was quickly-crushed and by the next day the officers had the disturbance under control[4]. Though the relationship of the dissatisfied troops to the Soviet and insurgents was not hostile, it was hardly cordial. On December 3, the 'Soldiers' Committee' categorically refused to give arms to the workers' militia and it told factory representatives 'not to interfere in our affairs'[5]. Vasil'ev-Yuzhin has pointed out that support among, and connections with, the troops were weak, not only because of insufficient material means, but because the Committee had given little prominence to the land question – which would have attracted the soldiers to its side[6].

An attempt was made to form a Soviet of Soldiers' Deputies which met on 3 December. At its first and only meeting, representatives from the Ekaterinoslav, Rostov, Troitse-Sergiev and other regiments attended together with men from the two factions of the RSDLP and the Socialist-Revolutionaries[7]. A report in *Vpered* (Moscow) said,

[1] V. A. Petrov, *Ocherki po istorii revolyutsionnogo dvizhenii v Russkoy armii v 1905 g.* (M.L. 1964), p. 102.

[2] K. Rosenblyum, *Voennye organizatsii bol'shevikov 1905-07 gg.* (M.L. 1931), p. 102.

[3] B. Gavrilov, *Moskovskie bol'sheviki v bor'be za armiyu v 1905-07 gg.* (1955), p. 93. An official report into disturbances in the armed forces defining the regiments concerned and their activity is printed in K.A. No. 51 (1932), pp. 215-223, the Moscow units – p. 221.

[4] See Keep, p. 246 and *1905: armiya v pervoy revolyutsii* (M.L. 1927), pp. 127-61.

[5] B. Gavrilov, *Moskovskie bol'sheviki v bor'be za armiyu v 1905-07 gg.* (1955), pp. 97-98.

[6] Vasil'ev-Yuzhin, *Moskovski sovet...* (M. 1925), p. 46.

[7] *Vpered* (Moscow), No. 3, Dec. 1905.

Peasants, *meshchane,* workers, handicrafts-men and *sluzhashchie*	705
Students and pupils	21
Chinovniki	23
Merchants	17
Doctors	5
Barristers	2
Engineer	1
Literator	1
Deakon	1
Artist	1
Unknown occupation	11

788

Byuro Meditsinskogo Soyuza, cited by P.V.Kokhmanski, *Moskva v dekabre 1905 g.* (M. 1906), p. 190.

'From the speeches of the soldier deputies it was clear that the temper of all the regiments was rising: all were sympathetic to the revolutionary movement, they might join the people's uprising – on all accounts they would not fire on their brothers'[1]. This kind of report probably led many Moscow Social-Democrats to exaggerate the support they would get from the garrison. In the armed uprising an insignificant part of the armed forces took part, though many of the garrison were sympathetic. None joined the revolt, and only 27 sailors returned from the Far East joined a workers' detachment[2].

The fighting detachments (*boevye druzhiny*) were in a very rudimentary form in 1905. In terms of numbers, Garvi has estimated that there were not more than a thousand at the time of the uprising – from 200 to 300 in each three of the party groups[3]. Griva, a Bolshevik, confirms this rough estimate: 250 *druzhiny* were under the Moscow Bolsheviks, half of whom were well armed, the Mensheviks had 200 (of whom 150 were printers), the Socialist-Revolutionaries 150, and a non-party student group 250, in addition there were some other *druzhiny* organised by factory owners[4]. There can be no doubt

[1] *Ibid.*
[2] Gavrilov, p. 112.
[3] P. A. Garvi, *Vospominaniya sotsialdemokrata* (N.Y. 1946), p. 639.
[4] *Pervaya konferentsiya voennykh i boevykh organizatsiy RSDRP* (1906), p. 57.

that the Bolsheviks were badly organised: '...in the days of the December uprising no firm fighting organisation existed. The attempt of the Moscow armed uprising shows that our party was completely unprepared to lead a revolution. No plan of armed uprising existed'[1]. The separate detachments numbered from 15 to 50 men, who were armed mainly with revolvers, though there was a small number of bombs and explosives[2]. One should not lightly dismiss the uprising nor the havoc it caused, for with sufficient support, relatively small groups of well organised armed men can occupy a very large number of troops.

11. Summing-up

As in St. Petersburg, the Social-Democrats in Moscow were very weak in 1904, when the *Zubatovshchina* was strong. The leading role of the Social-Democrats in the uprising of 1905, therefore, is unlikely to be due purely to the *organisational* methods of the RSDLP, of which, at least in Moscow, the practice of Bolsheviks and Mensheviks was alike. The non-party workers' clubs and benevolent funds (*kassy*) were weaker in Moscow and operated solely on a workshop basis. The Shidlovski Commission in St. Petersburg promoted unification on a city basis of these more spontaneous workers' groups, thereby giving them more coherence and preparing the ground for the Soviet in the autumn. This coherence was lacking in Moscow where the political parties, and particularly the Social-Democrats, provided the organisational forms for uniting the workers. Hostility between management and men was probably greater in Moscow due to the structure of its industry. Much of the working class was linked to the villages here and this had two main sets of consequences. Firstly, many of the newer factory workers regarded the Tsar as a 'protector' and therefore tended to hold the factory management (or owners, if these aspects can be separated) responsible for their grievances. The actions of the autocracy, particularly the shooting of the St. Petersburg workers in January 1905, tended to weaken this faith and led to the identification of the autocracy with the factory owners. Secondly, the factory workers influenced some of the peasantry from whom they were recruited – we saw in the introduction to this section that a large proportion came from Moscow province – and the workers in the factory settlements outside Moscow city. Though

---

[1] Speech of Z, *Pervaya konferentsiya voennykh i boevykh organizatsiy RSDRP* (1906), p. 56.
[2] S. M. Pozner (ed.), *Boyevaya gruppa pri TsK RSDRP (b) 1905-07 gg.* (M.L. 1927), p. 152.

this did not result in a Social-Democratic *movement* in the rural areas, it helped to create a number of supporters or sympathisers. On the other hand, the clustering of many semi-proletarians in the textile mills tended to favour the Socialist-Revolutionaries. In Moscow, during the upheavals of 1905, the Bolsheviks provided the leadership for the uprising. This illustrates the way in which a relatively small group of men can quickly mushroom into quite a formidable opponent to the incumbent powers under conditions in which the wider population suffer grievances and the policies of alternative groups neither offer a solution to their problems nor provide a means to achieve their aspirations. In such cases leadership is an important factor. The Bolsheviks' main support in Moscow lay among the less skilled and underprivileged workers though they had some support among other social strata. Such workers were more homogeneous by nationality and economic condition than in many other areas of Russia. The Bolshevik Moscow leadership realised that many of these men were prepared for armed action. In this respect they probably had their finger more on the pulse of the Moscow proletariat than did their Menshevik opponents: but in this they were not unique, the Socialist-Revolutionaries also provided an impetus to revolutionary action.

chapter five

THE STRUCTURE AND ACTIVITY OF
SOCIAL-DEMOCRACY IN IVANOVO-VOZNESENSK

1. Social and Economic Background

At the beginning of the twentieth century Ivanovo-Voznesensk, with a population of fifty-four thousand, was the largest town in Vladimir province. The province itself had just over one and a half million people of whom under five thousand were not Great Russians[1]. The dominating industry of town and province was textiles which, in 1905 employed 136,831 of the 155,037 industrial workers[2]. It was one of the oldest industrial areas of Russia, having been a textile centre long before 1861[3]. It has been estimated that in 1904-05 from 26,771 to 29,667 people were employed in the Ivanovo-Voznesensk (town) textile industry[4].

The Vladimir area was, even in 1905, one of the chief, though technically less advanced, textile areas. The greater capital intensity of the Polish and St. Petersburg industries may be shown by the ratio of men employed to spindles (see Tables 27 and 28). In 1900, in Petrokov, 32,358 men were employed working 14.4% of the total number of spindles, compared to 84,256 men in Vladimir working only 18.2%. The ratio of weavers to spinners (see Table 28) was also higher in the central economic area, illustrating its greater economic backwardness.

Ivanovo, being an industrial town, had no Zemstvo servants and few administrative workers, who sometimes provided the middle

---

[1] *Vseobshchaya perepis' naseleniya 1897 g.* (*Obshchi svod*), Vol. II, pp. 20-37.

[2] *O rabochem dvizhenii i s.d. rabote vo Vladimirskoy gub. v 1900-kh godakh* (*sbornik*) (Vladimir 1925), Part II, pp. 7-8, hereafter cited as *RD Vladimir*.

[3] See, for example, 'Ekonomicheskaya karta evropeyskoy Rossii nakanune reformy 1861 g.', in K.V. Bazilevich, *Atlas istorii SSSR* (M. 1949), Part II, p. 16.

[4] A. V. Shipulina, 'Ivanovo-Voznesenskie rabochie nakanune pervoy russkoy revolyutsii. Usloviya ikh trud i byta', in *Doklady i soobsheheniya instituta istorii*, No. 8 (M. 1955), p. 50; O. A. Varentsova et al, *1905-y god v Ivanovo-Voznesenskom rayone* (Ivanovo, 1925), p. 4 – this source gives most detail and is probably the most reliable.

Table 27. Textile Spindles in Various Provinces of the Russian Empire, 1900

	% of Empire	Number
Moscow	22.8	1,295
Vladimir	18.2	1,224
Petersburg	15.0	1,074
Petrokov (Lodz')	14.4	745
Estlyand	7.0	–
Yaroslavl'	5.4	–
Tver	5.4	–

'Materialy dlya statistiki v khlopchatobumazhnoy promyshlennosti' (1901), cited by A. Pankratova, 'Tekstil'shchiki v revolyutsii 1905-07', in *Proletariat v revolyutsii 1905-1907* (M. 1930), p. 53.

Table 28. Textile Workers in Russian Empire by Area, 1900

			Total
Moscow:	spinners	27,614	
	weavers	41,639	69,253
Vladimir:	spinners	25,417	
	weavers	58,839	84,256
Petrokov:	spinners	15,784	
	weavers	16,574	32,358
Petersburg:	spinners	9,794	
	weavers	8,288	18,082

A. Pankratova, pp. 56-57.

class support of the Social-Democrats. Apart from the industrial workers, the other main social group was formed by the traders and factory owners. A number of foreign skilled workers, many of them Lancastrians, came to set up, and occasionally supervise, work in the textile mills, but no foreign firms put down roots in Ivanovo, where ownership was Russian.

The Ivanovo workers had been recruited from among the landless peasants of the nearby areas, and it is important to determine how close were their links with the land. A survey of 5,723 factory workers in Shuya *uezd* in 1899 showed that 'over half' were of (*otnositsya*) the farming peasantry: of these, 27% of the married and 41% of the single belonged to families which continued to work the land in the village. On average, 80.6% of the surveyed workers had broken off economic links (i.e. *khozyaystvennye svyazy*) with the village. According to factory inspectors' reports for 1897, only 12.5% of the men and 7.9% of the women working in the factories of Vladimir *guberniya* went to the villages in the summer[1]. This does not rule out the possibility either that during times of high employment larger numbers went to the villages, or that a higher proportion went there at holiday times. Over half of the peasant householders in Shuya *uezd* worked both on their own plots and for a wage[2]. We shall see below that in Tver, the links between the urban workers and the local peasantry were firm, but in Ivanovo this was not so. The amount of money sent by the factory worker to his home in the village is an indication of the strength of the ties. Of 5,061 workers surveyed (and excluding 662 who did not know how much they sent home), 80.1% (or 4,083) claimed that they sent nothing from their pay to their village[3].

The attitudes of these workers to the soil are important. Obviously, the more 'urban' they felt, the more likely were the Social-Democrats rather than the Socialist-Revolutionaries to influence them. The background of F. Samoylov, who later became an active Social-Democrat, is in may ways typical of the uprooted peasants forming the Ivanovo working class. He had lived in the village until 1895 when he was thirteen and then moved to the town. His parents were completely illiterate and he was only partly literate, his attendance at the village school seven *versts*[4] away had been infrequent[5]. His father had insufficient land to maintain the family and he worked as a weaver in the town. When Samoylov went there he thought 'at first that all seemed better than in the village. Although there was no cow's milk, on holidays there was white bread and despite

[1] Cited by A. V. Shipulina, 'Ivanovo-voznesenskie...', p. 48.
[2] Shipulina, p. 49.
[3] 'Materialy dlya otsenki zemel' Vlad. *gub.* – Shuya *uezd* (Vladimir 1908), pp. 100-101, cited in O. A. Varentsova et al, *1905-y god v Ivanovo-Voznesenskom rayone*, pp. 8-9.
[4] One Russian *versta* is 1.06 kl. or 0.66 miles.
[5] The factory workers in Vladimir *guberniya* were on average much better educated than the population at large: one estimate is that out of 65,815 male workers, 26,982 were literate: I. M. Koz'minykh-Lanikh, *Fabrichno-zavodski rabochi Vladimirskoy gubernii (1897 g.)* (Vladimir 1912), pp. 8-9.

the tiring factory work, urban life seemed more interesting and attractive'[1]. Later, however, he recalls that he longed for village life '...the aroma of the fields, woods and air'[2]. Economic necessity kept him in the town, though he frequently returned to the village, some twenty *versts* (21 km.) away, for holidays. His brother having reached the age of fifteen, also came to the factory when their father gave up such work to return to the village. For such a family the attitude to town was ambivalent: sentimental attachment to village life, but awareness of the opportunity and challenge of the town. One or the other may have been predominant at different times. In the village these adventurers may have had much prestige – they were better-educated, more worldly and richer[3].

Industrial discipline among the Ivanovo proletariat was poor and compared even to textile workers in other areas wages were low. The average wage for all-Russia from 1901 to 1904 was 206 rubles, while in Vladimir province it was 138.88 rubles[4]. Compared to the Polish and St. Petersburg textile workers, those in Ivanovo were worse off: the average textile worker's wage in Russia in 1900 was 180 rubles, while in Vladimir province it was 139 rubles 36 copecks[5].

For those who were employed, money wages rose slightly in Vladimir province from 1900 to 1904 – for textile workers from 139 rubles 36 copecks to 142 rubles 48 copecks, though some trades had a fall in wages[6]. At the same time prices rose: real income fell. A price index of ten basic foods rose from 100 in 1900 to 106.5 in 1903 and 105.1 in 1904[7]. Not only were wages lower in Ivanovo but the cultural level was also inferior to the textile workers in Poland, who were more literate, being recruited from handicraft workshops[8].

---

[1] F. N. Samoylov, *Vospominaniya ob Ivanovo-Voznesenskom rabochem dvizhenii*, Part I (M. 1922), p. 9.

[2] *Ibid.*, p. 9.

[3] This conclusion is supported by S. Nowakovski, writing about Poland before 1939: 'Peasants who settle in towns have the feeling of social promotion. In pre-war Poland there was an abysmal difference in living standards between town and country and the impoverished peasants, who found it very difficult to leave their over-populated villages, developed a myth of happy and easy life in town'. 'Aspects of social mobility in postwar Poland', in *Transactions of the Third World Congress of Sociology*, Vol. III (1956), p. 336.

[4] K. A. Pazhitnov, *Polozhenie rabochego klassa v Rossii* (Spb. 1906), Vol. III, p. 47; Vladimir senior factory inspector's reports for 1901-04, cited in *O rabochem dvizhenii i S.D. rabote vo Vladimirskoy gub. v 1900-kh. godakh*, Part II (Vladimir 1925), p. 18.

[5] *Ibid.*, p. 18. Cf. Table 19, p. 95.

[6] *Ibid.*, p. 19.

[7] Based on factory inspector's reports, cited in 'O rabochem dvizhenii...', p. 20.

[8] A. Pankratova, 'Tekstil'shchiki v revolyutsii 1905-07 gg.' in *Proletariat v revolyutsii 1905-07 gg.* (M. 1930), p. 72.

2. The Early History of Social-Democracy

Populist propagandists had arrived in Ivanovo in 1875, but were arrested after a few months work. These intellectuals worked in the factories as weavers and distributed books to the workers, but left no permanent groups in existence[1]. A Populist circle of about 30 was formed in 1885 which was composed mainly of intellectuals and school pupils, though some textile workers also took part. In the 1890's the circles discussed Populist literature and socio-economic questions. They had some links with the factories and put out at least one proclamation (in 1891)[2].

Generally, the attempts of the Populists to form stable organisations met with little success, and Ivanovo was no exception. This suggests that the migrated peasantry had no wish for a communal land-centred way of life. As M. A. Bagaev, a member of these early Populist groups, has recalled: 'the Populist propaganda of the 'peasant revolution' on the basis of a socialised peasant *obshchina* was alien to the Ivanovo workers. Though they were linked to the villages, the small amount of land and exhaustion of the soil could only give them some assistance on top of their basic factory wages'[3].

In the 1890's groups with elements of Social-Democratic policy began to develop and to displace the purely Narodnik circles of the 1880's. One of the first of such groups, which lasted about eighteen months, was lower middle class in social composition and had very few workers among its members[4]. In 1892, a Social-Democratic group of workers was organised by F. A. Kondrat'ev who had earlier been a member of the Brusnev circle in St. Petersburg. Kondrat'ev made contacts with workers by giving lessons in his flat. The first Social-Democratic circle was composed of five textile workers, a night watchman and an unskilled railway worker – very few intellectuals. The members paid 2% of their wages as subscriptions, probably indicating that the group contributed to members' welfare during sickness or unemployment. These circles helped the general education of their members: books and pamphlets were read, discussions on social, political and religious themes took place[5]. In

---

[1] S. P. Sherternin, *Rabochee dvizhenie v Ivanovo-Voznesenskom rayone* (Geneva 1900), p. 21.

[2] A. M. Stopani and O. A. Varentsova, commentary to 'Doklad delegata Severnogo Rabochego soyuza' in N. Angarski, *Doklady sotsial-demokraticheskikh komitetov vtoromu s'ezdu* (M.L. 1930). p. 279; O. A. Varentsova and M. A. Bagaev, *Za 10 let* (Ivanovo 1930), pp. 16-18, further details of the early circles are given in *XXV let RKP (b.) Vospominaniya Ivanovo-Voznesenskikh podpol'shchikov* (Ivanovo 1923), pp. 15-34.

[3] O. A. Varentsova and M. A. Bagaev, p. 18.

[4] N. Maslov (memoir) in *XXV let RKP (b)* (Ivanovo 1923), pp. 29-30.

[5] 'Materialy po istorii rabochego dvizheniya v Ivanovo-Voznesenske', in *XXV let RKP (b)*, p. 35.

1895 after a May Day meeting, the Ivanovo-Voznesensk Workers' Union was formed which was of a purely economistic character[1]. The Union's agitators spoke to crowds during strikes, and were sometimes called 'students' because of their wider theoretical knowledge, though in fact they were simple workers. Strikes at this time advocated a reduction in hours and were more often against the reduction of wage rates than for an increase in them[2]. Though the Ivanovo-Voznesensk Workers' Union was autonomous, it had links with Moscow and St. Petersburg Social-Democratic groups from which it sometimes received money during strikes[3]. From 1895 to 1898 the police was well informed of members' movements, knew of the links of the Union with outside, and frequently arrested activists[4]. In 1897, Afanas'ev was exiled from St. Petersburg to Ivanovo and he and his brother Egor at the Burylin factory set up a Social-Democratic group twenty strong[5]. In 1898, the Union declared itself the Ivanovo-Voznesensk Committee of the RSDLP on receiving its Manifesto[6]. At this time the Committee numbered a few hundred men[7].

By 1900, the Ivanovo-Voznesensk Social-Democratic Committee was organised in three districts – town, suburb and factory (*mekhanicheski*). It had a library, some contacts with the intelligentsia (such as existed in Ivanovo), and, according to the police, 'a wide organisation among the workers'[8]. This declined after the police arrests which afflicted the Ivanovo Social-Democrats. Many of the ordinary workers, however, were unaware of the existence of such political groups. Samoylov, following the arrest of a weaver at his machine has recalled: 'Afterwards a crowd of weavers gathered in the corridor. Somebody said that the arrested was a man who did not acknowledge the Tsar and God. But what these people wanted nobody from those gathered could explain. After this...I strongly wanted to know: who are these people and what do they want?'[9]

By 1901, the Ivanovo-Voznesensk Committee had organised two different kinds of circles: one of a political character for militants

[1] Angarski, p. 279.
[2] S. P. Sherternin, *Rabochee dvizhenie v Ivanovo-Voznesenskom rayone za poslednie 15 let* (Geneva 1900), pp. 15-17.
[3] Varentsova and Bagaev, p. 41.
[4] Varentsova and Bagaev, pp. 44, 71, 82 (police archives cited).
[5] 'Materialy po istorii rabochego dvizheniya v Ivanovo-Voznesenske' in xxv *let RKP* (b), p. 39.
[6] S. P. Sherternin, p. 27.
[7] *Ibid.*
[8] Varentsova and Bagaev, pp. 94-97.
[9] F. N. Samoylov, p. 15.

and another of a 'trade union' type for the masses[1]. The circles each consisted of five to six men. Two years later, in Ivanovo there were up to ten circles, in Shuya and Kokhma one each, in Yaroslavl were groups in the chief factories[2], in Tomna and Puchezh there were 'weak' groups[3].

The Social-Democratic Committees of Yaroslavl, Kostroma, Ivanovo and Vladimir formed the Northern Workers' Union in August 1901 and, by 1903, its membership included groups in Murom, Kovrov and Orekhovo-Zuevo. It was, in theory, controlled by a central committee with powers to organise activity in the region and to carry on relations with outside. The members of the central committee were to work in the localities thereby having knowledge of local conditions[4]. Not all of these groups were amenable to central control and in 1901 some of them had 'economistic' characteristics[5]. The Kostroma and Yaroslavl Committees claimed contacts with the workers in the chief factories in their areas[6]. In Yaroslavl there were circles in the boys' and girls' grammar schools and the seminaries[7] and one lycee had its own Social-Democratic committee. From 1900 to 1901, *Iskra*, *Rabochaya Mysl'* and *Rabochee Delo* were distributed in Ivanovo and among members of the other Committees of the Union. Literature both of Social-Democrats and Socialist-Revolutionaries also reached factory groups in 1902[8].

In 1903 the membership of the Northern Union was about one hundred and fifty men, Ivanovo having about fifty[9]. An organiser's report to the Third Congress said that during the summer of 1903 things in Ivanovo were 'quite miserable', the circles were isolated, little literature was distributed and no mass agitation was carried on[10]. This inactivity was in no small part due to the police and may underestimate the latent support for Social-Democracy. In 1902, continual arrests had taken place and the organisation was reformed

[1] 'Doklad delegata severnogo Rabochego Soyuza...', *II S'ezd RSDRP (Protokoly)*, p. 653.
[2] *Ibid.*, p. 668.
[3] *Ibid.*, p. 668.
[4] 'Doklad delegata severnogo Rabochego Soyuza...', p. 665.
[5] 'Doklad delegata...', p. 664.
[6] 'Doklad delegata...', pp. 658, 660.
[7] *Ibid.*, p. 660.
[8] I. Dosarev, 'Dvatsat' let tomy nazad', in *XXV let RKP (b)*, p. 68.
[9] Another estimate, based on recollections of party workers, puts the number of 'organised' workers in April 1903 at from 80 to 100 ('Materialy po instorii rabochego dvizheniya v Ivanovo-Voznesenske', in *XXV let RKP (b)*... (Ivanovo, 1923), p. 49).
[10] 'Otchet severnogo komiteta RSDRP', in *III S'ezd RSDRP: Protokoly* (M. 1959), p. 602.

in January 1903[1]. Samoylov, however, recalls that he joined the Ivanovo party organisation in May 1903, 'when it was reformed after the police swoop of the autumn 1902'[2]. Possibly he was unaware of the earlier effort. Certainly all evidence emphasises the intensity of the police surveillance and the precarious position of the Social-Democratic groups. The story was similar in other areas of the Northern Union. Early in 1902 the police made many searches and arrests and seized literature[3]. By the autumn of 1903, however, two full-time party workers were organising and they had formed twelve circles[4].

We have seen that during the 1890's the Social-Democrats were concerned mainly with discussion circles. Later not only did these groups distribute propaganda and literature among the workers, they also promoted their political education generally[5]. One of the main tasks of the Northern Workers' Union was to divert the elemental strike activity into a wider revolutionary struggle[6]. From 1901 to 1903 the Social-Democratic Committee in Ivanovo lacked sufficient support to lead strikes and the arrests and deportations continually harassed their activity. Many of the Social-Democratic groups in the Ivanovo-Yaroslavl-Kostroma area had 'economistic' tendencies up to the party's Second Congress in 1903. The main activity was the distribution of leaflets, many in support of strikes.

The Northern Union was sympathetic to *Iskra*[7]. The Northern Union was not the only Social-Democratic organisation in Ivanovo, however, for in 1899 a group calling itself 'The Committee of the Social-Democratic Union of the Workers of Russian Manchester' existed. Little is known about it except that one of its aims was to organise a congress of all-Russian workers excluding the intelligentsia[8]. It was probably a union based mainly on economic agitation and may have been the Ivanovo counterpart of later anti-*Iskra* groups in other areas. Another group called *Volya* claimed to base itself

[1] Varentsova and Bagaev, p. 121.

[2] F. Samoylov, *Pervy sovet rabochikh deputatov* (M. 1935), p. 14.

[3] Yaroslavl – 13 searches and 12 arrests; Vladimir 12 searches 7 arrests; Kostroma 17 searches and 14 arrests, 'Otnoshenie prokurora Moskovskoy sudebnoy palaty v ministerstvo yustitsii, 3 Maya 1902', in K.A. 82 (1937), p. 179.

[4] 'Otchet severnogo komiteta...', p. 603.

[5] Samoylov, for example, recalls that he was approached by the Social-Democrats after being noticed reading library books and he was later taken to a flat where he was introduced to illegal books and Social-Democratic activity (Samoylov, *Vospominaniya*, p. 16).

[6] 'Doklad delegata severnogo Rabochego Soyuza...', p. 652.

[7] See Krupskaya's commentary to 'Doklad organizatsii *Iskry* II s'ezdu RSDRP v 1903 g.', N. Angarski, *Doklady sotsial-demokratichestikh komitetov II S'ezdu RSDRP* (M. 1930), p. 30.

[8] Varentsova and Bagaev, p. 89.

on Marxism, emphasised the importance of the peasantry in Russia and advocated a union between Socialist-Revolutionaries and Social-Democrats. It ceased to exist after the Second Congress of the RSDLP[1]. The Northern Union in 1901 'accepted the programme of *Iskra* as the basis of activity'[2]. This was not a unanimous decision by the Union. Certain groups were in favour of activity directed along more 'economistic' lines, and made a distinction between political and economic struggle[3]. Following the arrest of some members in opposition to *Iskra* in 1902, the Union was a firm supporter of the paper and its tactics.

3. The Ivanovo-Voznesensk Committee after the Second Congress

The Ivanovo organisation, both in 1903 and 1904, was solidly Bolshevik. 'All our party professionals...belonged to the Bolshevik faction. Among the rank and file members was not one Menshevik...'[4] The factional differences within the RSDLP were not clear to the Ivanovo members who had little interest in them[5]. Menshevik agitators, however, did appear in the spring of 1905 and spoke to striking workers. They were in Ivanovo a short time and Samoylov says that only one man, V. Ivanov, showed any Menshevik sympathies[6].

In March 1905, the Northern Union was disbanded and the local town groups became independent Committees[7]. At this time M. V. Frunze was the organiser of the Ivanovo Committee. In May 1905, when he arrived at Ivanovo, he found 'not less than 400-500 activists, nearly all from the local workers'[8]. A letter to *Vpered* written in the spring of 1905 claims 700 'organised' Social-Democrats[9]. In the summer of 1905, the Socialist-Revolutionaries, Mensheviks and even Anarchists, had groups in Ivanovo, and the Bolsheviks seem to have been dominant. Martov records that there were six hundred Bolshevik members making it the largest Committee in the central in-

[1] A. M. Stopani and O. A. Varentsova, commentary to 'Doklad delegata severnogo Rabochego Soyuza', in N. Angarski, p. 282.
[2] 'Doklad delegata severnogo Rabochego Soyuza II ocherednom s'ezdu RSDRP', *II S'ezd: (Protokoly)*, p. 663.
[3] *Ibid.*
[4] Samoylov, *Pervy sovet...*, p. 27.
[5] *Ibid.*, p. 28.
[6] Samoylov, *Vospominaniya*, pp. 36-37.
[7] 'Otchet...', p. 602.
[8] M. V. Frunze, 'K istorii sotsial-demokratii v Ivanovo-Voznesenskoy gubernii', *Sobranie sochineniy*, Vol. 1 (M.L. 1929), p. 507.
[9] 'Pis'mo Yu. Yu. iz Ivanovo-Voznesenska v redaktsiya gaz. *Vpered*', in K.A. 69-70 (1935), p. 131.

dustrial region[1]. The centre of Socialist-Revolutionary influence was Shuya. Frunze has explained that this was due to the *meshchansko-burzhuazny* character of this town and the earlier influence of Narodnik groups[2]. The *Zubatovshchina* did not exist in Ivanovo as it did in other regions. Frunze, as other commentators, points out the difference between Moscow and St. Petersburg, on the one hand, where the intelligentsia played an important role, and Ivanovo, on the other, where it 'had no significant influence...in the life of the local organisation'[3]. Among the local leaders was only one intellectual.

The Ivanovo Committee had links with other settlements in Kokhma, Shuya, Lezhnevo, Teykovo, Sereda and Rodniki, but they were 'very weak'[4]. In the summer of 1905, however, a separate district organisation was set up, with its centre at Shuya including all settlements outside Ivanovo, and by the summer of 1906 it had outstripped the membership of the Ivanovo Committee[5]. The Ivanovo Committee itself, in the summer of 1905, started peasant groups in the village, but there are no details of their membership or activity.

4. The May Strikes: the First Soviet of Workers' Deputies

In January 1905 the influence of the Social-Democrats was not yet sufficient to organise a general strike in support of their St. Petersburg comrades[6]. The number of strikes in January 1905 was only 13, involving 11,482 participants, compared to 70 in May, involving 53,476. The proportion of 'political' strikes was extremely high, 81% and 75% for the two months respectively, and an average of 76% for the year[7]. Based on the senior factory inspector's report for 1905, they may underestimate strikes having 'economic' causes, which might be attributed to his incompetence.

The May Day celebration was rather disappointing: it had not been properly organised, and was only attended by 200 people because 'many workers had not returned after the Easter holiday from the

[1] Yu. Martov, 'Sotsialdemokratiya 1905-1907 g.', *Obshchestvennoe dvizhenie v Rossii v nachale XX veka*, Vol. III (Spb. 1914), p. 573.
[2] M. V. Frunze, 'K istorii sotsial-demokratii v Ivanovo-Voznesenskoy gubernii', *Sobranie sochineniy*, Vol. I (M.L. 1929), p. 511.
[3] *Soch.*, I, p. 507.
[4] Frunze, *Soch.*, Vol. II, p. 510.
[5] Frunze, p. 510.
[6] Samoylov, *Pervy sovet...*, p. 28.
[7] *O rabochem dvizhenii i S.D. rabote vo Vladimirskoy gub. v 1900-kh. godakh*, Part II (Vladimir 1925), p. 136.

villages'[1]. On 11 May 1905, a party conference took place outside the town attended by factory and mill delegates. Seventy-two men took part: they discussed the militancy of the workers, drew up a list of twenty-seven mainly economic demands to put to the industrialists, and declared a strike for the next day[2]. By the evening of 12 May, some 30,000 men were on strike; they were mostly from the large textile factories, men of the smaller workshops joined the strike later[3].

The factory managements told the strikers, through the senior factory inspector, to hold discussions with them individually. They thereupon 'elected about 100 deputies to lead the strike, to carry on discussions in the name of all the strikers both with the management and with government representatives. In this way the Soviet of Workers' Deputies of Ivanovo-Voznesensk...was founded. This was between 13 and 15 May 1905'[4]. The deputies, each representing roughly 200 to 250 workers were openly elected by all workers, including women and children. About thirty different trades were represented in the Soviet, the largest single group being the weavers of whom there were thirty-two, followed by mechanics (*slesari*) of whom there were sixteen[5]. The title of the body was the 'Assembly of Deputies' (*Sobranie deputatov*) or the 'Soviet of Workers' Deputies'[6]. Being elected by place of work, the members were most probably elected on the basis of occupation. It was composed of about one hundred and fifty men, of whom about one third were Bolsheviks and the remainder non-party[7].

The Soviet included twenty-eight women, and the majority of the delegates were under twenty-five years of age[8]. The leaders of the strikers were all of the more highly qualified workers: a *graver*, three electricians and a photographer from one of the textile factories[9]. The Bolsheviks took a leading role in the Soviet. According

1 'Pis'mo Yu. Yu. iz Ivanovo-Voznesenska v redaktsiyu gaz. *Vpered*', K.A., 69-70 (1935), p. 131.
2 S. Sherternin, 'K tridtsatiletiyu Ivanovo-Voznesenskoy vseobshchey stachki', K.A. (1935), Nos. 69-70, p. 128. The history of this strike has already been fully described by O. Anweiler, *Die Rätebewegung in Russland 1905-1921* (Leiden 1958), pp. 49-51. Here I shall give only a brief outline.
3 Samoylov, *Vospominaniya*, p. 43.
4 Samoylov, *Vospominaniya*, p. 44.
5 E. Chernova, *Ivanovo-Voznesenski proletariat* (M. 1955), p. 35.
6 Samoylov, 'Pervy sovet rabochikh deputatov v 1905 g.' in P.R. No. 39 (1925), p. 128.
7 S. Sherternin, 'K tridtsatiletiyu...', p. 128. Chernova has put Bolshevik allegiance at two thirds of the total, probably too much (E. Chernova, p. 35).
8 V. A. Galkin, 'Ivanovo-Voznesenski sovet upolnomechennykh v 1905 g...' in *Doklady i soobshcheniya instituta istorii*, No. 8 (M. 1955), p. 30.
9 S. Balashov, 'Rabochee dvizhenie v Ivanovo-Voznesenske', P.R. No. 39 (1925), p. 167.

to Samoylov who was in the presidium, its decisions were 'dictated by the leadership of the town Social-Democratic organisation'[1]. Another more recent writer has gone even further: 'not a single gathering took place without party leadership'[2], probably an exaggeration. During the May-June strikes two Menshevik orators spoke, though most speakers were Bolsheviks[3].

The Ivanovo Soviet had no executive committee, only a permanent presidium[4], and compared to other Soviets, was distinguished by the absence of representatives from political parties other than Social-Democrats. Its main demands were for an eight-hour day, a minimum wage of 20 rubles per month, general improvement of conditions, freedom of speech and strike, and the inviolability of the person[5]. Requests to, and replies from the employers were transmitted by the factory inspectors, some of whom attended meetings of the Soviet[6].

On 16 May, the employers rejected the workers' requests, after which mass meetings with red flags and revolutionary songs took place. On 22 May, the employers agreed to see a five-man delegation from the Soviet to discuss the men's economic demands[7]. After their rejection, the workers appealed to the Minister of Internal Affairs[8]. These appeals and the presence of the factory inspectors at some of the meetings of the Soviet suggest that they had the confidence of the local workers, and show they were not always regarded as the accomplices of the factory management.

Until the end of May, the strikers had been quite peaceful, but on 3 June fighting between strikers and troops broke out, followed later in the month, when the Soviet admitted that it could no longer safeguard public order, by the pillaging of, and the setting fire to, shops. This suggests, contrary to the views of Samoylov and Kolesnikov above, that much of the workers' activity was elemental and outside party control, though it is probably true that organised activity came under the Bolsheviks, who gave direction to the men's grievances. The Soviet sanctioned the resumption of work on 1 July, but the management demanded a declaration by each worker that he would resume under the old conditions, which led to a prolongation of

[1] Samoylov, *Vospominaniya*, p. 45.

[2] F. V. Kolesnikov, 'Vystuplenie uchastnikov Ivanovo-Voznesenskoy stachki 1905 g.', in *Doklady i soobshcheniya instituta istorii*, Vyp. 8 (M. 1955), p. 67.

[3] Samoylov, *Vospominaniya*, p. 49.

[4] Samoylov, 'Pervy sovet rabochikh deputatov v 1905 g.', P.R. No. 39 (1925), p. 135.

[5] S. Sherternin, 'K tridtsatiletiyu...', K.A., Nos. 69-70, p. 129.

[6] Samoylov, *Vospominaniya*, p. 45.

[7] 'Pis'mo rabochego iz Ivanovo-Voznesenska v red. gaz. *Proletari* 8 iyuniya 1905 g.' in K.A., Nos. 69-70 (1935), p. 132.

[8] Anweiler, p. 50.

the strike until 18 July[1]. Anweiler points out that the Soviet did not make material conditions much better, though the strike may have prevented conditions from becoming worse, which often occurred at the Easter wages review.

The Soviet succeeded in closing the state liquor shops and claims to have maintained public order in the town[2], at least until June. Its chief role was that of a strike leader. Even after the Soviet dissolved in July, its former deputies continued to act as spokesmen with the management. There can be no doubt that the Bolsheviks were in a dominant position in the Soviet, but I cannot define the limits within which they worked. Though the Social-Democratic party was small in Ivanovo, it wielded influence out of proportion to its size in the Soviet. The Soviet did not lead an uprising and achieved only modest aims but it had a wide appeal: 'tens of delegations' from the areas around Ivanovo came with requests for material aid and asked for help with local problems[3].

The Ivanovo Soviet and the disturbances associated with it occurred earlier than in other areas. The fact that so many public disturbances took place in May and September coinciding with the Easter and Harvest Festivals, may be explained by the practice of many factories adjusting their wage rates in these months to meet changed market demand and labour supply conditions[4]. This may have had the effect of strengthening class solidarity and making class conflict 'institutional' coinciding with May Day. Perhaps the timing of uprisings in societies undergoing industrialisation may be partly due to the influence of the seasons and the importance they have for the worker from a rural background.

5. Summing-up

The Bolsheviks were dominant in Ivanovo. Their policies here found fertile soil among the workers in the depressed textile industry. Such workers were not able to fall back on village subsistence in bad times, due to the poor agricultural habitat. The Mensheviks were weak, probably because the working class was more homogeneous and poorer. The industrial structure of Ivanovo, composed almost exclusively of textile workers, gave rise to greater shared experience

---

[1] Anweiler, p. 51.
[2] Samoylov, P.R., No. 39 (1925), p. 129.
[3] Frunze, *Sochinenie I*, p. 509.
[4] N. I. Makhov (memoirs) cited in P. M. Ekzemplyarski, *Ocherki po istorii rabochego dvizheniya v Ivanovo-Voznesenske*, Vol. I (Ivanovo 1924), p. 20.

and the possibility of greater class cohesion. Pankratova, when discussing textile workers, has argued that their Socialist-Revolutionary allegiance was due to their backward and near-peasant nature, and I have shown in my study of Moscow, that this seems to be the correct explanation there. But this cannot be the complete explanation, as among the Ivanovo textile workers the Socialist-Revolutionaries were weak. The explanation lies in the nature of the industrial structure. In Moscow and St. Petersburg, with their more diverse industrial composition, the urban newcomers would tend to cluster in textiles which required less skilled labour. In this way 'islands' of peasant life and expectations might be sustained. In Ivanovo, the only industry being textiles, the newcomers were thrown much more into contact with the permanent urban dwellers and came more under their influence, making it much more difficult for them to form a separate stratum and making them shed more quickly any of their aspirations for a self-sustaining agricultural plot. The other difference which would reinforce this in Ivanovo was that the area of recruitment was so poor agriculturally that a high proportion of the peasants probably did not want a peasant way of life. Not only was the working population grouped into one industry, it was also homogeneous nationally, precluding nationality as a basis for support for a non-Bolshevik Social-Democratic faction. Class conflict was also increased by the homogeneity of the factory managers and owners: all being Russian and all feeling the competition from the more modern textile factories of St. Petersburg and the Polish provinces, and therefore all trying to keep down wage costs. In Ivanovo, hostility between management and men was more intense than in other areas, the autocracy was less important as a common enemy. The factory inspectorate acted as a channel for communication between workers and management. There was no uprising in Ivanovo. The significance of the Soviet lay not only in its role as a strike leader, but showed that the Social-Democrats by virtue of their party organisation were able, from quite a small base, to lead political protest.

chapter six:

THE STRUCTURE AND ACTIVITY OF
SOCIAL-DEMOCRACY IN TVER

1. Social and Economic Background

In 1905 Tver was a small town situated on the railway line between Moscow and St. Petersburg. Factories had been set up there from the 1850's, notably the large Morozov factory founded in 1857.[1] More important economic development, however, took place in the 1890's when carriage-building works and railway workshops were built. The working population doubled from 1890 to 1908, when it was 40,224[2]: about half was employed in the textile industry, twenty-seven mills engaged 22,030 men[3], a large carriage-building works 4,000 and several paper-mills another 5,000[4]. The number of firms halved in twenty years, falling from 389 in 1890 to 169 in 1908 leading to greater industrial concentration[5].

Wages varied between industries but overall were above those paid in Ivanovo: at the French wagon-building factory they averaged 340 rubles 35 copecks per year, at the Kuvshinov paper-mill they were 196 rubles 56 copecks, and at the Zalogin textile factory as low as 148 rubles 20 copecks[6].

The population was nationally homogeneous. At the 1897 census, not less than ninety-nine per cent of the inhabitants of Tver province were Great-Russian[7]. The factory workers were recruited from the local peasantry, who, as in Vladimir, found it difficult to maintain

---

[1] A. Dokuchaev, *Materialy po istorii professional'nogo dvizheniya Tverskoy gubernii 1883-1917 gg.* (Tver 1925), pp. 10-11.
[2] P. K. Aleksandrov, *Ocherk rabochego dvizheniya v Tverskoy gubernii 1885-1905 gg.* (Tver 1923), p. 3.
[3] Aleksandrov, *ibid.*
[4] A. Belov, 'Ocherk revolyutsionnogo dvizheniya v Tverskoy gub.' *1905 v Tverskoy gubernii (sbornik)* (Tver 1925), p. 22.
[5] Aleksandrov, p. 3.
[6] These figures are probably for 1904, A. Belov, p. 22.
[7] *Pervaya vseobshchaya perepis' naseleniya* (1905), Vol. II, p. 38.

themselves by agricultural work. In 1903, the post-office received money transfers to peasants in Tver amounting to 11,179,844 rubles, showing the firm links between town and country and the dependence of many peasants on the town[1]. In 1906-07, 31.5% of the population had passports to leave their place of residence[2]. Moreover, in Tver province many small factories had been set up in villages (for example in Vyshni-Volochok and Popov) again blurring the distinction between a rural and urban way of life[3].

2. The Early History of Social-Democracy

Socialist groups were formed in Tver in the 1880's and ideas put forward in Marx's and Plekhanov's works were discussed in the 1890's[4]. These early half-Populist half-Social-Democratic groups were composed of workers and intellectuals, high school pupils and seminarists. Political prisoners who had been detained in Tver contributed to the growth of Social-Democratic groups[5]. At the same time *kassy* or sickness and insurance funds existed legally from the 1890's among workers and *sluzhashchie*[6].

By 1901, despite arrests, socialist groups, as one might loosely call them, had grown in numbers: meetings of up to eighty men took place in Tver led 'chiefly by those exiled from St. Petersburg'[7]. It was not until March 1902 that the members of some of these circles formed the Tver Committee of the RSDLP[8]. The Tver Committee affiliated to the Northern Workers' Union officially from February 1903, but actually had been part of it from November 1902[9]. Affiliation lasted only until the Second Congress and, apart from providing contact between Social-Democratic organisations, did not contribute much to the life of the Tver Committee.

---

[1] 'Statisticheski obzor Tverskoy gub. za 1903, 1904', cited in 1905 v Tverskoy..., p. 19.

[2] 'Proletariat i krest'yanstvo v epokhu revolyutsii', P.R. 1926, 5 (52), p. 178.

[3] 'Doklad Tverskogo komiteta', in *II S'ezd RSDRP (protokoly)* (M. 1959), p. 607.

[4] 'Doklad Tverskogo komiteta', pp. 613-4.

[5] P. K. Aleksandrov, *Ocherk rabochego dvizheniya v Tverskoy gubernii 1885-1905* (Tver 1925), pp. 26-27. For names of activists see B. I. Nikolaevski's commentary to 'Doklad Tverskogo komiteta' in N. Angarski, *Doklady S.-D. komitetov vtoromu s'ezdu* (M.L. 1930), p. 302, for an account of a political prisoner see A. P. Smirnov, 'Zametki o Tverskoy organizatsii' in P.R. No. 12 (47) (1925), p. 117.

[6] A. Dokuchaev, *Materialy po istorii profdvizheniya Tverskoy gub.* (Tver 1925), p. 57: no details of these *kassy* are given in this work.

[7] 'Doklad Tverskogo komiteta', p. 611.

[8] A. P. Smirnov, p. 121.

[9] 'Doklad Tverskogo komiteta', p. 618.

Sources vary in their description of the numbers of Social-Democratic circles in Tver: it has been estimated that in 1902 from seven to fifteen circles existed, having from forty to a hundred members[1]. Socially, the circles were widely spread among the workers at the main factories, the students of secondary schools, the teachers and the *Zemstvo* 'Third Element'[2]. By 1903, Aleksandrov claims, there were sixteen circles in the factories alone, nine of which were at the Morozov works[3]. A fairly rapid turnover of members took place in these circles: 'a large number came regularly, others after attending once or twice left the circle'[4]. On the basis of these figures one might estimate a membership of about a hundred men in 1903 (assuming that each of the sixteen circles had six members).

Other groups were formed in the settlements near Tver: in Krasny Kholm, Kashin, Bezhetsk and Vyshni-Volochok and were composed mainly of the local intelligentsia. In the Vasil'evsk *volost'*, where half of the employed population worked in factories in Tver, a group made up mainly of ex-workers of the Morozov factory had formed a Social-Democratic group in 1902-03[5]. These village or settlement Social-Democratic circles are, as we shall see, one of the characteristic features of Tver province.

Up to 1903 the activity of the Tver Committee was based on circles, the intelligentsia lead discussions and carried out propaganda[6]. The Committee possessed its own printing machines and in May 1903, it claimed to have distributed 14,000 leaflets, including some to the army garrison.[7] The work of the Committee was increasingly concerned with strikes which, as in the 1880's were mainly for increases in wages and for reductions of working hours.[8] In circle discussions it was explained that strikes took place because of political conditions and that they required political action.[9] But the Social-Democrats were unable to take a very dominant role in strike activity. In 1902, their warning to the Morozov workers that withdrawing labour was premature and would serve no useful purpose, went unheeded. In 1903, strikes in Tver were largely of a 'non-

[1] 'Doklad Tverskogo komiteta', p. 618, and Aleksandrov, p. 31.
[2] 'Doklad Tverskogo komiteta', p. 618.
[3] Aleksandrov, p. 31.
[4] 'Doklad Tverskogo komiteta', p. 616.
[5] I. V. Tikhomirov, 'Vasil'evskaya volost'—ochag revolyutsionera' in *1905 v Tverskoy gubernii* (Tver 1925), p. 157.
[6] 'Doklad Tverskogo komiteta', p. 616.
[7] *Ibid.*
[8] A. Dokuchaev, *Materialy...*, pp. 22-25.
[9] 'Doklad Tverskogo komiteta', p. 616.

political' kind, accompanied by brawls and machine smashing.[1] The Social-Democrats gave support to the working class by printing leaflets in support of the strikes, and in May 1903, by calling for the release of arrested men.[2]

Unlike in some other areas, up to the Second Congress of the RSDLP there seems to have been little factional activity and opposition to *Iskra* in Tver. Attempts had been made to start trade unions based on *kassy* with benefits for members in times of unemployment or trouble. In 1902, one of these groups had twenty-five members, but such attempts were short-lived and failed due to police interference.[3] The Tver Committee's recognition of *Iskra* appeared in the journal in April 1902.[4]

3. Social-Democracy after the Second Congress

After the Second Congress Tver continued to be a member of the Bolshevik camp. The Committee wrote to the (Menshevik) *Iskra* in February 1904 supporting peace within the party and Lenin's formulation of Clause I[5], it supported[6] and attended the Bolshevik Third Congress. At party cell meetings internal party questions were hardly ever discussed[7]. A member of the Committee recalls that 'for nearly all the workers the split in the party was unclear and therefore they had a negative attitude to it, and our relations to other parties also were not quite defined... On the one hand, we disputed with them at meetings, but on the other, not knowing the substance of the disagreements...we considered them as comrades doing one and the same thing'[8]. There were, however, spirited discussions in the executive committee between Bolshevik and Menshevik supporters – the latter opposing the calling of the III Congress. The Mensheviks seem to have been in the minority in the Committee and, according to Platov, were mainly 'intellectuals'[9].

Smirnov, who was on the executive committee at that time, recalls that the Social-Democrats had much influence both among the workers and the peasants, among whom the Socialist-Revolutionaries

[1] 'Iz otcheta Tverskogo komiteta', *Protokoly: III S'ezd RSDRP* (M. 1959), p. 577.
[2] Leaflet printed in A. Dokuchaev, *Materialy...*, pp. 27-28.
[3] Aleksandrov, p. 31.
[4] *Iskra*, No. 24, April 1902.
[5] *Iskra*, No. 60, Feb. 1904.
[6] *Iskra*, No. 66, May 1904.
[7] 'Iz otcheta Tverskogo Komiteta', p. 580.
[8] A. I. Bulanov, 'V dni napryazhennoy bor'by', *1905 v Tverskoy gubernii* (Tver 1925), pp. 128-9.
[9] Platov, pp. 115-7.

had only about forty sympathisers[1]. Literature received included nos. 75-95 of *Iskra* (Menshevik), nos. 1-3 of *Sotsial-Demokrat* (Menshevik), nos. 1-12 of *Vpered*, and several leaflets of the Central Committee[2], indicating that one ought not to think of local groups in terms of a narrow factional allegiance. Mitskevich has recollected that from 1904 to 1905 the Committee and its 'periphery' were Bolsheviks, only one member of the Committee (Panov) being a Menshevik[3].

In 1904, strikes and revolts took place in Tver, which were sparked off by minor disputes between management and men. The Social-Democratic Committee agitated on the basis of these strikes and sought to exploit the causes of discontent. Following the strike at the Morozov factory on 19 February 1904, the Tver Committee's leaflet of 21 February demanded 'The eight-hour day; an increase of 50% in earnings; polite treatment; abolition of searches; dismissal of two foremen; good thread for the weavers; boiling water for all factories; and relief for the workers in the calico factory'. The leaflet ended with the slogans 'Down with the autocracy! Down with capitalism! Long live socialism'[4]!

One of the most important activities of the Social-Democratic circles was to publish and distribute leaflets[5]. The reference groups of the leaflets in 1905 were the general public, the workers, and the peasants, in that order[6]. They were copied from outside papers or composed by the local intelligentsia[7]. No printing press existed in Tver itself until 1904[8]. Literature was received from abroad and from the secret presses at Vyshni-Volochok and Rzhev[9], which printed the local proclamations of the Committee. Literature and the expenses of the press took a large proportion of the Tver Committee's income which in 1902 had averaged 75 rubles per month, the largest single source being the donations of the 'Third Element'. The chief outgoings were on the maintenance of full-time workers, literature and the running of the press[10]. By the summer of 1905, income had risen to 190 rubles per month, spent chiefly on subsistence of

[1] A. P. Smirnov, 'Zametki o Tverskoy organizatsii', P.R. 12 (47) (1925), p. 129.
[2] *Proletari* no. 6, June and no. 11, August 1905.
[3] S. I. Mitskevich, *Revolyutsionnaya Rossiya* (M. 1940), p. 316.
[4] Cited by P. K. Aleksandrov, p. 47.
[5] 'Doklad Tverskogo komiteta', p. 616.
[6] Based on leaflets collected in *1905 v Tverskoy gubernii*.
[7] P. K. Aleksandrov, p. 39.
[8] *1905 v Tverskoy gubernii*, p. 106.
[9] *Ibid.*
[10] 'Doklad Tverskogo komiteta', *II S'ezd (Protokoly)*, p. 617.

revolutionaries, support for the unemployed and production of literature[1].

In the spring of 1905, the town of Tver was divided into four districts each with a Social-Democratic group led by a district organiser, one of whom claims that 300 men were carrying out agitation among the workers in Tver[2]. But many of the workers who were sympathetic to the revolutionary movement did not like to show it, being afraid of arrest and imprisonment[3]. This is evidence to support my contention that the numbers taking part in the revolutionary movement may seriously underestimate its latent strength and support. The *Zemstvo* officers were, as noted earlier, left-wing and many were in the Social-Democratic party. In 1904, some had been dismissed for their involvement in Social-Democratic activity and others left in protest at their dismissal[4].

Social-Democratic groups continued to flourish in the settlements outside Tver: a circle of workers, railwaymen and cobblers was in Kimry; in Torzhok, a group was formed by the local school-teachers[5]; and by the summer of 1905, it was claimed, the Vyshni-Volochok group had six circles with sixty-two members[6].

Most of the members were young and closely connected with the villages. As shown earlier, large sums of money were transferred to the villages in Tver province which gave the town worker prestige and perhaps a potential for political leadership. A correspondent of *Iskra* reports in December 1903 that revolutionary and illegal papers were read in the villages in Tver where one could also hear revolutionary songs[7]. At Easter 1905, many demonstrations were held in the villages attended by anything between 25 and 150 persons[8]. Though Social-Democratic agitators spoke at these meetings and socialist leaflets were circulated, one cannot estimate how effective they were. At the Third Congress of the party it was claimed that the 'consciousness' of the town worker was being transferred to the village labourers[9]. Social-Democratic work was making progress here, despite the shortages of organisers, due to a weaker police force and the help of men exiled to their home village for revolu-

[1] *Proletari*, no. 6, June 1905.
[2] 'Iz otcheta Tverskogo komiteta', *III S'ezd RSDRP*, pp. 578-80.
[3] *Ibid*.
[4] S. I. Mitskevich, *Revolyutsionnaya Rossiya* (M. 1940), p. 312.
[5] Aleksandrov, p. 40.
[6] *Proletari*, no. 16, September 1905.
[7] *Iskra*, no. 55, December 1903.
[8] *Proletari*, no. 4, June 1905.
[9] 'Iz otcheta Tverskogo komiteta', p. 577.

tionary activity in the towns. But propaganda in the villages was mainly confined to the summer months with open-air meetings[1]. Social-Democratic groups in the villages were less sophisticated than those in the towns and relatively few villagers took part in the circles.

A. Khromov has recalled that Social-Democratic circles were not organised on a village but on a district basis, composed of members from different villages. In 1905 there were about 50 members in a district circle. Of course, not all villages welcomed agitators and sometimes the Social-Democrats had a hostile reception[2]. The Social-Democratic agitators utilised the village meetings to put their propaganda; this indeed may have been an effective institution for communication and allowed the Social-Democrats to play on peasant grievances and sentiments[3]. One should not, perhaps, lightly assume that the party was without support in the rural areas, even if such support sprung more from sympathy with revolutionary goals than with explicitly Social-Democratic ones. In 1905 the Social-Democrats were not the only party in the villages, the Peasants' Union and the Socialist-Revolutionaries too had groups, though Khromov says that they had little influence[4].

4. 1905 in Tver

Following the Gapon demonstration, police security in Tver increased and dampened revolutionary activity, though 600 men gathered for a meeting at the Morozov factory on 13 January[5]. This was not the only factor which may account for little revolutionary activity among the masses in Tver immediately after the Gapon massacre. The Committee was inactive, it had not succeeded even in getting out a leaflet, and some of the Committee were against taking strike action[6].

In March 1905, a strike occurred in the glass works, and school and seminary pupils took part in a demonstration[7]. Another wave of strikes followed in May. But these, together with a strike in August

---

[1] Ibid., p. 580.
[2] A. Khromov, 'Rabota v derevne', 1905 v Tverskoy gubernii, pp. 143-4.
[3] E. Morokhovets, 'Proletariat i krest'yanstvo v epokhu pervoy revolyutsii', in P.R. 5 (52) (1926), p. 179.
[4] Khromov, p. 148.
[5] V. S. Platov, Revolyutsionnoe dvizhenie v Tverskoy gubernii (Kalinin, 1959), p. 110.
[6] A. P. Smirnov, 'Zametki o Tverskoy organizatsii', P.R. 12 (47) (1925), p. 129.
[7] 1905 v Tverskoy gub., pp. 56-57.

(notable for the hostile presence of the Black Hundreds) were the only spasmodic outbreaks which foreshadowed the events of October.

After the publication of the October Manifesto demonstrations occurred in Tver. The Socialist-Revolutionaries wanted to free prisoners from the jail[1], and large crowds gathered which were dispersed by the police. At the same time (17 October) defenders of the Tsarist order attacked the *Zemstvo* offices and beat the officials, causing damage amounting to £3,700 (37,219 r.)[2]. The pogroms of 1905 in Russia were not only directed against Jews as such, but were against groups which were identifiable as being opposed to the autocracy.

On 18 October, the Social-Democrats published a leaflet calling on Tver workers to stop work, to come onto the streets and to demonstrate[3]. The demonstrations were followed by a strike lasting until 21 October. The Tver Soviet was formed from 20-23 October, under the initiative, according to Platov, of the workers at the Morozov works[4]. Each delegate represented about fifty workers, but no formal elections had taken place[5]. It had from 200 to 250 deputies and was led by a strike committee on which the Social-Democrats predominated[6]. The chairman recalls that the Soviet was composed of long-standing workers in the Social-Democratic organisation; at the town meeting of the Soviet there was only one Socialist-Revolutionary[7]. It passed a motion by 193 votes to 5, recognising the leadership of the RSDLP and accepting the constitution worked out by the local executive committee on 18 November[8].

The Soviet formed workers' detachments five to ten men strong and decreed that spirits were not to be sold. This abstemious order, it is said, was only obeyed in the factory district where the Soviet had most support[9]. The Soviet organised a canteen for the unemployed, legal aid and a strike fund, and operated a committee of 'self-help'[10]. A general strike was declared in Tver on 12 December and an uprising, which succeeded in expelling the police from the factory district, took place on 13 December. The telegraph office was

[1] A. I. Bulanov, 'V dni napryazhennoy bor'by', *1905 v Tverskoy...* p. 127.
[2] A. Belov, pp. 92-4.
[3] See *Bol'sheviki vo glave vserossiyskoy politicheskoy stachki v oktyabre 1905 g.* (M. 1955), pp. 449-50.
[4] V. S. Platov, *Revolyutsionnoe dvizhenie v Tverskoy gub.* (Kalinin, 1959), p. 159.
[5] Bulanov, *1905 v Tverskoy...*, p. 128.
[6] A. Belov, 'Ocherk rev. dvizh. v Tverskoy gub.', *1905 v Tverskoy gubernii* (1925), p. 72.
[7] A. P. Smirnov, 'Zametki o Tverskoy organizatsii', P.R. no. 12 (47) (1925), p. 132.
[8] A. Belov, *ibid.* See details, Platov, pp. 161-6.
[9] A. Belov, p. 75.
[10] P. Gorin, *Ocherki po istorii sovetov rabochikh deputatov 1905 g.* (M. 1925), p. 205.

destroyed, trams were overturned and barricades built[1]. The Morozov factory was under the control of the strike committee for a short time. But on 18 December, troops began an offensive and the insurgents were routed.

In the villages around Tver, during the urban upheavals, 'peasants' committees' were formed by the Social-Democratic organisers. In Tver, each village sent a delegate to the committee (which is sometimes called the 'Soviet') which met in November. The agenda was not concerned with the seizure of power, but considered the election of a member to the Tver (town) Soviet, the question of illegal chopping of wood by peasants and the provision of help to arrested men[2]. Village meetings during October were addressed by Social-Democrat orators. Judging by Khromov's account, they were well aware of peasant problems; they spoke about the liberation of the serfs and their subsequent difficulties – particularly the possession of the best land and woods by the landlords. They advocated the unity of worker and peasant in the struggle against the autocracy[3]. The Social-Democrats' work in the villages also exploited the peasants' wishes to be exempt from paying taxes and from conscription[4].

The performance of the peasants' committee in the uprising culminated in the seizure of a railway station at Kulitskaya. Collections were made in the villages for the strikers and, as a sign of solidarity, bread and potatoes were sent to the town[5]. Just how much is not known but probably it was small in quantity. Though public meetings were held in the countryside, there were no 'comings-out' on a *volost'* level. The village soviet lasted a little longer than the town one but petered out in December[6].

5. Summing-up

The history of the party in Tver shows that the Social-Democrats, again small in numbers before 1905, were able to have considerable influence in the disturbances in the autumn of that year. A characteristic of the Tver Committee was the support given to the Social-

[1] A. Belov, pp. 83-4.
[2] Khromov, 'Rabota v derevne', in *1905 v Tverskoy*..., p. 147. Khromov was the secretary of this committee and a Social-Democratic organiser in these rural areas.
[3] Khromov, p. 146.
[4] A. P. Smirnov, 'Zametki o Tverskoy organizatsii', in P.R. 12 (47), p. 132.
[5] Khromov, pp. 149-152.
[6] Khromov, pp. 159-161.

Democrats by the *Zemstvo* officials, though they did not play a dominant role in the Committee, their sympathy and material help was important. In Tver the Bolsheviks were supreme and no formal Menshevik 'Group' was in existence at this time. This did not preclude the circulation of Menshevik literature nor the discussion of the causes of the party split. Such discussion, however, was the business of the leading figures in the Committee, the rank and file were unconcerned with the causes of the split and were content to follow their leaders. The Social-Democrats' work in the villages was significant. In the factory settlements the party had both members and activists. In this very poor agricultural area many in the rural districts had links with the towns: though it is an exaggeration to say that the Social-Democrats had much organised membership in the countryside they were not without groups of sympathisers. The prestige and influence of the Social-Democrats may be regarded as a spill-over from the prestige given to the migrant peasant, now a more or less regular bread-winning factory worker. The support given to Russian Social-Democracy in these cases was probably not just based on the belief of the rightness of a socialist society but on the preference for an urban as against a rural way of life.

chapter seven:

THE STRUCTURE AND ACTIVITY OF
SOCIAL DEMOCRACY IN EKATERINOSLAV

1. Social and Economic Background

The Donbass industrial complex, in which Ekaterinoslav was situated, was one of the largest and fastest growing industrial areas of the Russian Empire at the beginning of the twentieth century. Coal output had grown from 15.6 million puds[1] in 1870 to 671.7 million puds in 1900, and iron smelting from 2.0 million puds in 1885 to 50.6 millions in 1900[2] when it accounted for over a quarter of Russian total iron smelting. The steel, metal-working, chemical, engineering and food industries also developed during the late nineteenth century. Donbass industry was modelled on the practice of western Europe, and many of the factories were owned and managed by British, German and French entrepreneurs. More than half of the mines were under Franco-Belgian ownership, and only one of the nine blast-furnaces was completely Russian-owned[3]. The Donbass factories were larger in size, smaller in number, and utilised a greater proportion of horsepower per worker than factories in other Russian areas. For example, in 1900 Donbass output per worker in the ferrous metal industry was 2,315.3 puds compared to 398.2 puds in the Urals[4].

A corollary to the growth in industry was the growth of the working class. The numbers of workers in the coal and metallurgical industries increased from 32,825 in 1892 to 107,673 in 1900[5]. Such rapid growth of highly technological industries required skilled workers and engineers. Many of these came from abroad: John Hughes, for example, brought with him 70 experienced British

---

[1] One Russian *pud* equals 16.3 kilogrammes or 36.1 British pounds.
[2] S. I. Potolov, *Rabochie Donbassa v XIX veke* (M. 1963), pp. 80-1.
[3] Potolov, pp. 88-9.
[4] Potolov, p. 86.
[5] Potolov, p. 99.

Table 29. Numbers of Selected Nationalities in the Donbass, 1897

Province	National Groups (ooo's)											
	Great Russians		Ukrainians		White Russians		Poles		English		Jews	
	Male	Female	Male	Female	Male	Female	Male	Female	Male	Female	Male	Female
Ekaterinoslav	202.5	162.4	736.8	719.4	8.3	5.6	7.3	5.0	.209	.160	50.6	48.5
Kharkov	225.8	215.1	1,004.3	1,005.0	4.9	5.3	4.0	1.8	.031	.034	7.0	5.6
Don Army	858.6	854.2	336.4	353.1	5.0	4.1	1.9	1.3	.048	.038	7.4	7.6

Pervaya vseobshchaya perepis'...., (Spb. 1905), vol. II, pp. 20, 23.

workers. At the beginning of the twentieth century the Donbass was a magnet for workers from western Europe, the central and western provinces of Russia, Silesia and Westphalia. These industrial immigrants affected the structure of the population making it very heterogeneous. The numbers in selected national groups are shown on Table 29. It shows that in the Ekaterinoslav Province two out of nine men were Great Russians, the proportions being one in six in Kharkov, and eight in eleven in the Don area. The large difference between the male and female Great Russian population in Ekaterinoslav implies that many were immigrants and the large number of Poles, White Russians and Englishmen there (compared to other areas) shows its mixed national composition[1].

The qualified workers were foreigners or came from the Bryansk, Tula or Petersburg Provinces. The bulk of the labourers and un-skilled workers were of peasant background and a few came from handicraft strata[2]. The national composition of the industrial working class was different from that of the mainly Ukrainian popu-lation in the area. Generally, Russians outnumbered the local Ukrainians, rather like the English-speaking industrial migrants in South Wales. In coal-mining, 74% of the workers were Russian and 22.3% Ukrainian, in metallurgy and metal-working 69% were Russian and 20.2% Ukrainian. In the chemical industry there were relatively more Ukrainians – 37.2% of the work force. There were also small numbers of White Russians, Moldavians, Cossacks, Poles and Jews among the industrial workers[3].

In 1880 Ekaterinoslav town was known as the 'capital' of the southern mining area of Russia, in 1887 the population was 48,000 and by 1900 had grown to 156,000[4]. By social status the majority of inhabitants were townsmen (meshchane) (55%) a large proportion of whom were Jews, followed by peasants (33%) a category including the newcomers to the factories who had not lost their legal peasant estate. The town was an important trading centre, there were 1,800 shops, having a yearly turnover of forty million rubles[5]. In the town of Ekaterinoslav were over 200 industrial enterprises, many of which were small handicraft workshops, producing finished consumer goods.

[1] For area breakdown see, *Rossiya* (Spb. 1910), vol. XIV, map facing p. 176.
[2] M. A. Rubach, *Istoriya Ekaterinoslavskoy sotsial-demokratischeskoy organizatsii 1889-1903* (Ekateri-noslav, 1923), p. xxxii.
[3] S. I. Potolov, p. 132, see also *Pervaya vseobshchaya perepis'... 1897 g.*, vol. XII (Spb. 1905), vol. XLVI (Spb. 1904).
[4] *Rossiya*, vol. XIV (Spb. 1910), p. 556.
[5] *Rossiya*, vol. XIV, p. 557.

2. The Early History of Social-Democracy

In the 1890's in south Russia as elsewhere, Marxist groups began to take the place of the Populist circles. In 1894-95, attempts were made to create links between workers and intellectuals in Ekaterinoslav, and a circle of twelve existed among the workers at the Bryansk factory[1].

Some of the leading activists in the late nineties were handicraftsmen from Vilna and Minsk who formed an important part of the newly recruited working class in south Russia. They formed their own Sickness and Injury Funds, as had been their practice in the western provinces[2]. At the Dneprovsk factory (Kamensk village), for example, the majority of workers engaged in revolutionary activity were skilled Polish workers. The national groups tended to form Social-Democratic groups along national lines. Piatnitsky recalls that in the western provinces no workers' union was open to men of all nationalities[3]. This tendency, as we shall see, was to fragment Social-Democracy in Ekaterinoslav.

I have shown that the population in south Russia was highly mobile. This movement was not only internal but resulted also in emigration. The estimated number of Russian emigrants from 1898-1903 was about one million, of whom the overwhelming majority went to the U.S.A.[4] No divisions are given by *guberniya*, but it is likely that the majority came from the western or southern areas, thereby providing other avenues of change for potential revolutionaries. A Bolshevik activist, discussing the Social-Democratic circles which existed around Vilna, recalls that many of the participants improved their general education in them, some took examinations and became teachers and others 'possibly the best part' emigrated to America[5]. D. Treadgold[6] has suggested that Russian emigration (to Siberia) in the late nineteenth century was similar in many respects to the American frontier which served as a political 'safety valve' in the formation of the U.S.A. Ukrainian emigration (both to Siberia and abroad) had such a political effect making the area less prone to extremist elements.

[1] M. A. Rubach, *Istoriya Ekaterinoslavskoy sotsial-demokraticheskoy organizatsii 1889-1903* (Ekaterinoslav 1923), p. XVII. For the early history see S. I. Potolov, *Rabochie Donbassa v devyatnatsatom veke* (1963), pp. 187-200, p. 219, and Rubach, p. XIX.

[2] Rubach, p. XXI.

[3] O. Piatnitsky, *Memoirs of a Bolshevik* (London n.d.), p. 26.

[4] *Ezhegodnik Rossii 1905 g.* Tsentralny statisticheski komitet M.V.D. (Spb. 1906), pp. 140-41.

[5] S. I. Mitskevich, *Revolyutsionnaya Moskva* (M. 1940), p. 160.

[6] D. W. Treadgold, 'Russian Expansion and Turner's American Frontier', *Agricultural History*, vol. 26 (no. 4) October 1952.

The Ekaterinoslav Committee of the RSDLP was formed in 1898, and partly grew out of the Ekaterinoslav Union of Struggle for the Liberation of the Working Class which had been started in 1897 by Lalayants, Petrusevich and Babushkin[1]. At the same time Social-Democratic groups were being formed in other areas of the Donbass. The Don Committee was formed in 1898[2]. Other groups became the basis of the Social-Democratic Miners' and Metal-workers' Union which was founded in January 1902[3] and, from 1903, became known as the Donets Union of the RSDLP. Most of the Union's activity was directed at miners and factory workers. But it was not narrowly industrial: links with the countryside existed, though only on a small scale, and attempts were made to organise the handicraftsmen, the village middle classes – especially the teachers[4]. The Union claimed that it was 'one of the few organisations in Russia where the workers play a predominant and highly influential role'[5].

In 1903, the Union is claimed to have had thirty circles with about five hundred members[6]. In Ekaterinoslav in 1899 the Committee of the RSDLP claimed twenty-five circles with a membership of two hundred men[7]. By 1903 the total membership of Social-Democratic groups had grown to about one thousand[8]. The *Iskra* group, it has been claimed, numbered only thirty-five at this time, composed partly of men from the large factories, but mostly of handicraft workers[9]. M. Khinoy has argued that the membership of the anti-*Iskra* group was seven hundred and fifty. The social basis of this group were the Jewish workers who had been in contact with the Bund in Vilna, Minsk, Vitebsk and Gomel and groups of metal workers from Poland. The core of the opposition to *Iskra* were groups with a non-Russian national background[10]. This evidence confirms what I have

[1] Potolov (1963), p. 229.

[2] 'Doklad sotsial-demokraticheskogo soyuza gornozavodskikh rabochikh yuga Rossii', in *II S'ezd RSDRP (Protokoly)* (M. 1959), p. 545.

[3] 'Doklad S.-D. soyuza...', p. 547.

[4] 'Doklad S.-D. soyuza...', p. 554.

[5] *Ibid.*, p. 550.

[6] I. Moshinski, 'K voprosu o S.-D. (Donetskom) Soyuze Gornozavodskikh rabochikh', in P.R. no. 5 (65) (1927), p. 233.

[7] Rubach, *Istoriya Ekaterinoslavskoy S.-D. organizatsii*, p. xxvi.

[8] I. B. Polonski, 'Vospominaniya' in Rubach, p. 360.

[9] V. Nogin, 'Vospominaniya', in Rubach, p. 363, see also 'Tov. Makar (V. P. Nogin)' in P.R. no. 7 (30) (1924), p. 148. According to police records, only one man was known to be unemployed, five were students or teachers, ten were handicraftsmen (cobblers, stocking-makers, bookbinders, seamstresses, etc.), nine were factory workers, two had no definite occupation and five had various other jobs (Police report dated 23 May 1903, in Rubach, pp. 377-80).

[10] M. Khinoy, *U istokov men'shevizma* (N.Y. 1960), pp. 5-6, 19.

said about nationality being the basis for factional division in Part One.

In Ekaterinoslav prior to the Second Congress the Social-Democrats concentrated on leaflet and agitational work. Though strikes had been frequent from 1892 to 1901, the Social-Democratic Union of Mining and Metal Workers was mainly concerned with organising circles and distributing propaganda[1]. In Ekaterinoslav, propaganda called for the abolition of the autocracy and the capitalists[2]. Though the agitators spoke to large crowds during strikes, the Social-Democrats generally did not take a dominant role.

The police were a hazard in the south, though in Ekaterinoslav they do not seem to have dislocated the organisation of the Social-Democrats as much as in Moscow or Ivanovo.

Internal factional dispute was much more important. At the end of the 1890's a circle (the 'Group' of the RSDLP) disagreed with the official Committee over its emphasis on political agitation[3]. This disagreement was the forerunner of a more important split based on the principles of 'electiveness' (*vybornost'*) and 'nomination' (*naznachenstvo*). One of the leaders of the 'electiveness' faction, N. Drokhanov (who became a Menshevik in 1905) has argued that the executive committee was out of contact with the masses, and was not fulfilling the demands of party workers for proclamations, propaganda and political leadership[4]. Under his leadership they formed a separate 'Workers' Committee' in the autumn of 1901. Wildman has suggested that this division also represented a social split between the intelligentsia and the working class because of antagonism between them[5]. This is probably correct: Krasnoshchekov recalls that in 1901 the Committee was mainly composed of intelligentsia having no contacts with the masses, and Drokhanov says that 'in 1901 the workers in Ekaterinoslav took the leadership into their own hands'[6]. This opposition tried to organise other anti-*Iskra* circles in the neighbouring Committees of Nikolaev, Odessa, Kharkov, Voronezh and in the area of the Union of Metal and Mining Workers[7]. On the

[1] The Union, for example, up to 1903 had printed eighteen leaflets, altogether 10,000 copies and had distributed many more: 'Doklad sotsial-demokraticheskogo soyuza gornozavodskikh rabochikh...', p. 543.

[2] See proclamation, *Iskra*, no. 17, Feb. 1902.

[3] Rubach, p. XXVI.

[4] Cited by Rubach, p. XXXIII.

[5] A. K. Wildman, *The Proletarian Prometheans: The Young Social-Democrats and the Workers' Movement, 1894-1901*, Ph. D. Thesis (Chicago, 1962), pp. 131-4.

[6] 'Na zare', in Rubach, p. 256.

[7] 'Materialy o sosial-demokraticheskikh organizatsiakh v Rossii nakanune II s'ezda RSDRP', V.I. KPSS, No. 9 (Sept. 1963), p. 82.

eve of the Second Party Congress there were two Social-Democratic organisations in Ekaterinoslav: the *Iskra* Committee and the 'Opposition' or the 'Workers' Committee'. In the south generally, opposition to *Iskra* was quite strong, though the latter had succeeded in obtaining many declarations of support. By 1 February 1903, the Organisational Committee of *Iskra* had the support of the Kharkov, Kiev, Rostov, Ekaterinoslav, Odessa and Nikolaev Committees for calling the Second Congress and all, with the exception of Odessa and Nikolaev, had granted *Iskra* the right to compose general party leaflets[1]. The Union of Metal and Mining Workers (with one dissenter on the executive committee) recognised *Iskra* and the line of 'What is to be done?' – though it wanted *Iskra* to be in more popular language and the practical leadership to be in Russia and not abroad[2]. In May 1903, the Ekaterinoslav Committee declared 'its full solidarity on all questions of the programme, tactics and organisational views of *Iskra* and *Zarya* and recognised them as the leading organs'[3]. Khinoy recalls that this Committee was in a minority in the area and 'packed' with *Iskra* men[4].

3. The Structure and Activity of Social-Democracy in Ekaterinoslav 1903 to 1905

In chapters one and two I have already shown that south Russia was an area of Menshevik influence. There were, however, pockets of Bolshevik supporters. Of the towns in the Donbass, only Lugansk remained firmly under Bolshevik control. It was a new Committee of the RSDLP having been founded only in 1903 and, even at the beginning of 1905, it was 'weak' though it could on occasions call mass meetings attended by up to a thousand men[5]. It is claimed that the Mensheviks' support was mainly among the town handicraftsmen[6], though this is not the whole picture for the large factory settlement of Yuzovka in April 1905 was Menshevik. In many other places (Mariupol' and Krivoy Rog for example), it has been reported that there were few Social-Democrats[7].

In view of the opposition to *Iskra* and the diverse nature of Social-

---

[1] Krupskaya, K.A. no. 59 (1933), p. 44.
[2] 'Doklad sotsial-demokraticheskogo soyuza...', pp. 548-9.
[3] *Iskra*, no. 40, May 1903.
[4] M. Khinoy, *U istokov Men'shevizma* (N.Y. 1960), pp. 16, 20.
[5] 'Pamyati tovarishcha' (Lu. Lutimov), L.R. no. 3 (1925), pp. 181-2.
[6] G. Shklovski, P.R. no. 4 (51) (1926), p. 6.
[7] Letter no. 4 (April 1905), P.R. no. 4 (51) (1926), p. 15.

Democratic groups in Ekaterinoslav before the Second Congress, it is not surprising that rival Menshevik and Bolshevik Committees were set up[1]. An activist in Ekaterinoslav in 1904 has recalled that at this time 'both among the Bolsheviks and Mensheviks were factionalists to the extent of fanatics...' the differences between them arose out of organisational and tactical matters[2].

By the autumn of 1903 the membership of the Committee was estimated at 350[3] though it is doubtful whether many of these men had much knowledge about the split. In October 1903, a Bolshevik cell was founded at the Bryansk factory just outside Ekaterinoslav, and after discussions with the existing 'Workers' Organisation' during November and December a joint group was formed[4].

A member of the Ekaterinoslav Committee in 1904 has recalled that the Committee had circles among the student youth, and an organiser was especially responsible for the factory district[5], where the Bolsheviks had made some headway. At this time the Bolsheviks also had a group among the railwaymen living in the settlement[6]. They had, however, no group in the town district where in November 1904 a resolution was passed protesting against the calling of the Third Congress by the Bolsheviks[7].

In the villages around Ekaterinoslav the Social-Democrats probably had less support than the other revolutionary groups. Before the Second Congress, circles linked to the Ekaterinoslav Committee existed, mainly led by the village school-teachers[8]. These circles were probably not firmly committed to Social-Democracy: they debated different policies and, many being dissatisfied with the Social-Democrats' agrarian policy, joined Socialist-Revolutionary groups[9]. The activists in the villages (both Social-Democratic and Socialist-Revolutionary) were drawn from the village school-teachers,

[1] I. B. Polonski, 'Vospominaniya' in M. A. Rubach, *Istoriya Ekaterinoslavskoy sotsial-demokraticheskoy organizatsii, 1889-1903 (Dokumenty)* (Ekaterinoslav 1923), p. 360.
[2] Dyadya Vanya, 'Russko-Yaponskaya voyna', in *Materialy po istorii Ekaterinoslavskoy S.D. organizatsii bol'shevikov i revolyutsionnykh sobytiy 1904, 05, 06* (Ekaterinoslav 1924), p. 2. Cited hereafter as *Ekat. Mat.* (1924).
[3] V. Nogin, 'Vospominaniya', in Rubach, p. 370.
[4] 'Materialy o sotsial-demokraticheskikh organizatsiakh nakanune II s'ezda', V.I. KPSS (September 1963), p. 82.
[5] A. Fabrichny, 'Pered grozoy', in *Ekat. Mat.* (1924), pp. 4-5.
[6] These were railway workers in the workshops, not footplatemen, I. Volkov, 'Iz vospominaniy zheleznodorozhnika', in *Ekat. Mat.* (1924), pp. 147-9.
[7] Cited by police agent in his report in *Ekat. Mat.* (1924), p. 81, see also: Brandenburgski, 'Iz vospominaniy', in *Ekat. Mat.* (1924), p. 9.
[8] E. Kogan, 'Iz istorii selyanskogo' dvizheniya na Ekaterinoslavshchine nakanune 1905 g.', in L.R. no. 5 (1926), pp. 107-10.
[9] Kogan, p. 110.

school-pupils and the *Zemstvo* officials. Kogan says that in 1904 there were Social-Democratic cells in six villages, though the *Krest'yanski Soyuz* and Socialist-Revolutionaries, as one would expect, claimed the allegiance of most of the 'organised' villagers[1]. Social-Democratic activity in the villages was at the discussion-circle level, a few activists distributed leaflets (particularly about the land question) and occasionally meetings were held, addressed by agitators from the towns.

In the town of Ekaterinoslav other parties were quite strong. In the railway workshops a large number of the men were Socialist-Revolutionaries – this may be explained by the large number of workers recently recruited from the countryside – and in the town district the *Bund* and *Poale Tsion* had many members[2]. The Black Hundreds and *Zubatovshchina* were also well-organised and provided the police with accurate information about Social-Democratic activities. Dyadya Vanya recalls that through the Zubatovites the police were able to record Socialist-Revolutionary supporters and the Bolsheviks and Mensheviks among the Social-Democrats. Half of the arrests, he estimates, were due to information received from such informers[3]. The police reports confirm their awareness of the movements of the Social-Democrats of both factions[4]. The police, however, stressed the role played by Jews in these anti-government groups: they emphasised the role of Jewish youth in disturbances and the 'large proportion of Jews who took part in the strikes of school pupils in 1905'[5]. No doubt the more 'open' forms of Menshevik organisation helped the police at least in the larger factories, though possibly less so in the small workshops. A significant, even if not large, proportion of the population was probably hostile to the Social-Democrats, and was prepared to co-operate with the authorities. Before 1905, as we have seen in St. Petersburg and Moscow, workers at the Bryansk factory were hostile to the slogan, 'Down with the autocracy' and argued that the Tsar was not responsible for the bad position of the workers, rather the *chinovniki* and capitalists were[6].

The work of the Social-Democrats in 1904 consisted, as in other

[1] Kogan, pp. 113, 126-29.
[2] I. Zakharenko, 'O moey rabote v partii (za 1904-05)', in *Ekat. Mat.* (1924), p. 128.
[3] Dyadya Vanya, 'Russko-Yaponskaya voyna', *Ekat. Mat.* (1924), p. 3.
[4] See reports in *Ekat. Mat.* (1924), dated 21/i/1904, p. 54; 10/xi/1904, p. 81; 16/vi/1905, 7/vii/1905, pp. 176-7.
[5] See reports dated 4/v/1905, p. 232; 26/vi/1905, p. 261; 21/x/1905, p. 324; 9/xii/1905, p. 354, in *Ekat. Mat.* (1924).
[6] G. I. Petrovski, 'Shtrikhi', in *Ekat. Mat.* (1924), p. 111.

Committees, of agitation and propaganda. The Bolshevik delegate to the Third Congress reported that in January 1904 there were 450 members of the Committee, but that by the summer membership had fallen[1]. In 1904, the Bolsheviks had organised their members into three districts: the largest of which was the 'factory district' having seven propaganda groups, the 'town district' only had one such group, the numbers of cells in the 'Lower Dnieper' and in the separate students' section are not known[2]. In March 1904 at the Yuzovka settlement, which was most probably Menshevik-controlled, there were nine propaganda circles (four in the settlement and five in the works)[3]. Activity at the level of the factory cell in 1904 consisted of the study of some set books (including *The Communist Manifesto*) on which members were required to prepare written answers to questions put by the Social-Democratic propagandist. At larger agitational meetings, attended by about thirty men, a participant has recalled that lively speeches were made and poetry was recited, showing the emotional atmosphere in which Social-Democratic ideas were communicated and which may have played a part in attracting men to the cause[4].

In January 1905, the leaders of both Menshevik and Bolshevik factions were arrested, and the control of the Committee remained with the Mensheviks[5]. The police, well aware of the split in the ranks of Ekaterinoslav Social-Democracy, noted that 'the leadership went from the Bolsheviks to the Mensheviks and then back'[6]. The factional activity no doubt diverted attention away from other activities. The Ekaterinoslav Bolshevik delegate to the Third Party Congress complained that his Committee was regarded by many as a 'small group of intellectuals occupied with discussion, not action'[7].

In 1905 membership and activity of all parties increased, and the Social-Democrats in Ekaterinoslav were no exception. By the end of May 1905, the Bolshevik local secretary wrote: 'Nearly all the factory district (Bryansk mill) is in our hands, in the town district, where earlier we had nothing, there are now sixty of our own men'[8].

[1] 'Otchet Ekaterinoslavskogo Komiteta RSDRP', in *III S'ezd* (*Protokoly*) (M. 1959), p. 622.

[2] 'Otchet...', p. 622 and 'Letter no. 5', in P.R. no. 4 (51) (1926), p. 15.

[3] 'Proval Yuzovskoy gruppy RSDRP', in *Ekat. Mat.* (1924), p. 93.

[4] I. Merinkov, 'Vospominaniya Brantsa', in *Ekat. Mat.* (1924), p. 118-9.

[5] 'Pis'mo chlena Ekaterinoslavskogo bol'shevistskogo komiteta III partiynomu s'ezdu o Ekaterinoslavskoy partynoy organizatsii', in *III S'ezd RSDRP* (*Protokoly*) (M. 1959), pp. 690-2. See also A. M. Pankratova, K.A. 73 (1935), p. 93.

[6] Police report dated 7 Feb. 1905, cited in S. Kramer, 'Yanvarskie dni 1905 g. v Ekaterinoslave i Donetskom basseyne', in L.R. no. 1 (1925), p. 188.

[7] 'Otchet Ekaterinoslavskogo Komiteta RSDRP', *III S'ezd* (*Protokoly*), p. 625.

[8] Letter no. 9 (30 May 1905), P.R. 4 (51) (1926), p. 18.

It has been estjmated that, in the factory district, the Bolsheviks had from fifty to sixty men in their branches[1]. By the summer of 1905, the Ekaterinoslav Bolsheviks claimed to have had two hundred organised men and their own press[2]. No doubt the Mensheviks had many more.

The factional disputes did not prevent joint action between Bolsheviks, Mensheviks and Bundists. In July an agreement was made over collections for an armed uprising and over a general plan of activity[3]. Yaroslavski, one of the Bolshevik local leaders working in the Chechelev area in the summer of 1905, recalls that the Bolsheviks had a joint organisation with the Mensheviks who had 'many talented orators' though they were in a minority – three-quarters of the organisation being Bolshevik. This did not prevent each faction from meeting separately and having different policies. Merinkov points out that in 1904 the factions differed in their attitude to a provisional government, and to a centralised or more democratic form of Social-Democratic organisation[4] showing that differences at the top of the party were also reflected in the local Committees.

The RSDLP had competition from other revolutionary groups: the Bundists among the handicraftsmen; the Socialist-Revolutionaries who, according to Yaroslavski, had their support among the intellectuals; and the Anarchists who carried out work among the masses and had many followers among the unemployed[5]. Ravich-Cherkasski in his memoirs paints a similar picture: the Socialist-Revolutionaries, of whom 90% were *sluzhashchie*, were several thousand strong; the Bund had a membership of 500 Jewish workers and a small part of the intelligentsia[6].

4. 1905 in Ekaterinoslav

As in the other Committees I have described, revolutionary activity increased after the St. Petersburg shootings in January. The initial response seems to have been spontaneous: in Ekaterinoslav members of different revolutionary groups convened meetings, without the

---

[1] E. Yaroslavski (memoir), 'Posle Stokgol'mskogo s'ezda v Ekaterinoslave', in L.R. nos. 3-4 (1926), p. 144.

[2] Letter no. 11 (15/VI/1905), P.R. 4 (51) (1926), p. 20.

[3] Letter no. 17, dated 26/VII/1905 in P.R. 4 (51) (1926).

[4] I. Merinkov, 'Vospominaniya Brantsa', in *Ekat. Mat.* (1924), p. 119.

[5] E. Yaroslavski, 'Posle Stokgol'mskogo s'ezda v Ekaterinoslave', L.R. nos. 3-4 (1926), pp. 143-9.

[6] M. Ravich-Cherkasski, 'Moi vospominaniya o 1905 g.', L.R. nos. 5-6 (1925), p. 315.

sanction of their executive committees. Mensheviks, Bolsheviks, Socialist-Revolutionaries and Anarchists took part in discussions and many called for unity against the common enemy[1]. But industrial action did not take place until 17 January[2].

Leaflets had been distributed at the Bryansk factory one or two days after 9 January. In these strike leaflets the demands were mainly 'economistic': an eight-hour day, the increase of wages by 30%, reduction of work by two hours on Saturdays, government insurance (to be paid by the employers), polite treatment, the improvement of medical aid, certain measures to improve safety, and the dismissal of several foremen. At Bryansk, delegates were elected on a workshop basis to confer with the administration. The management made some concessions to the workers at this time and many of their specific economic demands were met[3]. Of the delegates' group of eight which bargained with the administration only two were party men (Merinkov and Molitvin). Not only did this group succeed in winning some 'economic' concessions, it also prevented the dismissal of twenty-three men[4]. The cooperation of the management seems clear: they even provided the delegates with a room for their meetings[5]. Strikes generally were for higher pay and better conditions as reflected in the demands cited above[6]. The police regarded the January strikes as being solely of an 'economistic' character: 'political questions were not touched'[7]. It is not possible to evaluate the results of all these strikes, but at one factory, of twenty demands, fifteen were fulfilled by the management[8].

The relatively weak political protest in January, the emphasis on 'economistic' demands and the greater acceptance of the workers' trade-union type organisations show the differences with the other areas studied and help explain why the Mensheviks were more successful here than in the central areas.

We have seen that the Donbass mining industry had grown rapidly.

---

[1] Shevchenko, 'O revolyutsii 1905 g.', in *Ekat. Mat.* (1924), pp. 130-3.

[2] Report of MVD cited in S. Kramer, 'Yanvarskie dni 1905 goda v Ekaterinoslave i Donetskom basseyne', *Letopis' revolyutsii* (Kharkov), no. 1 (1925), p. 170.

[3] I. Merinkov, S. Andronov, N. Miller, N. Troshin (collective recollections), 'Bryanski zavod v 1905 godu', L.R. nos. 3-4 (1926), pp. 165-6.

[4] I. Merinkov, 'Vospominaniya Brantsa', *Ekat. Mat.* (1924), p. 121.

[5] I. Merinkov et al, L.R. 3-4 (1926), p. 168.

[6] Another list of demands is in S. Kramer, L.R. no. 1 (1925), pp. 180-2. As a general rule there were no political demands, save for slogans advocating the abolition of the autocracy, and the creation of a democratic republic coupled with the need for freedom of speech, press (and so on) (Kramer, pp. 182-3).

[7] Police report dated 24 January 1905, L.R. 1 (1925), pp. 210-1.

[8] Kramer, L.R. no. 1 (1925), p. 182.

The miners' demands were similar to those of the workers in Ekaterinoslav: better wages and conditions, the eight-hour day, workers' control (elected workers to consider wages, the causes of dismissal of workers) and civil rights[1]. As early as 1900, the miners had asked for parity of conditions between Russian and foreign workers[2], and at one mine this was repeated in 1905 – miners wanting an increase to Belgians' rates, who received two to three times as much as the Russians[3].

The miners presented a special problem for organisation and the Bolsheviks had set up a union among them in 1905 to counter the Menshevik 'Donets Union' which had much influence in the Donets basin[4]. The miners were difficult to organise, a police report sums up the situation: '...the miners present the lesser danger compared to the factory workers who are more inclined to disorders, more receptive to different kinds of propaganda, are more literate, intelligent and at a significantly higher cultural level'[5]. In the autumn of 1905, they did not play a very prominent part in the uprisings.

In the industrial area of Ekaterinoslav spasmodic strikes took place from the spring to the summer of 1905[6]. But the days from February to October were generally quiet. May Day passed peacefully. The only strike was a short one in July[7]. Compared to the strikes of metalworkers in St. Petersburg and the Polish provinces, such activity was much weaker in the south of Russia[8].

5. The October Disturbances

The quiet summer period ended at the beginning of October when demonstrations began to take place. One might expect outbreaks in the autumn with the return of peasants from summer working on the land when wage-rates tended to fall. But in 1905, the disturbances reached large proportions. Crowds (one of 3,000 strong is reported

[1] V. Sof'ev, 'Gornorabochie v 1905-07 g.', in *Proletariat v revolyutsii* (M. 1930), p. 198.
[2] Sof'ev, p. 196.
[3] Kramer, L.R. 1 (1925), p. 182 (footnote).
[4] Sof'ev, p. 202.
[5] General Keller, 'Zapiska po rabochemu voprosu v Ekaterinoslavskoy gubernii', cited by A. M. Pankratova, K.A. 73 (1935), p. 92.
[6] At the Dneprov factory (Kamensk) in July every shop put forward its requests for better conditions and for the dismissal of some engineers. (T. Skubitski, 'Rabochee dvizhenie na Dneprovskom zavode (1895-1905)', L.R. no. 6 (1926), p. 167).
[7] A. M. Pankratova, K.A. 73 (1935), p. 93.
[8] F. Semenov, 'Metallisty v revolyutsii 1905-07 gg.', in *Proletariat v revolyutsii 1905-07 gg.* (M. 1930), p. 20.

by the police) were harangued by orators demanding action to ameliorate the hardship of their lives. Red flags, banners and revolutionary songs (often the Marseillaise) helped to create solidarity among the participants. They may have given the impression of more solidarity and unity to observers than might in fact have been the case[1].

Having heard rumours of the events in Moscow and St. Petersburg, a demonstration and strike took place in Ekaterinoslav on 10 October, and on the next day barricades were erected in the Chechelev district[2]. A police telegram sums up the position: 'Factories, *sluzhashchie* of the railway, the railway workshops and depot continue to strike; the school-pupils are absent, the shops are closed and a general strike of all the working people is expected. The trams are not working. There is an armed demonstration, barricades have been built, shooting has occurred between troops and insurgents causing casualties on both sides'[3]. Thirty-one were killed, and twenty-one were taken to hospital[4].

On 12 October, a general strike took place[5], followed on the next day by clashes between police, cossacks and strikers. In Aleksandrovsk, strikers took over the post-telegraph offices and stopped work[6]. The strike, accompanied by street fighting and disorders, continued for several days. Again support for the insurgents was wide: 'On the barricades were people of all ages and positions – workers, peasants, *sluzhashchie*, intelligentsia, young and old men'[7].

The workers' settlement at Chechelev was badly policed and here, according to local newspaper accounts, were held the 'most grandiose' meetings. On 19 October, a crowd gathered all day and 'speakers from many parties and groups spoke in five or six places in the auditorium'[8]. Such dispersed groups show the multi-party and heterogeneous nature of the demonstrations and political leadership. The strike did not last long: on 20 October, the workers in the large Ekaterinoslav factories went back to work, though in Nizhnedneprovsk they held out[9]. From 21 October, pogroms against the

---

[1] See police telegrams 29/ix/1905 to 10/x/1905, in K.A. 73 (1935), pp. 97-103.
[2] Shevchenko. 'O revolyutsii 1905 g.', *Ekat. Mat.* (1924), p. 134.
[3] Police telegram, Ekaterinoslav, dated 11/x/1905, in *Ekat. Mat.* (1924), p. 299.
[4] 'Spisok...', in *Ekat. Mat.* (1924), pp. 301-2.
[5] Police telegram dated 12/x/1905 in *Ekat. Mat.* (1924), p. 303.
[6] Police telegram, dated 13/x/1905, in K.A. no. 73 (1935), p. 103.
[7] *Byulleten' boevogo stachechnogo komiteta* (Ekaterinoslav), no. 7 (22 Oct. 1905). See also contemporary journalists' account, 'Volneniya v Ekaterinoslave' in *Ekat. Mat.* (1924), pp. 310-20.
[8] Article 'Mitingi', *Pridneprovski Kray* (20/x/1905), in *Ekat. Mat.* (1924), p. 321.
[9] Police report in K.A. no. 73 (1935), p. 122.

Jews took place[1]. The Jews were not just a convenient scapegoat for the police, they figured prominently in revolutionary activities and may genuinely have been thought one of the causes of trouble.

The peasantry and agricultural workers took neither a very active part in Social-Democratic activity nor in the uprisings, though an agitational-propaganda group was sent to the villages to ask for support[2]. In the villages, it addressed large crowds but, apart from the sympathy of some peasants in Bryansk, little support was received.

The uprising continued during October and November and, unlike in the northern areas, in Ekaterinoslav the consuls of Britain, France, Belgium and Germany brought pressure for the protection of their nationals and their property[3]. The existence of foreign owners was probably a cause of greater social and political distance between the government and manufacturers than existed in the Moscow and St. Petersburg areas. We have seen that in January the employers had given in to some of the workers' demands and it is probable that factory administrations might have abetted their workers in political anti-Tsarist protest, while at the same time seeking police protection for the security of their property.

The insurgents had a wide social base of support. In January 1906, an engineer from the Bryansk factory was a member of the finance commission of the Coalition Fighting and Strike Committee, and factory directors are reported to have given large donations to it: one of 4,000 rubles, another of 2,000 rubles and a third 300 rubles. Two German engineers at the Bryansk factories were Social-Democrats and, it is alleged, stirred up the workers[4]. The revolutionaries were not composed solely of factory workers, though they were predominant at demonstrations. The Bryansk factory's 'Delegates' Council' (obshchedelegatskoe sobranie) was led by an intellectual, and sums of money were collected from the intelligentsia for the unemployed and for an uprising[5].

Among the troops, many of whom had returned from Manchuria, meetings took place, revolutionary leaflets were circulated and, according to the Byulleten' boevogo stachechnogo komiteta, some were willing to assist the strike committee[6]. In fact, the troops did not

[1] Police reports 22/x, 23/x and 25/x in Ekat. Mat. (1924), pp. 331-3.
[2] Merinkov et al, 'Bryanski zavod v 1905 g.', L.R. 3-4 (1925), p. 175.
[3] See police messages 20/x: p. 323; 26, 27/x: p. 333; 3, 13/xi: p. 333, in Ekat. Mat. (1924). Requests from the consuls were made more than once.
[4] Police report dated 9 January 1906 in Ekat. Mat. (1924), p. 388.
[5] Merinkov et al, L.R. 3-4 (1926), pp. 172, 174.
[6] Byulleten'... (Ekaterinoslav), no. 1 (11 Dec. 1905), no. 3 (13 Dec. 1905).

play a very active role in support of the revolutionaries. Rosenblyum has estimated that only 65 soldiers 'took part' in Social-Democratic activity (in 1906) compared to 250 in Moscow[1].

The insurgents did not face a united ruling class in Ekaterinoslav. The factory administration was dependent on the Tsarist power to maintain law and order and its own property but it supported in general terms those forces in Russian society which strove for a liberal-democratic political order. The political action taken by the insurgents tended to separate the capitalists from the workers' organisations and strengthened the links of the former with the autocracy.

The 'Delegates' Councils' of workers' deputies which had bargained with the management earlier in 1905 became the main organ of political expression for the workers from October. A report of a Delegates' Council in November shows the pragmatic attitude of one of these groups. Its agenda was not concerned with revolutionary action, but with the pay due to some of its members after the closing of a factory, with the need to give aid to the unemployed and other workers, and with the problems of forming trade unions. On the first item it is interesting to note that the meeting discussed the management's obligations in terms of the 'agreement book' (*dogovornaya kniga*), which, according to them, said that the workers were entitled to two weeks' pay when the factory closed[2]. This shows that institutional bargaining took place between management and men and that a standard of reference had been set[3]. In view of this, one cannot argue that it was an absence of *channels* of communication or of workers' representatives that caused friction in this area.

It was not until the beginning of December that these factory-based committees formed a town organisation called 'The Deputies' Council of Ekaterinoslav Workers', or later (popularly) the 'Soviet of Workers' Deputies'[4]. The Social-Democrats were dominant on the executive of the Soviet, all seven members being in the RSDLP. The Socialist-Revolutionaries and other parties argued that a system of proportional representation should have been used, from which

[1] K. Rozenblyum, *Voennye organizatsii Bol'shevikov 1905-07 gg.* (M.L. 1931), p. 102.

[2] 'V delegatskom sobranii Ekaterinoslavskikh rabochikh' (Report) in *Ekat. Mat.* (1924), pp. 380-1.

[3] Merinkov recalls that when he was in the executive committee of the Metalworkers' Union (in 1906), it sent to Germany for material on trade-union activity, showing that a 'western' form of union activity was thought of as a model by many of the activists (Merinkov et al, L.R. 3-4 (1926), p. 126.

[4] A. Fabrichny, 'V vikhre revolyutsii', *Ekat. Mat.* (1924), p. 280.

we may infer that the other parties were of significant but smaller size[1]. As in St. Petersburg, 'the Mensheviks played the predominant role...(and) took the initiative in the organisation of the Soviet. Both chairmen of the Soviet (Nikifor and Pavel Pavlovich) were members of the Menshevik committee...'[2] The Soviet was replaced as the leading organ of the insurrectionists by a much wider body formed in December called the 'Coalition Fighting and Strike Committee'. It was composed of the seven members of the executive committee of the Soviet (four Bolsheviks and three Mensheviks); of representatives from the political parties: three Bolsheviks, three Mensheviks, two from the Bureau of the Provincial Organisation (Mensheviks), two Bundists, three Socialist-Revolutionaries; and of four trade-union delegates, two from the railway union, and two from the post-telegraph union[3]. This gave the Mensheviks a majority.

There can be no doubt that the revolutionaries had a great deal of popular support. A police report estimated that about one-twelfth of the workers were 'organised'. Though many of these were in

Table 30. *Voting in the Workers' Curia to the II Duma in Ekaterinoslav Province*

Name of Factory	Electors and Faction	Total Vote	Bols.	Independent S.D.	Mens.	S.R.	Right-wing
Ezau	1 S.D. Men.	130	–		112	15	3
Parovozn. masterskaya	2 S.D. Men.	800	–		650	–	–
Parovozn. depo	1 S.D. (no faction)	230	–	230	–	–	–
Gvozdil'ny	1 S.D. Bol.	250	250		–	–	–
Truboprokatny	1 S.D. Men.	200	–		195	–	5
Bryanski rel'soprok	4 S.R.	1100	–		300	800	–
10: 4 Mensheviks 1 Bolshevik 1 Independent S.D. 4 S.R.'s		2710	250	230 Total S.D. 1737	1257	815	8

Proletari, no. 13 (Feb. 1907), reprinted in 'Nekotorie dannye o vyborakh po rabochey kurii na yuge Rossii', V.I. Lenin, *Soch.* (IV Ed.), vol. 12, p. 76.

[1] Shevchenko, 'O revolyutsii 1905 g.', in *Ekat. Mat.* (1924), p. 140.
[2] A. Fabrichny, *Ekat. Mat.* (1924), p. 281.
[3] Shevchenko, 'O revolyutsii 1905 g.', *Ekat. Mat.* (1924), p. 140, and correction note p. 529.

societies of an 'elemental' kind, the majority of workers was not opposed to the revolutionaries, and the Jews were singled out as being particularly revolutionary[1].

As to the relative support of the revolutionary parties, some results of factory elections to the Second Duma in Ekaterinoslav have been published in *Proletari*. Whilst the figures are only a rough indication, Table 30 shows that the Social-Democrats had twice as many votes as the Socialist-Revolutionaries (1,737 to 815): the Socialist-Revolutionaries, as in St. Petersburg, again did extremely well in the large factory (the Bryansk factory having 4,350 workers). The election results confirm the factional strength of the Mensheviks in this area and among the factory workers.

The climax of the insurrection was in December 1905, following the arrest of the members of the St. Petersburg Soviet. A general strike was declared, and the railway stopped. At a meeting at Bryansk, some Social-Democrats wanted moderation so that repression would not follow from the government. They recommended a general strike, and a financial struggle with the government including the withdrawal of money from the banks[2]. During December, the local strike committee seized control of the stations, the railway and railway telegraph and organised special 'delegates' trains' for the strikers[3].

On 14 December, the authorities were again in charge of the town but the workers' settlement was still under the control of the insurgents and became popularly known as the 'Chechelev Republic'[4]. In the settlement the strike committee put on meals in the factory canteens, organised workers' detachments, controlled the bakeries and the waterworks, and ordered the workers not to pay taxes[5].

This state of affairs lasted for a week or so when the strike committee decided that it had insufficient arms to continue the struggle and decided to end the strike[6]. On 28 December, the 'Republic' was finally taken, with little resistance, by government troops[7]. In January, arrests of the revolutionary activists began to take place. The uprising was over, though strikes and minor disturbances continued in 1906.

---

[1] Police report, dated 9/xɪɪ/05, *Ekat. Mat.* (1924), p. 354.
[2] Police report, 9 December 1905, *Ekat. Mat.* (1924), p. 355.
[3] Police report, 'Delo 23, 1906 g.' in *Ekat. Mat.* (1924), pp. 450-1.
[4] Police telegram, dated 15/xɪɪ in K.A. no. 73 (1935), p. 118.
[5] Shevchenko, 'O revolyutsii 1905 g.', in *Ekat. Mat.* (1924), p. 142.
[6] Merinkov et al, p. 176.
[7] Police telegram, 28/xɪɪ, in *Ekat. Mat.* (1924), p. 371.

6. Summing-up

Social-Democracy in Ekaterinoslav was heterogeneous and reflected the mixed occupational and national groupings of the population in the town. Of the two factions of the RSDLP, the Menshevik was dominant. The chief Menshevik support lay among the more highly skilled workers. There can be no doubt that the workers from other areas brought their political traditions with them which helps to explain the factional nature of activities. Many of the Mensheviks were Jews though there were also some supporters among the Great Russians. The absence of detailed Menshevik source materials makes it difficult to define exactly their support. However, it is tempting to suppose that, as the majority of the immigrant factory workers were Russians and as the Bolshevik's strength lay here rather than among the native handicraftsmen, the Bolsheviks were mainly but not exclusively recruited from Great Russian immigrants. This inference is in keeping with some of the conclusions of Part One. The uprising in Ekaterinoslav shows that the non-Bolshevik groups did not lack revolutionary energy, but the town fell relatively easily to the government forces, with only Chechelev putting up much resistance. This again could be explained by the greater homogeneity and class consciousness of the working class in the settlement outside the town. Factory managements in the new big firms were more 'progressive' in Ekaterinoslav than in the other areas studied so far. They were more like western European factory management in practice and had institutionalised channels for dealing with their employees. Though worker-management relations were not smooth, it seems probable that there was much less conscious class antagonism here than in say Moscow or Ivanovo. The foreign-owned and foreign-managed factories, the proprietors of which were used to the free-market, non-interference in business activities and the civil liberties of western Europe, might well have encouraged the popular struggle against the autocracy. Bendix has argued, and it is widely held, that the nature of management in Russian industry was dominated by patriarchal relations and police interference[1], but he like some other writers ignores the importance of non-Russian firms in Russia and their attempts to accommodate their employees. The *dogovor* (agreement) in the Ukraine showed a considerable degree of worker-capitalist agreement. Bargaining with the employers was not only institutionalised but also gave tangible benefits to the workers which helps to explain why the Mensheviks found support here for their more 'trade-union' type policies.

[1] R. Bendix, *Work and Authority in Industry* (N.Y. 1956), pp. 117-190. Bendix throughout relies too heavily on factory rules and regulations quoted by Pankratova and virtually ignores the *process* of industrial relations.

THE STRUCTURE AND ACTIVITY OF
SOCIAL-DEMOCRACY IN THE CAUCASUS, (BAKU)

1. Social and Economic Background

The area now known as Azerbaydzhan was ceded to Russia from Persia at the beginning of the nineteenth century. Of a total population of 827,000 inhabitants in Baku province in 1897, 485,000 were Tatars (*Tatarskoe naselenie*), 89,000 Tats (*Tatskoe naselenie*), Great Russians numbered 74,000, Armenians 52,000, Kurds 48,000, Jews 8,000 and Georgians 1,500[1].

The population of Baku (town) rose very quickly in the late nineteenth century, from 14,000 in 1860 to 207,000 in 1900. According to a census of 1903, from 75,000 to 80,000 men were employed: 30,000 were oilmen, 8,720 metalworkers (including those in the shipbuilding and oil industries), 5,376 were in building, 3,184 were in the gas, electric and coal industries and 7,056 were in transport[2]. *Azerbaydzhantsy* and Tatars[3] composed about 54% of the employed, Russians 20.3%, Armenians 20.5% and other nationalities 6.5%. Among the skilled workers (mechanics, turners) Russians predominated, being 48.5%, followed by Armenians – 24% and by '*Azerbaydzhantsy*' – 15%[4].

Immigrants were an important part of the labour force. Persian Azerbaydzhan issued 312,000 passports to workers going to Russia from 1891 to 1904, and many of these found work in Baku[5]. In addition, skilled workers and many of the administrative and tech-

---

[1] *Pervaya vseobshchaya perepis' naseleniya*, vol. II (Spb. 1905), pp. 38-55.

[2] 'Baku po perepisi 22 Okt. 1903 g.' (1909), cited in *Rabochee dvizhenie v gody pervoy russkoy revolyutsii (Dokumenty)* (Baku 1956), p. X. Cited hereafter as *R.D. Baku*.

[3] There is ambiguity in the literature on the definition of Tatars; some writers lump together Tatars, Tats and *Azerbaydzhantsy* under the generic term 'Tatars' or *Azerbaydzhantsy*. Where possible I shall distinguish between these races.

[4] A. M. Pankratova, 'Rabochi klass i rabochee dvizhenie', in *1905* (M. 1925), p. 435.

[5] Ibragimov, *Revolyutsiya 1905-07 gg. v Azerbaydzhane* (Baku 1955), p. 33.

nical personnel were from western Europe: Germans, French and Englishmen.

The main industry was oil, which was developed by western European and American firms and which had grown rapidly from 1870 when Baku oil production was 1,482,000 puds to 671,706,000 puds in 1901 (a good year) – accounting in that year for more than half of world output[1]. In 1900 there were 158 firms, the output of the six largest accounted for half of the total production.

The oil industry's growth was uneven and during years of crisis workers were laid off. The Baku Congress of Oil Producers gives the following statistics:[2]

Year	Number employed
1898	20,500
1901	37,000
1904	27,700
1907	50,000

Output fell during 1905 to 410 million puds compared to 615 millions in 1904[3]. The oil-worker, especially the unskilled, was faced with uncertainty about the tenure of work.

Wage differences between skilled and unskilled were strongly marked in Baku and, according to Ibragimov, were greater than in central Russia[4]. Annual wages in 1900 ranged from 62 rubles 40 copecks to 187 rubles 20 copecks at the Kedabesk factory (calculated on 20-60 copecks per day rate), from 62 r. 40 c. to 93 r. 60 c. at the Shushin, and from 124 r. 80 c. to 156 r. 0 c. on the Elizavetpol' railway. Workers from western Europe received much more than their Russian counterparts: (*Rossiyskie*) engineers received only half the rates of western Europeans. Cultural, social, economic and – as I shall show later – political differences in Baku were determined by the national composition of the population.

Georgians and Russians, and to a lesser extent Armenians, formed the cadres of more skilled workers. *Masterovye* (foremen) formed only 5.4% of the oil workers in Baku: but 19.4% of Georgians and 13.4% of Russians were in this category (figures for 1909). Average earnings for different national groups varied: the average

[1] D. D. Gadzhinski, *Promyslovye i zavodskie komisii v Bakinskom neftepromyshlennom rayone v gody pervoy russkoy revolyutsii* (Candidate's dissertation, Baku 1962), p. 28. (One pud equals 16.38 kilograms or 36.11 imperial pounds).
[2] Cited by A. N. Guliev, *Bakinski proletariat v gody novogo revolyutsionnogo pod'ema* (Baku 1963), p. 30.
[3] *Ibid.*, p. 12.
[4] Ibragimov, pp. 37-8.

yearly income at oil establishments was 361.67 rubles: the average for Georgians was 444.69 r., Russians 400.57 r., Armenians 371.09 r., and local 'Tatars' 325.76 r[1]. The ranking is the same where education is concerned: considering again only single men, 26.7% were literate: the figure for Georgians was 83.8%, Russians 51.3%, Armenians 34.9% and Persians 5.5%[2].

2. The Early History of Social-Democracy

Marxist circles in the Caucasus developed as elsewhere in the 1890's – though later in Baku than in Tiflis. The group *Mesame-dasi* was formed in 1893 (one of its leaders was N. Zhordaniya, the future Menshevik), it had its own newspaper and influence in Georgia. *Mesame-dasi* existed alongside other groups, among them the railway workers' circles in which Stalin was active in 1898[3]. Already by the middle of the 1890's it has been estimated that twenty Marxist circles existed in Tiflis[4]. The workers' papers *Musha*, *Skhivi* and *Gantiadi* had come out in *Guriya* from 1889 to 1892[5]. Plekhanov's work had been translated into Georgian at the turn of the century and a Social-Democratic press existed in Baku at the same time[6]. According to Makharadze, workers' activity at this time in Georgia was led almost exclusively by the Social-Democrats[7].

After the First Party Congress in 1898 self-styled Committees of the RSDLP existed in Tiflis, Batumi, Kutais, Chmatur and in 1899 one was formed in Baku. In 1901 the Baku Committee had links with the St. Petersburg Union of Struggle, *Yuzhny rabochi*, and *Iskra*. Whilst one faction supporting *Iskra* was grouped around the press and Ketskhoveli, other factions supporting the *Bund*, the *Economists* and *Yuzhny rabochi* also existed[8]. Though, perhaps incongruously, this press reprinted *Yuzhny rabochi* and copies of *Listok Rabotnika*, its main activity was in support of *Iskra*. Editions were printed by the press in both Russian and Georgian. At the same time, in Tiflis under the

[1] Single men's wages only, A. M. Stopani, *Neftepromyshlenny rabochi i ego byudzhet* (M. 1924), pp. 124-5.
[2] *Ibid.*
[3] V. G. Esaiashvili, *Ocherki istorii kommunisticheskoy partii Gruzii*, Ch. I (Tbilisi 1957), p. 33.
[4] N. Badriashvili, *Tbilisi* (Sakhelgami 1957), p. 63.
[5] V. G. Esaiashvili, p. 20.
[6] A. Enukidze, 'Istoriya organizatsii i raboty nelegal'nykh tipografiy RSDRP na Kavkaze za vremya ot 1900 po 1906 god', in P.R. no. 2 (14) (1923), pp. 110-1.
[7] F. Makharadze, 'Partorganizatsiya Zakavkaz'ya nakanune i posle II s'ezda', in P.R. no. 2 (1933), p. 74.
[8] Enukidze, P.R. no. 2 (14) (1923), p. 117.

influence of Zhordaniya, *Brdzola* and *Kvali* were printed and resisted unification with the *Iskra* Baku press[1].

Enukidze recalls being sent as a railwayman from Tiflis to Baku in 1898, at which time there 'was not even a circle but only individual comrades – some deported from Russia (the majority being from Moscow) and others returned from emigration abroad'[2]. With the aid of his Tiflis comrades, Enukidze began organising underground circles and by 1899 two circles among the oil workers had been started. In 1900, according to Sturna's memoirs there were seventy members of the Baku group with many cells among the workers[3]. By 1901, the local police noted a 'significant development of Social-Democratic workers' circles'[4]. At the same time, the Tiflis police chief, Zvolyanski, reported that Social-Democratic propaganda and support was growing and that searches and arrests were not sufficient to prevent the growth of revolutionary cells[5]. In this early period the participants in the circles of the Baku Committee were workers who had been deported from south Russia and from Tiflis[6].

Before the Second Congress, the Baku Committee was organised into five districts, in which the local organiser claimed many cells among the workers. Support among the Persians and Azerbaydzhanis in the oil industry was weak[7]. In terms of membership for the nine months prior to the Second Congress there had been 25 to 30 circles with from 10 to 15 men attending meetings[8]. This would give a minimum of 250 persons in the circles and allowing for a fairly rapid turnover, about a thousand men would have taken part in discussions at one or two meetings. Six other circles were conducted for the more class-conscious workers, where discussions about socialism and the history of the workers' movement took place – involving, say, about fifty men[9].

The main problems in the Caucasus for the RSDLP groups was the assimilation of the Armenian, Georgian and Tatar populations into their organisations, and their relationship with the existing nationalist parties. The Socialist-Revolutionaries had groups in Baku but were

[1] Enukidze, P.R. no. 2 (14) (1923), p. 120.
[2] Enukidze, p. 109.
[3] O. Makharadze, P.R. 2 (1933), p. 82.
[4] Z. Ibragimov, *Revolyutsiya 1905-07 gg. v Azerbaydzhane* (Baku, 1955), p. 45.
[5] K. A. no. 82 (1937), p. 176.
[6] 'Doklad Bakinskogo komiteta' in *II S'ezd: (Protokoly)* (M. 1959), p. 515.
[7] 'Doklad Bakinskogo...', pp. 515-7.
[8] 'Doklad Bakinskogo...', pp. 521-2.
[9] J. Keep's estimate is that about 2,500 men, mostly Russians, were in the Caucasian Union at this time, *The Rise of Social Democracy in Russia*, p. 101.

said to be small in numbers[1]. The Armenian nationalist party, however, was widely and firmly based in Baku[2]. The numerous languages also made it difficult for the Social-Democrats to communicate with the non-Russian speaking groups. The Armenian Social-Democratic paper *Proletariat* as well as leaflets in Armenian were printed but the bulk of the leaflets were in Russian, relatively few proclamations were in Tatar[3]. The Tatars were the most difficult group to organise being 'far from the ideas of political agitation', but the Social-Democrats did succeed at one stage in forming a circle sixty strong (probably meaning that this number attended a few meetings) in which propaganda in the native language was carried out[4]. In Batum a similar situation confronted the Social-Democratic Committee.

There were no significant groups of the *Zubatovshchina* either in Batum or in Baku[5]. As in Baku it was the presence of Georgians, Armenians, Persians, Greeks and Turks that presented the greatest organising obstacle[6]. In Batum the Committee had much more support among the peasants than had the Baku Committee. It had organised a special 'commission' in Georgia for village work. It claimed to have had circles in 'nearly all the villages', many of the members, as we have seen in Tver Province, were returned urban workers[7]: from 1901 to 1903, the administration had sent 15,000 men from the towns back to the villages[8]. The Batum Committee claimed forty circles in 1903. If one assumes an average membership of seven per circle, the town membership would have been 280, and in the villages on the basis of nine circles, another sixty-three[9].

Though the multi-racial composition of the area created difficulties for the Social-Democrats, it also had its advantages – the opposition to the Tsarist autocracy being reinforced by nationalist sentiment. As we have noted, the Zubatovites did not succeed in setting up a firm group in Baku, though they had made attempts before 1903[10]. It was reported that the police in Baku was badly organised, not having caught one member of the Committee in the first nine months of its

[1] 'Doklad Bakinskogo...', p. 519.
[2] M. Leman, 'Iz proshlogo kavkazskikh bol'shevistskikh org.' in P.R. no. 5 (40) (1925), p. 12.
[3] 'Doklad Bakinskogo...', pp. 516, 523.
[4] *Ibid.*, p. 517.
[5] 'Doklad Batumskogo komiteta' *II S'ezd: Protokoly* (M. 1957), p. 681 and 'Doklad Bakinskogo komiteta', p. 518.
[6] 'Doklad Batumskogo komiteta', p. 684.
[7] 'Doklad Batumskogo komiteta', pp. 682-5.
[8] Ibragimov, *Revolyutsiya 1905-07 gg. v Azerbaydzhane*, p. 51.
[9] 'Doklad Batumskogo komiteta', p. 683.
[10] D. Gadzhinski, *Promyslovye i zavodskie komissii v Bakinskom neftepromyshlennom rayone v gody pervoy russkoy revolyutsii*, Candidate of Science Dissertation, (Baku 1962), p. 96.

existence[1]. The demonstrations held in May 1903 were not hindered by the police and the garrison was undermanned. At one demonstration a crowd of two thousand gathered and twelve open meetings were held – attended by from one hundred to eight hundred men[2]. The Committee's organiser thought that police activity would increase, and it would be erroneous to regard it as non-existent: in March 1902, '... an almost complete collapse of the Baku Committee had taken place, with 86 members being arrested'[3]. Possibly these two factors – the relative weakness of the police and the hostile national groups – explain the relatively more open nature of the revolutionary groups in Baku.

As elsewhere, circle and discussion groups had been the main activity in the 1890's. Prior to the Second Party Congress much propaganda was distributed (at least it was printed): from December 1902 to June 1903, the Baku Committee printed twenty-six thousand copies of leaflets in Russian, six thousand eight hundred in Armenian but only two hundred and fifty in Tatar[4]. In the autumn of 1901 and the winter of 1902, the tempo of Social-Democratic activity increased and by the summer of that year mass meetings were held outside the town[5]. In 1902, May Day was celebrated at meetings with Red Flags, anti-capitalist and anti-government slogans[6]. On May Day 1903, fifteen thousand workers took part in a demonstration at Baku, and in July started a general strike involving forty-five thousand workers. The demands were for increases in wages, the eight-hour day, improvement of conditions, the abolition of fines and overtime and the freeing of men arrested in the strikes of March and April 1903. According to a report of General von Val, the Baku strike '...had undoubtedly a political character, and was created by the Baku Committee of the RSDLP'[7]. Once again we must be on our guard against accepting uncritically statements by the police, but they help to show that the Social-Democrats were being recognised as sources of trouble by the authorities.

As in Ekaterinoslav there was considerable opposition to *Iskra* in the Caucasus, though before the Second Congress there were fewer

[1] 'Doklad Bakinskogo...', p. 515.
[2] 'Doklad Bakinsgogo...', pp. 524-5.
[3] Enukidze, 'Istoriya organizatsii...', P.R. 2 (14) (1923), p. 124.
[4] 'Doklad Bakinskogo komiteta', p. 523.
[5] A. Enukidze, 'K dvadtsatiletiyu Bakinskoy organizatsii', in *Dvatsat' pyat' let Bakinskoy organizatsii bol'shevikov* (Baku 1924), p. 13.
[6] V. Sof'ev, '1905 v Baku', in *Proletariat v revolyutsii* (M. 1930), p. 212 and see proclamation in K.A. no. 82 (1937), pp. 185-7.
[7] Cited by Ibragimov, *Revolyutsiya 1905-07 gg. v Azerbaydzhane*, p. 54-5.

disagreements over the recognition of *Iskra* in Baku and Batum than in Tiflis[1]. Makharadze reports that the Social-Democratic organisations in the Caucasus, even prior to the Second Congress had nationalist internal divisions[2]. The Caucasian Union, joining together the main Social-Democratic Committees (Tiflis, Baku, Batum), was formed in March 1903. The Union supported the *Iskra* programme by as many as fourteen votes to one[3], giving the Union the right to send delegates to the Second Congress. How representative the Union was of Social-Democratic groups is open to question. The Tiflis Committee issued a statement rejecting its right to send delegates to the Congress on the grounds of its short period of existence and the absence of statutes[4]. Some opposition was based on the grounds that *Iskra* did not recognise the autonomy of the Caucasus. One might fairly confidently conclude that amongst the Social-Democrats a considerable amount of opposition existed to the *Iskra*-dominated Caucasian Union, and that this was especially so in Tiflis.

3. The Structure of Social-Democratic Groups 1903-1905

There can be little doubt that inter-factional rivalry was very intense in the Caucasus. Though Baku was to be predominantly a Menshevik area of influence, immediately after the Second Congress the Baku Committee was formally in Bolshevik hands. It was not until February/March 1904 that the Baku Committee came under Menshevik control[5]. The Caucasian Union had been set up by the Bolsheviks to unite their small groups and, not surprisingly, it refused to recognise the new Menshevik leadership in Baku and set up another Committee led by Dzhaparidze, Fioletov and Stopani[6].

The factional alignment in Baku was complicated by the existence of what one might loosely call a 'workers' union' led by the Shendrikov brothers. This group was recognised by the Mensheviks as a constituent part of the party and with the other Mensheviks adopted the name of the *Organizatsiya* (or, sometimes, the *soyuz*) *Balakhanskikh i Bibi-Eybatskikh rabochikh*. The Union agitated mainly on the everyday

---

[1] 'Doklad Bakinskogo komiteta', pp. 525, 528-9, 'Doklad Batumskogo komiteta', p. 682.
[2] F. Makharadze, p. 93.
[3] 'Doklad III s'ezdu RSDRP o deyatel'nosti Kavkazskogo soyuza za 1903-05 g.', in *III S'ezd RSDRP (Protokoly)* (M. 1959), p. 607.
[4] Statement of the Tiflis Committee of the RSDLP, K.A. no. 59 (1933), p. 66.
[5] V. I. Nevski, 'Yanvarskie dni 1905 g. na Kavkaze', P.R. no. 27 (1924), p. 55.
[6] 'Kratki konspekt dlya doklada na III partiynom s'ezde Bakinskogo komiteta RSDRP' in *III S'ezd RSDRP (Protokoly)* (M. 1959), p. 610.

needs of the workers. Its leader, Shendrikov, was recognised, even by the Bolsheviks, as a brilliant speaker, though he was regarded by them as being in the pay of the oil companies, an assertion which I cannot verify with the sources available[1]. This accusation did not affect the popularity either of Shendrikov or the Union. By the spring of 1904 the Mensheviks had 'quite strong organisations among the workers'[2]. The Shendrikovs were mainly supported, according to the recollections of a local worker, by the most highly qualified workers but also had much influence and support among the masses[3].

The issues which separated these main socialist factions were, in the eyes of the Mensheviks, that the Bolsheviks ignored the workers' demands and acted in their own interests. Evidence of this, argued the Mensheviks, was the narrow membership of the local Bolshevik executive which was composed mainly of intellectuals, whereas the Menshevik committee was composed of workers[4]. There is some evidence to substantiate the latter more concrete point. Barsov (Tskhakaya), at the Third Party Congress acknowledged that the representation of workers in the Bolshevik executive of local committees and at congresses in the Caucasus was 'irrefutably' small[5].

I have not found precise data on the structure and membership of the Menshevik faction, but the evidence points to a widely based organisation. As far as the Bolsheviks are concerned, up to December 1904, the Baku Committee claimed to have 50 circles with twenty to thirty propagandists[6]. Assuming a minimum membership of ten men to a circle, membership would have been about 500, though this is most probably an optimistic total. Even if it were half of this figure, membership here would have been greater than in the central economic region, another indication of the more open society and less stringent police control, which again would have been to the advantage of the Mensheviks, with their notion of a wide party organisation.

Perhaps the most significant aspect of Social-Democratic organisation in Baku was the attempt by the Bolsheviks to set up groups among the non-Russian 'native' population. A special group called

---

[1] Nevski, P.R. 27 (1924), p. 59, and letter of Stopani to Lenin/Krupskaya in P.R. no. 40 (1925), pp. 19-20.

[2] M. Vasil'ev Yuzhin, 'Reznya 1905 g. i vystuplenie nashey organizatsii', in 25 let Bakinskoy organizatsii bol'shevikov (Baku 1924), p. 55.

[3] A. Khachiev, 'Tri perioda raboty v Baku', in 25 let..., pp. 139-40.

[4] Letter Stopani-Lenin/Krupskaya (Jan. 1905), P.R. no. 40 (1925), p. 24.

[5] Speech, III S'ezd (Protokoly) (M. 1959), p. 330.

[6] 'Kratki konspekt dlya doklada na III partiynom s'ezde Bakinskogo komiteta RSDRP', in III S'ezd RSDRP (Protokoly) (M. 1959), p. 611.

Gummet was formed[1], which had separate representation at the IV Congress of the Caucasian Union, showing that its members did not participate in the same basic cells as Russian-speaking members. But work among them in 1905 was held up because of the absence of literature in their native languages. Particularly, literature on peasant questions was lacking[2]. Makharadze has recalled that one of the main defects of the work among the Persians and *Azerbaydzhantsy* was the absence of links with the villages[3].

The income of the Baku Bolshevik Committee amounted to 7,054 rubles (£705) for the nine months ending in February 1905, on average an income of 783 r. per month. Of this 266 r. per month was spent on the press, 158 r. on maintenance of professional revolutionaries, and 105 r. to support men on strike. Subscriptions from workers were the 'least part' of the income and did not come to more than 10% of it, the chief sources were public collections and funds 'from the factories' (*s predpriyatiy*)[4]. To launch and maintain the Baku press, Enukidze has recalled that the ordinary income was insufficient and that a comrade, Ketskhoveli, was able to get some money from his brother (ostensibly to continue his education) which was used to finance the typography. Later a further sum of 800 rubles was collected with the help of Krasin, Kazerenko and Kits[5] – presumably this money came from rich sympathisers.

During the summer of 1905 the Bolsheviks were most probably in a minority. Later in 1906 and 1907 the Mensheviks were to predominate on the Baku committee, though the Bolsheviks claimed support in the workers' districts[6]. There were Social-Democratic circles in the area around Baku: in Elizavetpol', Shusha, and Nukha. Propagandists went to the villages and, as one would expect, leaflets were circulated[7]. Though the workers deported to the villages were

[1] F. Makharadze, 'Partorganizatsiya Zakavkaz'ya nakanune i posle II s'ezda', P.R. no. 2 (1933), p. 83.
[2] Dzhaparidze's speech, *III S'ezd (Protokoly)* (M. 1959), p. 396.
[3] Makharadze, *ibid.*
[4] 'Kratki konspekt dlya doklada na III partiynom s'ezde Bakinskogo komiteta RSDRP', in *III S'ezd RSDRP (Protokoly)* (M. 1959), p. 614. Of the income in February 1905 it has been estimated that only 3% came from workers' subscriptions, the 'subscription lists' being filled mainly by middle class contributors. V. I. Nevski, 'Istoriya RKP', p. 284, cited in A. Raevski, *Bol'shevizm i Men'shevizm v Baku* (Baku 1930), p. 178.
[5] A. Enukidze, 'Istoriya organizatsii i raboty nelegal'nikh tipografiy RSDRP na Kavkaze za vremya ot 1900 po 1906 g.', P.R. no. 2 (14) (1923), pp. 111, 114.
[6] A. Enukidze, *op. cit.*, p. 14, and S. Ordzhonikidze, 'Bor'ba s men'shevikami' in *25 let...*, p. 43.
[7] Ibragimov, *Revolyutsiya 1905-07 gg. v Azerbaydzhane*, pp. 127-9.

a source of support, it is doubtful whether there was much allegiance there to the Bolsheviks[1].

In neighbouring Georgia, where police activity was weak, the Mensheviks had much support among the Georgians[2]. Circles existed among the railwaymen, factory workers and students[3]. Police activity, however, was strong enough to lead to the arrest of a hundred members of the Tiflis party organisation on 5 and 13 January 1904[4]. Aladzhalova, in her memoirs, recalls that the Mensheviks broke up her meetings, opposing Lenin's formulation of Clause 1. They cried, 'The Bolsheviks oppose workers being in the party. They want to rule over us as Nicholas II. Down with them!'[5] In Tiflis, the (Menshevik) Committee left the Caucasian Union, refused to recognise it and claimed possession of the press[6]. A letter from Tiflis in March 1905 said that the Bolsheviks there were like a general staff without an army, but that the Mensheviks had a widely based organisation[7].

In Batum, the RSDLP had two committees: the Batum and the Georgian. V. Taratuta has recalled that Social-Democracy there had considerable support from the population, especially in the villages where the police had little control over the Georgians[8]. But the Social-Democrats in the villages had little class consciousness and were 'barely acquainted with party affairs'[9]. Mainly the supporters were Georgians and Taratuta was one of the first Russian propagandists among them.

J. Stalin, in a letter to the Bolshevik foreign centre, has summed up the factional division in the Caucasus in May 1905 as follows: 'Tiflis is nearly completely in the hands of the Mensheviks, half of Baku and Batum is also with the Mensheviks. The other half of Baku, a part of Tiflis, all Elizavetpol', all the Kutaissi district, Chiatur and half of Batum is with the Bolsheviks'[10]. There can be no doubt of the success of the Mensheviks among the Georgians. This may be due to

---

[1] Ibragimov, p. xxix.

[2] M. Leman, 'Iz proshlogo Kavkazskikh bol'shevistkikh organizatsiy', P.R. no. 40 (1925), pp. 15-17.

[3] N. N. Aladzhalova, *Iz bol'shevistskogo podpol'ya (vospominaniya)* (Tbilisi 1963), p. 9.

[4] Z. A. Akubzhanova, *Kavkazski soyuz RSDRP (1903-06 gg.)* (Candidate's dissertation, Tbilisi 1962), p. 58.

[5] N. N. Aladzhalova, *Iz bol'shevistskogo podpol'ya (vospominaniya)* (Tbilisi 1963), p. 20.

[6] M. Leman, P.R. no. 40 (1925), p. 14.

[7] Letter signed *Tari* dated 8 March 1905, in P.R. no. 40 (1925) p. 48.

[8] 'Kanun revolyutsii 1905 g. na Kavkaze', P.R. no. 1 (48) (1926), p. 210.

[9] *Ibid.*, p. 213.

[10] Letter cited in Z. A. Akubzhanova, *Kavkazski soyuz RSDRP (1903-1906 gg.)* (Candidate's dissertation, Tbilisi 1962), p. 128.

two factors: the higher social and economic status of the Georgians in the Caucasus among which social groups the Mensheviks recruited elsewhere; and the Mensheviks' greater emphasis on local control was much more in keeping with nationalist sentiment. Given the national and social segmentalisation, once identification with the Mensheviks had begun, it was carried on by its own momentum.

4. Social-Democratic Activity

In Baku one of the most important events in 1904 was the general strike which took place in December. The Bolsheviks considered that the best time for the strike was in the spring. But – presumably due to the demands of the workers and the other political groups – a strike was called for 13 December. The general political demands printed by the press of the *Balakhanskie i Bibi-Eybatskie rabochie* (dated 1 December 1904), called for full freedom of assembly, speech, press, unions, and strike; affirmed opposition to the Tsar and called for the immediate creation of an All-Russian Constituent Assembly, equality of rights and the ending of the war[1]. The strike took place on 13 December. On 19 December the oil producers made an offer meeting some of the demands[2], which was rejected by the strike leaders. During this time the influence of the Shendrikovs increased[3]. On 30 December, the conditions offered by the employers were accepted by the workers' representatives, and what is usually regarded as the first collective agreement in Russia between management and workers was signed. It gave the workers a working day of nine hours, increases in wages and payment during illness, abolition of overtime, the provision of free fuel and other improvements[4].

The significance of the collective agreement lies in the kind of employer-employee relationship it presupposes. In the Caucasian oil-fields the employers were prepared and willing to recognise a 'responsible' workers' movement, and to bargain with it on pay and conditions. The legal attempts in 1903 to regularise relations

---

[1] The most important demands were for an eight-hour day, reductions of working time (before holidays and so on), better conditions of work (7 points), higher wages (13 points), conditions of dismissals and fines (6 points), improved living and social conditions (schools and hospitals), and other points on employer-employee relations (polite treatment), holidays and unemployment. (V. I. Nevski, 'Dekabr'skaya zabastovka 1904 g. v Baku', P.R. no. 25 (1924), p. 57.) The leaflet is printed in full, *ibid.*, pp. 77-84.
[2] See document of 35 points in *R. D. Baku*, pp. 22-5.
[3] Sof'ev, '1905 g. v Baku', in *Proletariat v revolyutsii*, p. 215.
[4] The twenty-three points in the original document are printed in full in *R. D. Baku*, pp. 34-36.

between workers and management through the *starosty* elected to the *Institut fabrichnykh starost*, set up by the Nobel' company, involved only a few hundred men[1], but they were important in showing a path of cooperation to many workers. (It is interesting to note that mainly Russian workers took part in the election in 1903). The fact that the workers could press their claims successfully and reach agreement with the management (even if this was later abrogated) had important implications for the Social-Democrats. It favoured the wider kind of workers' party envisaged by the Mensheviks and helps to explain the support they received in these parts.

In the strikes of 1904 and 1905 workers' *promyslovye* and *zavodskie* commissions also developed during strikes and carried on discussions with the factory management[2]. The demands of these mainly non-party groups impinged on management functions, for they sought control over the hiring and dismissal of workers. Later, in an agreement negotiated by the Shendrikovs in September-October 1905, the commissions were officially recognised as a channel of communication[3].

The possibility of a regularised and relatively harmonious relationship between factory management and men did not mean that either the Shendrikovs or the working class as a whole had a cooperative attitude to the autocracy. The leaflet which I have already cited above (see p. 186) shows hostility to the Tsar. The local representatives of the Imperial government played on nationalist sentiment to gain support, and 1905 in the Caucasus witnessed clashes between different nationalist groups resulting in pogroms.

January 1905 in Baku was quiet though in other areas of the Caucasus strikes took place in sympathy with the St. Petersburg events[4]. But from 6-9 February a number of pogroms, particularly Tatars against Armenians, took place. The Bolsheviks called for the abolition of the autocracy, for an all-Russian uprising, for the 'international unity of all workers', and for the 'brotherhood of nations'[5]. Such emphasis put by the Bolsheviks on the international ties of the working class may have cost them supporters in an area where national antagonisms existed. The support of the Mensheviks among the more highly-skilled Russian-speaking strata probably made it more im-

---

[1] Gadzhinski, *Promyslovye i zavodskie komissii v Bakinskom neftepromyshlennom rayone v gody pervoy russkoy revolyutsii* (Candidate of Science dissertation, Baku 1962), pp. 70, 89-91, 101.

[2] D. D. Gadzhinski, p. 113.

[3] Gadzhinski, pp. 131, 138.

[4] V. Nevski, 'Yanvarskie dni 1905 g. na Kavkaze', P.R. no. 27 (1924), p. 47.

[5] Leaflet dated 10 February 1905, in *R. D. Baku*, p. 99, *Vpered* 11, March 1905 extract in *R. D. Baku*, p. 105.

portant for the Bolsheviks to organise the less-skilled and non-Russian workers. One would also, on theoretical grounds, expect this to be the policy of the Bolsheviks, who stressed the homogeneity of the working class, and had referred to the Mensheviks on some occasions as representing the petite-bourgeoisie and better-off workers. The Bolsheviks too advocated forming industrial as opposed to craft trade-unions[1].

During the spring and early summer more strikes broke out in Baku, especially on May Day, but they did not last long[2]. In May again some establishments showed willingness to give concessions and granted a nine-hour day[3].

In August, the Bolsheviks wanted to call a general strike[4], though the Mensheviks and the other parties (*Gnchakists* and *Droshaks*) opposed it arguing that the strike would provoke pogroms[5]. Though some factories came out, the strike was poorly supported and was not a success[6].

The late summer in Baku saw oil outlets set on fire, clashes between nationalist groups and the streets paraded by groups of the Black Hundreds. The firing of the oil wells led to closures of many wells and to unemployment. About forty-five thousand people left Baku at this time[7]. The oil producers met the Minister of Finance in September from whom they received pledges of financial support and the strengthening of the Baku garrison and police.

In October and November revolutionary meetings took place in Baku. Not only did parading workers unfurl red flags, but groups of the Black Hundreds demonstrated with portraits of the Tsar[8]. Some revolts occurred in the armed forces, especially in the navy[9]. These, however, as in other areas did not cause the authorities much trouble. Though revolutionary propaganda among the troops had had some success among all ranks[10] there is not much evidence to suggest that the Social-Democrats had very strong organisations among them.

Trade unions were formed on the base of the *zavodskie* and *promyslovye* commissions. Among these the Bolsheviks had not carried out much

---

[1] Sof'ev, '1905 v Baku' in *Proletariat v revolyutsii* (M. 1930), p. 224.

[2] Police report on May Day strike in Baku, in *R. D. Baku*, pp. 144-5.

[3] *Proletari*, no. 6, June 1905.

[4] *Proletari*, no. 15, August 1905.

[5] Letter of a member of the Baku Committee in *Proletari*, no. 18, Sept. 1905, reprinted in *R. D. Baku*, pp. 225-8.

[6] *R. D. Baku*, p. xix.

[7] Gaz. *Kaspiy*, no. 181, Sept. 1905, extract in *R. D. Baku*, p. 230.

[8] Telegram dated 21 Oct. 1905, in *R. D. Baku*, pp. 262-4.

[9] See official report in *R. D. Baku*, pp. 262-4.

[10] Official report in *R. D. Baku*, p. 341.

work and they were for the most part under the influence of the Shendrikovs[1]. By 1906, in Baku, were about a score of trade union associations with a membership of from eleven thousand to thirteen thousand men[2]. Many of these associations, even the professional ones, were not concerned only with 'trade-union' type activities. At a meeting of the Lawyers' Union on 11 December, for example, heated speeches on the need for revolution and an armed uprising were reported[3].

By the end of October a group of workers' representatives (probably from the factory commissions) was beginning to meet to discuss the political situation and to formulate a policy on such problems as compensation for damage caused during pogroms, and on the setting-up of employment exchanges for the unemployed[4].

At a meeting on 25 November these deputies declared themselves the Soviet of Workers' Deputies. It was composed of 226 men, including representatives from the *promyslovye* and *zavodskie komissii*, and was dominated by the Shendrikovs and their Menshevik supporters[5]. The Soviet arranged discussions with the employers, and tried to reach agreement over such topics as compensation for damage during pogroms[6]. The Soviet had wide support, a police report written in February 1905 said that many people went to it because they regarded it as 'a defender of their economic needs and interests'[7].

At a workers' meeting at the end of November a resolution was passed calling for the formation of armed detachments and for the civil authority in Baku to be formed from representatives, not only of the town council and the Congress of Oil Producers but also of the Soviet. The meeting also demanded the payment of full compensation during the time of political strikes.[8] These resolutions were endorsed at the Soviet's meeting of 28 November. Both these last two recommendations show the similarity of interest between workers and bourgeoisie and their mutual hostility to the autocracy.

The Shendrikovs were supreme in the Soviet, its chairman being

[1] A. A. Abdurakhmanov, 'Pervy Bakinski Sovet rabochikh deputatov', *Trudy Azerbaydzhanskogo filiala IMEL pri TsK KPSS*, vol. XIX (1955), p. 123.

[2] 'Krasnaya letopis'', nos. 2-3 (1922), p. 3. Cited in *R. D. Baku*, p. XXXIII.

[3] 'Gaz. Kaspiy', no. 240 (13 December) and police report, cited by Ibragimov, p. 162.

[4] 'Gaz. Kaspiy', no. 223, Nov. 1905, in *R. D. Baku*, pp. 281-2. All workers could attend these meetings ('Gaz. Kaspiy', no. 220, Nov. 1905, in *R. D. Baku*, p. 278).

[5] Gadzhinski, pp. 159-61.

[6] 'Gaz. Kaspiy', no. 230, Nov. 1905, in *R. D. Baku*, p. 285 and Sof'ev, '1905 v Baku', in *Proletariat v revolyutsii* (M. 1930), p. 220.

[7] Report dated 21 Feb. 1906 in *R. D. Baku*, p. 356.

[8] 'Gaz. Baku', no. 177, Dec. 1905, in *R. D. Baku*, pp. 286-7.

Lev Shendrikov, and one of his supporters, Kas'yan, edited the *Izvestiya*[1]. The Bolsheviks had a few members forming their own faction (Dzhaparidze and Montin)[2], but their influence in the Soviet was small. December was the climax of the Baku Soviet's activities and it provides us with another example of a Menshevik Soviet's activities.

On 8 and 9 December the Caucasian railway was on strike and controlled by its workers. On 13 December, the Soviet called a general political strike which lasted from 14 to 22 December. The Soviet's nine specific demands were: the immediate creation of a Constituent Assembly based on democratic rights, an eight-hour working day, state insurance (paid by the capitalists), free children's education (paid by the state), the immediate fulfilment of the soldiers' demands for a two-year period of service and higher pay, the fulfilment of the post-telegraph and railway workers' demands, the release of all political prisoners, the end of police brutality, the return of cossacks to their homes, and the satisfaction of peasant demands[3]. During the time of the strike all the factories, power stations, the railway, telegraph and telephone services and the press were not working[4].

Bolshevik writers assert that the Menshevik leaders (especially those of the Soviet) did not call for an uprising in Baku. But a police telegram dated 21 December noted that 'the local press is calling for an armed uprising and the local administration is powerless'[5]. The insurgents formed local organs of revolutionary government to weaken the authority of the Tsarist order. In the words of the Baku *Okhrana*, the Soviet 'in fact took power into its own hands and turned itself into an organ of provisional revolutionary government'[6].

This strike, however, did not lead to an armed uprising, though clashes between strikers and government forces took place. The Soviet did not lead an armed uprising, its objectives were achieved without one. By 19 December, the railway station was again under police control. Mass arrests of strikers and members of the Soviet took place, the *druzhiniki* were rounded up, the stations and railway taken over by the police, and on 27 December the railways were re-started. The period of insurrection in Baku was over.

[1] V. Nogin, '1906 god v Baku', in *25 let...*, p. 18.
[2] Ibragimov, p. 154.
[3] 'Gaz. Baku', no. 184, Dec. 1905, in *R. D. Baku*, pp. 310-1.
[4] *R. D. Baku*, p. xxviii and a letter from the Nobel' firm in Baku to St. Petersburg on the political strike, *ibid.*, pp. 328-9.
[5] Telegram, 21 Dec. 1905, in *R. D. Baku*, p. 329.
[6] Cited by Ibragimov, pp. 154-5.

5. Summing-up

Though the Bolsheviks were relatively stronger in Baku than else-where in the Caucasus, they had few members and little popular support. This was because of two main factors: the multi-national composition of the area and the highly stratified occupational structure. These factors cannot be untwined, the national groups had strong solidarity based on common race, religion and language to which their economic status was closely linked: Russians and Georgians occupying the more highly paid jobs, *Azerbaydzhantsy* the less well-paid. If we ignore national differences, Menshevik support was similar to that in the other areas studied, being composed of the better-off workers. In Baku they were well-organised and ably-led in 'trade-union' based groups. While the Mensheviks were able to capitalise and reinforce their support along national lines, the op-posite applied to the Bolsheviks. The lower-paid status groups were non-Russians having strong national solidarity and hostility to the Russians. The Bolsheviks, rejecting their Social-Democratic op-ponents' policies for the more privileged workers, were forced to find support among such lower strata. In this, not only did they face tremendous organisational problems and difficulty in communicating a class policy, but they may also have lost support among the lower-paid Russian-speaking workers. It is well known that such 'poor white' groups become the most militant opponents of policies which associate them with culturally lower, and what they regard as inferior, racial strata. The Bolshevik slogan of international brotherhood, their policy of forming general unions and their em-phasis on a class party, did not strike home in Baku. As in Ekaterinoslav, the policies of western firms were important in influencing the formation of the organised working class. In Baku many oil firms had attempted to institutionalise conflict through recognised workers' commissions and bargained with workers on 'trade-union' conditions. This policy had the support of a large number of workers and led to the creation of a Menshevik-type movement. Though the Shendrikovs may not have been 'in the pay' of the oil producers, for bargaining to have taken place between the parties, a common basis and at least tacit agreements must have been reached.

chapter nine

THE STRUCTURE AND ACTIVITY OF
SOCIAL-DEMOCRACY IN SIBERIA (OMSK)

1. Economic and Social Background

When discussing Siberia one must bear in mind that the great distances between towns made the work of the Social-Democratic Committees more independent of one another and political-social life more self-contained than in the geographically more compact areas of European Russia. Here I shall outline the general features of Social-Democracy in Siberia and give in greater detail the Committee organisation in Omsk.

The population of Siberia had grown due to the arrival of settlers and deportees from the west. It had been a penal colony from the seventeenth century, though in the nineteenth rapid growth and development had taken place. Even by the beginning of the twentieth century, Siberia was still relatively undeveloped, the main railway construction, which opened up the area, had taken place only in the 1890's. From 1890 to 1899, it has been estimated that nine hundred and forty-two thousand emigrants settled in Siberia, followed by four hundred and forty-seven thousand between 1900 and 1905[1].

In 1897, its population (excluding Akmolinsk and Semipalatinsk oblasts) was 5.760 millions (Russians being 4.651 millions and other nationalities 1.109 millions). By 1911 the population was 9.366 millions of which nearly eight millions were Russians[2]. The urban population (i.e. settlements with more than 999 inhabitants) in 1897 was 326,280, only nine towns having over ten thousand inhabitants, the largest being Tomsk (52,210), Irkutsk (51,473) and Omsk (37,376)[3]. Omsk was in Akmolinsk province where two-

---

[1] Obolensky, *Mezhdunarodnye i mezhdukontinental'nye migratsii*, p. 90, cited by D. W. Treadgold, *The Great Siberian Migration* (Princeton 1957), p. 255.

[2] P. I. Lyashchenko, *Istoriya narodnogo khozyaystva SSSR*, vol. II (M. 1952), p. 519.

[3] *Sibirskaya sovetskaya entsiklopediya*, vol. I (M. 1929), p. 23.

thirds of the population was Kirgizian, the other third was mainly Russian (Great Russians 174,000, Ukrainians 51,000)[1]. The Russians were mainly clustered in the urban settlements.

Industrial production, even by 1908, was small compared with that of the European Russian provinces: there were 19,300 workers in Western Siberia producing 65.8 million rubles worth of goods[2]. In 1905 in Omsk there were about 100 industrial enterprises. Half of the factory-mill workers were concentrated in four enterprises (including a tobacco factory and two breweries), the remainder were handicraft workshops[3]. Others were employed in shops and some 3,000 men worked in the railway workshops[4]. At the beginning of the twentieth century the social structure of Omsk had a bias towards the trading classes of the population, *meshchane* amounted to 43%, nobles and *chinovniks* to 23.7%, army lower ranks and their households to 15%, peasants only to 11.5% and cossacks to 2.8%[5].

2. The Early History of Social-Democracy

In Siberia, socialist circles grew up around the settlers and exiles from European Russia. The origins of the Social-Democratic circles may be traced back to the 1880's. In the formative years of the eighties and nineties discussions took place in ostensibly Narodnik groups between the 'young Marxists and the older Narodniks[6]'. A government report on revolutionary activities in Siberia found secret circles in Irkutsk and Krasnoyarsk and by 1901 an 'anti-government committee' existed in Irkutsk[7]. Not only exiles spread Marxist ideas, settlers' children attending universities were also a source. Baranski has recalled that his sisters, when on holiday from St. Petersburg, introduced him to Marxist ideas and that later his views were reinforced by a student from Tomsk University[8]. In Irkutsk in 1899, the secret circles had only ten members – two village school teachers, a pupil of the military school, a worker and an

[1] *Pervaya vseobshchaya perepis'*, 1897, vol. II (Spb. 1905), pp. 38-55.

[2] Lyashchenko, p. 529.

[3] 'Obzor Akmolinkoy oblasti za 1907 g.' (Omsk 1908), p. 3, cited in *Omskaya organizatsiya RSDRP 1905-07* (Omsk 1956), p. 5.

[4] *Ibid.*

[5] *Rossiya* (Spb. 1903), vol. XVIII, pp. 372-3.

[6] N. Baranski – a participant in the circles – 'Kratki ocherk istorii Sibirskogo Soyuza RSDRP', in *Sibirski soyuz RSDRP* (M. 1935), p. 12.

[7] *Obzor revolyutsionnogo dvizheniya v okruge Irkutskoy palaty za 1897-1908 gg.* (Spb. 1908), pp. 1-5.

[8] N. Baranski, *V ryadakh Sibirskogo S.-D. soyuza* (Novonikolaevsk 1923), p. 9.

aristocrat[1]. The local native inhabitants were not amenable to anti-government action[2]. Of the groups in opposition to the autocracy the Social-Democrats were among the most important. In 1901, circles existed in Omsk, Tomsk, Krasnoyarsk, Irkutsk[3] and Chita[4]. The exiles, together with the local intelligentsia of Irkutsk, formed the Irkutsk Committee of the RSDLP in 1901[5].

The Siberian Union of the RSDLP was formed in the spring of 1901[6]. Its aims were to found Committees in the larger settlements, to organise the delivery of literature, to print the journal *Sibirski rabochi* together with books and pamphlets, and to maintain contact with Russian Social-Democracy[7]. At least until 1903, the Union exercised little, if any, control over the individual Committees which carried out their work independently[8]. By 1903 the Union had groups in Tomsk – working among the printers and other workers, at Krasnoyarsk – mainly among the railwaymen, and at Irkutsk where propaganda was carried out among railwaymen, building workers, bakers, tailors and soldiers[9]. At Tomsk, Krasnoyarsk and Irkutsk were circles for discussion and the training of revolutionaries[10]. Until 1903 the membership of the revolutionary circles was relatively small. Although no firm statistics are available to us, on the basis of three to four circles in the five main towns, each with seven members, one might estimate membership of the Siberian Union at about a hundred.

These early circles not only studied illegal literature but also tried to start strikes, as among the Krasnoyarsk railwaymen in February 1899[11]. Among the workers and exiles illegal sickness and welfare funds were organised[12]. By the eve of the Second Congress the Social-Democrats were taking an active part in strike activities. In Tomsk the Siberian Union had called for a strike and demonstration on 20 February[13]. The Committees in Tomsk, Krasnoyarsk and Irkutsk had

[1] *Obzor rev. dvizh...*, p. 5.
[2] *Ibid.*
[3] 'Doklad Sibirskogo Soyuza', in *Protokoly II s'ezda RSDRP* (M. 1959), p. 674.
[4] *Revolyutsionnoe dvizhenie v Zabaykal'e 1905-07 gg.* (sbornik) (Chita 1955), p. 10.
[5] For an account of life among the exiles see, V. Mandel'berg, *Iz perezhitago* (Davos, 1910), pp. 28-29.
[6] *Iskra*, no. 6, July 1901.
[7] B. I. Nikolaevski, commentary to 'Doklad Sibirskogo Soyuza', *Doklady S.-D. komitetov vtoromu s'ezdu* (M.L. 1930), p. 315.
[8] V. Mandel'berg, *Iz perezhitago* (Davos 1910), p. 31.
[9] 'Doklad Sibirskogo Soyuza', *II S'ezd: Protokoly* (M. 1959), p. 678.
[10] *Ibid.*
[11] *Obzor rev. dvizh...*, p. 5.
[12] N. Baranski, *V ryadakh Sibirskogo sots.-dem. soyuza*, p. 10.
[13] 'Doklad Sibirskogo komiteta', p. 678.

started circles for agitators, and demonstrations in all these places had taken place on May Day 1903 causing police and military intervention[1]. Propaganda was well-developed in Siberia. The Committees of Tomsk, Krasnoyarsk, Irkutsk and Chita all had their own printing machines and by the middle of 1902, 100 proclamations had been printed – a total of thirty thousand sheets[2].

The attempts of *Iskra* to unite the disparate groups in Siberia and to be recognised as the leading organ of the movement met with opposition, mainly over the question of local autonomy. A separate *Iskra* group, 'The Siberian Group of Revolutionary Social-Democracy' was formed in 1902[3]. By January 1903 *Iskra* was recognised as the leading organ, and a motion of solidarity with the paper was passed[4]. 'The Siberian Union *as a Committee of the party* (their italics) aims to be the agent of an all Russian centre... it does not see any basis for the independent existence of regional organisations'[5]. It was not, however, to be a firm supporter of the Bolshevik faction. One of its delegates to the Second Congress was L. Trotsky, who considered the Siberian delegation to be 'soft'[6] and the area was to be one of Menshevik influence.

3. The Structure of Social-Democracy

Despite police arrests, after the Second Congress and especially during 1905, the membership of the Siberian Social-Democratic Committees increased. Membership in 1903, as I have said, was about a hundred. In terms of numbers of organised Committees, Baranski says that there were five in July 1903, seven in June 1905, eleven in October 1905, fifteen in June 1906 and thirty-four in the winter 1906-07[7]. By July 1905, the first issue of *Rabochaya Gazeta Sibirskogo Soyuza* claimed 500 party workers in Siberia[8].

[1] *Ibid.*, p. 679.
[2] *Ibid.*
[3] *Sibirskaya sovetskaya entsiklopediya*, vol. 1 (1929), p. 372.
[4] 'Doklad Sibirskogo Soyuza', p. 677 and *Iskra*, no. 35, March 1903.
[5] 'Doklad Sibirskogo Soyuza', *II S'ezd RSDRP*, p. 680.
[6] L. Trotsky, *Otchet Sibirskoy delegatsii vtoromu s'ezdu* (Geneva edition, 1903), p. 11.
[7] N. Baranski, *V ryadakh Sibirskogo sotsial-demokraticheskogo soyuza* (Novonikolaevsk 1923), pp. 66-7.
[8] *Obzor revolyutsionnogo dvizheniya v okruge Irkutskoy sudebnoy palaty za 1897-1908 gg.* (Spb. 1908), p. 8. At the Third All-Siberian Conference of the RSDLP in 1907 there were claimed to be 3,500 men in the organisation: the largest organisations being Kransoyarsk with 390 members, followed by Omsk (300), Irkutsk (270), Chita (250), and Tomsk (225) ('Izveshchenie o tret'ey obshchesibirkoy konferentsii RSDRP', in *Sibirski soyuz RSDRP* (M. 1935), pp. 118-9).

After the Second Congress, Siberia was predominantly an area under Menshevik influence. By June 1905, at the First All-Siberian Conference, the Union refused to recognise the 'so-called Third Party Congress' which the Bolsheviks had called; voting for the resolution were sixteen, three were against and seven abstained, giving a good indication of the factional strength[1]. In 1905, according to A. A. Anson and B. Z. Shumyatski only in Krasnoyarsk and Chita did the Bolsheviks have any influence over the Committees[2], but in Kharbin a separate Bolshevik-controlled 'Workers' Group of the RSDLP' was founded in opposition to the Menshevik Committee[3]. In the other areas, the two factions worked in the same Committees though most of them seem to have been Menshevik-controlled. For example, in the summer of 1905, of eleven men on the Tomsk Committee, only two were Bolsheviks, on the sub-committee thirty strong were only six Bolsheviks, 'the general alignment was Menshevik'[4]. At the Second Siberian Conference in May 1906, the majority of the eleven delegates (from eight Committees) were Mensheviks[5]. The editor of *Omskaya Organizatsiya RSDRP 1905-07* explains that the predominance of Mensheviks at this Conference was due to the arrest of leading Bolsheviks, though in other areas we have seen that the arrest of leading Bolsheviks did not prevent them from being replaced by other Bolsheviks. Other writers have suggested that the existence of Menshevik Committees in Tomsk and Irkutsk can be explained by the large proportion of intelligentsia in the population (students, school pupils and public servants) which the Mensheviks tended to attract[6]. Baranski has estimated that in the Tomsk Committee in 1904-05 there were 300 students[7]. In the case of Kharbin again, Vetoshkin has asserted that the Mensheviks consisted largely of the intelligentsia, and the Bolshevik group was composed of railway workers and navigation workers (*sudovodnye rabochie*)[8]. There is evidence that even in the 'Bolshevik' Committees, the Mensheviks were significant. In Krasnoyarsk some Mensheviks were on the committee, the journal *Krasnoyarski Rabochi* was run by

[1] N. Baranski, 'Ob oktyabr'skikh dnyakh 1905 g. v Tomske', P.R. 5 (52) (1926), p. 205.

[2] Article in *Sibirskaya sovetskaya entsiklopediya*, vol. I, pp. 373-4.

[3] M. Vetoshkin, 'Bol'sheviki i Men'sheviki v 1905 g. na Dal'nem Vostoke', P.R., 4 (51) (1926), p. 159.

[4] N. Baranski, P.R. 5 (52) (1926), p. 206.

[5] *Omskaya org. RSDRP*, p. 250.

[6] A. Mil'shtein, 'Proletariat v revolyutsionnom dvizhenii Sibiri', *Proletariat v revolyutsii 1905-07 gg.* (M. 1930), p. 319 and Baranski, P.R. 5 (52), p. 205.

[7] Baranski, 'Kratki ocherk istorii Sibirskogo Soyuza RSDRP', in *Sibirski Soyuz RSDRP* (M. 1935), p. 16.

[8] Vetoshkin, P.R. 4 (51) (1926), pp. 159-60.

them, and the leading members of the Krasnoyarsk Soviet of 1905 were Mensheviks[1]. Likewise the Chita Committee had both Menshevik and Bolshevik members[2].

The alignment of the factions in Omsk during the 1905 Revolution is difficult to determine. Recent Bolshevik writers have claimed that in 1905 the two sub-committees of the party were organised by different factions: the 'town' being Menshevik and the 'railway' being Bolshevik, though sometimes both sub-committees are said to have been Bolshevik-controlled[3]. This applies to the soldiers 'organisation which probably had no clear factional identity. V.V. Kuybyshev recalls that the 'majority' of the Omsk Committee were Bolsheviks. Of the West Siberian Conference in September 1906, he says: 'only three to four delegates belonged to the Mensheviks'[4]. It is possible, of course, that this meeting was only a factional one. Whilst one cannot discount the Bolshevik presence in Omsk, one cannot be sure of its strength and it is possible that power passed from one faction to another, generally the Mensheviks dominating the 'town' and the Bolsheviks the 'railway'.

The organisational scheme of the Omsk Committee is shown in Chart 6. A joint committee was formed from the representatives of two sub-committees (*podkomitety*) and the troops (but to 8 March 1906 no representative from the latter had attended)[5]. The joint committee and the sub-committees (of the districts) had executive commissions, which carried out day-to-day administration, and gave weekly reports to the committees[6]. The two sub-committees were organised on the basis of 'town' and 'railway'. Below these were groups in workshops of between 100-200 men; other small worksshops were joined – on the basis of trade – to make up a group. The clerks and telegraphists had their own special organisation. The students also formed a separate administrative group with the right to put out pamphlets. Each of the town and railway groups had 'agitational groups' of 20 to 25 men each. They met weekly and discussed specific questions (the State Duma, the election law, the eight-hour day, trade unions), discussion papers were also read.

The Committee's report claims that it needed four full-time or-

[1] A. Mil'shtein, p. 320.
[2] Mil'shtein, pp. 338-9.
[3] *Omskaya org. RSDRP*, pp. 9-11.
[4] V. V. Kuybyshev, *Izbrannye proizvedeniya* (M. 1958), p. 18. The delegate, Popov, to the Fifth Party Congress (1907) was also a Bolshevik, *V S'ezd RSDRP (Protokoly)* (M. 1963), p. 624.
[5] 'Otchet o rabote Omskogo komiteta RSDRP s 15-go fevralya po 8-e marta 1906 g.', in *Omskaya org. RSDRP*, p. 105.
[6] *Ibid.*

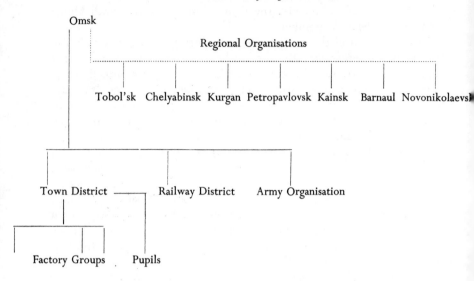

Chart 6. West-Siberia Party Organisation 1906

ganisers but only had two. In March 1906, there were claimed to be eighteen propaganda groups (four being among the pupils and two among the troops) having a membership of 180 men. They had links with all parts of the army but were weakest among the cossacks[1].

Like the Krasnoyarsk Committee[2], the Omsk Committee had an interrupted existence: a police raid led to its collapse between June 1903 and winter 1904. By July 1905, it had five circles of grammar school pupils and up to forty 'organised workers'[3]. During this time its main activities were to carry out agitation and to print leaflets. The propagandists were local school pupils[4].

Besides organisation in the town of Omsk itself, the other Social-Democratic circles in West Siberia were subordinated to it. The reports presented to the September (1906) Conference of the West-Siberian party groups give a relative measure of membership: Kurgan 260, Petropavlovsk 147, Kainsk 60, Novonikolaevsk 120, Barnaul

[1] 'Otchet o rabote Omskogo kom. ....', pp. 106-7.
[2] The Krasnoyarsk Committee ceased to function from October 1903 to the summer of 1904. Obzor rev. dvizh..., p. 14.
[3] 'Sibirski sotsial-demokraticheski listok', no. 1, July 1905, p. 4, cited in Omskaya org. RSDRP, p. 48.
[4] Omskaya org. RSDRP, p. 6.

103, Tobol'sk 55, Chelyabinsk 168. On the basis of delegates at the Conference (one for fifty members), the Omsk Committee had 500, though this may be too many, for at the All-Siberian Conference in 1907, the Omsk Committee claimed 300 members only[1].

The report of the Omsk delegate to the September Conference of West Siberian Committees points out that the Social-Democrats among the troops had strongest links with the sappers and the signallers[2]. The Omsk Committee had weak links with the peasantry, though leaflets were addressed to them. Novikov writes that Social-Democratic activity in the villages was 'extremely weak'[3]. The West Siberian Conference recognised the importance of the work among the peasants (and cossacks) and called for special organisations to be formed under party control in the villages'[4].

In Part One I have already dealt with the social composition of Russian Social-Democracy. As the Siberian Social-Democratic movement had 'separatist' tendencies before the October Revolution, I have carried out a separate survey of the Social-Democratic activists appearing in the *Sibirskaya sovetskaya entsiklopediya*[5]. Twenty-seven biographies were found – only three were clearly Mensheviks, five undefined, the remainder Bolsheviks. The information on the social backgrounds was very sparse except for age and place of birth. Only three out of sixteen were born outside Siberia – a rather small proportion considering the number of exiles. The age distribution confirms the conclusions of Part One: the 'typical' Siberian Social-Democrat in 1905 was aged between 21 and 25, of the entries in the Encyclopaedia only four recorded being members of Populist organisations. It is probable that most of the men recorded in this source were prominent either before or after the revolution.

As to the active supporters, one may confirm the analysis of the biographies of Part One by considering other sources. In Irkutsk in 1904 many members of the Committee were very young, some in the senior class at school[6]. To 1905 the support in Irkutsk, according to the police, came from the intelligentsia and the student youth[7]. In the same year in Tomsk among the typographers were supporters, as were the railway workers in Chita, but the police claim that the chief support for the party lay among the intelligentsia and school

1 'Protokoly zasedaniy zapadno-sibirskoy konferentsii', in *Omskaya org. RSDRP*, pp. 152-172.
2 'Protokoly...', p. 155.
3 *Omskaya org. RSDRP*, p. 14.
4 'Protokoly...', pp. 169-70.
5 M. 1929-32, 3 vols. The fourth and final volume was not published.
6 *Obzor rev. dvizh.* (Spb. 1908), p. 57.
7 *Obzor...*, p. 62.

pupils[1]. Baranski, who was active in different Siberian groups, recalls that in Tomsk the organisation had strong connexions with members of the intelligentsia, but that in Chita the Committee was a 'pure proletarian organisation... the intelligentsia played a completely insignificant role in it'. In Irkutsk, the Committee was composed mainly of intelligentsia, the majority of whom supported the Mensheviks[2].

The Duma elections confirm that extensive support was given to the Social-Democrats in Siberia. Fifteen out of twenty-eight deputies elected to the Second Duma in Siberia were Social-Democrats[3]. In Omsk, a Menshevik had been elected to the First Duma for Akmolinsk *oblast'* in 1906. The election to the Second Duma in Omsk was contested by four parties: Octobrists, Cadets, Social-Democrats, and Socialist-Revolutionaries – the Socialist-Revolutionaries forming a bloc with the Cadets. Of 4,987 on the electoral role only 44 per cent voted[4]. There were four deputies to be elected. The four Social-Democrats received 1127, 972, 968 and 964 votes, the progressive bloc (Socialist-Revolutionaries and Cadets) from 728 to 909 and the Octobrists were bottom of the poll with from 176 to 252[5]. The Bolshevik A. K. Vinogradov was one of the men elected[6]; as Bolshevik sources are silent on the factional allegiance of the other three Social-Democrats they were probably Mensheviks. From these facts we may fairly safely conclude that the Social-Democrats had very wide support from the population.

The Menshevik predominance in Siberia needs some explanation. I have argued in Part One that the factional basis was related to economic and national factors. How relevant, it may be asked, were they in Siberia? There is no doubt that the Siberian settlers were better-off. Treadgold has estimated that the 'average emigrant family more than tripled its possessions in 11 years'[7]. By 1912 the proportions of households without a horse ranged from 7.2% to 10.4% in various Siberian provinces, compared to 33-40% in the

[1] *Obzor...*, p. 10.

[2] N. Baranski, *V ryadakh Sibirskogo sots.-dem. soyuza*, p. 23.

[3] V. I. Lenin, 'Vybory v dumu i taktika russkoy sotsial-demokratii', *Sochineniya* (4th Ed.), vol. 12, p. 171.

[4] MVD report, 'O pobede sotsial-demokratov na vyborakh vo vtoruyu gosudarstvennuyu dumu', in *Rev. dvizh. v Omske*, pp. 210-11.

[5] 'Golos sotsial-demokrata' (Tomsk, March 1907), no. 2, p. 4. Cited in *Omskaya org. RSDRP*, p. 209.

[6] He had only joined the Social-Democratic party in 1906 and attended the Fifth Party Congress as a Bolshevik delegate: *V S'ezd RSDRP*, p. 841.

[7] D. W. Treadgold, 'Russian Expansion and Turner's American Frontier', *Agricultural History*, vol. 26 (no. 4) (October 1952), p. 150.

central agricultural region and 60-65% in the south-west of European Russia[1]. Treadgold, in his study of Siberian migration, does not consider the national origins of the migrants[2], though he states that 13% of the Ukraine's population moved to Siberia between 1896 and 1915[3]. W. Kubijowytsch has estimated that the following percentages of the total migrant population came from the Ukrainian provinces: 1891-1900, 36%; 1901-1910, 49%[4]. Though the above evidence must be considered with caution, we can see that the factors operating in European Russia may also have been at work in Siberia.

4. Finance

Turning to the finance of the Omsk Committee, the total income for March and April 1905 was 232 rubles (only about £12 per month)[5]. There were no large individual donations: the largest (75 r.) coming on credit from the Siberian Union, from a 'group' came another 50 r., on different 'collection lists' were about 40 r., monthly subscriptions (*vznosy*) brought in only 12 r., small donations came to 16.25 r[6]. and another large sum of 22 r. also probably came from a sympathiser. The chief expenses were 71 r. spent on two professional revolutionaries, 'conspiracy' 46 r., cost of journeys 35 r., printing 13 r. and 'special outgoings' 25 r. This shows a rather small budget, compared to other areas: rather more on 'professionals' and less on propaganda, much of which probably came free from the Siberian Union.

By June 1905, total income was 146 r[7]. This was made up of a very large number of individual subscriptions: 28 out of 41 contributions were 3 r. or less – under such headings as a 'patriot', a 'proletarian', a 'revolutionary'. The largest single amount came from 'group no. 1' (25 r.) – possibly one of the sub-groups of the Commit-

[1] P. I. Lyashchenko, *Istoriya narodnogo khozyastva SSSR*, vol. II (M. 1952), p. 523.

[2] D. W. Treadgold, *The Great Siberian Migration* (1953), p. 8.

[3] D. W. Treadgold, 'Russian Expansion and Turner's American Frontier', p. 150.

[4] W. Kubijowytsch, *Siedlungsgeschichte, Bevölkerungsverteilung der Ukraine* (Berlin 1943), cited by Treadgold, *The Great Siberian Migration*, p. 9n.

[5] 'Otchet kassy...', in *Omskaya org. RSDRP*, p. 47. The Krasnoyarsk Committee from September 1904 to February 1905 had an income of 1,100 rubles (*Obzor...*, p. 15), an average of 183 rubles a month. In Irkutsk, the Committee had an annual income of 1,595 rubles from 1 August 1902, an average of 133 rubles per month (*Obzor...*, p. 61).

[6] From some soldiers came a donation of 8 r., from students 2.25 r., from a teacher 3 r. and from a sympathiser 3 r.

[7] 'Otchet kassy...', in *Omskaya org. RSDRP*, pp. 49-50.

tee, and another 16 r. came from the 'Congress' ('*so s'ezda*'). Out-goings consisted of payments of 37 r. on conspiracy, 33 r. on literature and 30 r. on printing.

For October total income had risen to 437 r[1]. The largest sums came from sympathisers who contributed 79 r., the Siberian Union gave 50 r., from collection lists came 81 r., grammar-school pupils contributed 12 r. and from another sympathiser came 30 r. The largest expenses were on premises (50 r.), delegates to conferences (45 r.), the Siberian Union's agent (30 r.), on a sick comrade (25 r.) and a loan to the Union (presumably a repayment) (25 r.). The account for November shows a rise in income to 478 r.,[2] 103 r. were contributed direct to the strike fund, probably from sympathisers, the remaining money was from small donations mostly under 10 r., though a collection for the 'Russian workers' brought in 75 r. Most of the expenses were on printing and literature (173 r.) the mainte-nance of 'professionals' came to 54 r.

The accounts for December 1905[3] and January 1906[4] show a similar pattern – individual subscriptions and collections at meetings being the most important sources of income. In the December account there is the first payment for 'self-defence' – 231 r. in all for arms in that month, and another 40 r. followed in January. In January, too, the Committee spent some of its funds to help the arrested and their families (251 r.) – but the largest expenditure was still on 'organisation' (392 r.), press expenses came to 144 r. and outgoings for the upkeep of 'professionals' came to 58 r.

Taking the accounts as a whole, one's attention is again drawn to the wide support given to the Social-Democrats. Though quite a small part of the income came from regular members, a large number of small donations came from sympathisers. No large donations came the way of the RSDLP in Omsk where they probably went to other political groups. More expenditure was devoted to the maintenance of professional revolutionaries than I have shown to be the case elsewhere, possibly because fewer men with large private means were party symathisers in Omsk and costs may have been higher as distances were greater. Payments for arms were small and had about the same priority as 'self-help'. Later, in March, the Committee even donated 338 rubles to the Red Cross',[5] not what one would expect from a revolutionary class-conscious party.

[1] 'Otchet kassy…', in *Omskaya org. RSDRP*, pp. 66-7.
[2] 'Otchet kassy…', in *Omskaya org. RSDRP*, pp. 71-3.
[3] 'Otchet kassy…', in *Omskaya org. RSDRP*, pp. 73-6.
[4] 'Otchet kassy…', in *Omskaya org. RSDRP*, pp. 93-7.
[5] 'Otchet kassy…', in *Omskaya org. RSDRP*, pp. 120-3.

5. Social-Democratic Activity in 1905

After 1903, the Siberian Union had organised strikes, especially along the railway lines, and the Committees in Tomsk, Krasnoyarsk and Irkutsk had begun to form groups of agitators to foment them. By 1905, the Committee in Irkutsk had influence among the railwaymen which, in the view of the police, led to their striking[1]. From April 1905, the Siberian Union called for a general strike to emphasise the solidarity of the working class. 'All the workers are on strike, fighting...for the interests of all the working class, fighting against... the whole bourgeoisie'[2]. But appeals for united class action did not result in it. In the summer of 1905 the strikes were sporadic. 'At the beginning of August, one after another the railway workshops and depots of the Siberian railway went on strike'[3]. On 16 August, a strike took place in the railway workshops but was not wholeheartedly supported. After the arrest of twelve leaders on that night, the workers began to drift back to work and by 18 August the strike was broken[4].

In October, the Omsk Committee called upon the workers to join the all-Russian strike and from 19-21 October, meetings and demonstrations took place in the town for a 'democratic republic', 'the eight-hour day' and so on. The Social-Democrats addressed large crowds, estimated to have been from four to five thousand strong[5], though it is impossible to know to what extent the RSDLP was responsible for organising the outbursts. During October, the railwaymen formed a fighting detachment, and in November the Omsk Committee of the RSDLP called on the workers to take arms and revolt: 'To arms! Long live an armed uprising!' At a Social-Democratic meeting on 6 December, reported in the local press, speakers pointed out the contradictions in the existing capitalist order, and called for revolutionary action. Two soldiers spoke in support of the Social-Democrats, they not only called for increased wages for the troops but emphasised the importance of the proletariat as revolutionary activists. The crowd of six hundred, it is reported, received the speakers with loud applause[6].

In December 1905, the railwaymen's general strike took place

---

[1] *Obzor rev. dvizh*, p. 63.

[2] 'Vseobshchaya stachka', in *Omskaya org. RSDRP*, pp. 27-8.

[3] 'Sotsial-demokrat' (Menshevik), no. 14, Sept. 1905 in *Omskaya org. RSDRP*, p. 54.

[4] Police report, 'O zabastovke rabochikh Omskikh zh.d. masterskikh i depo', in *Revolyutsionnoe dvizhenie v Omske*, pp. 54-5.

[5] 'O vseobshchey zabastovki Omskikh zheleznodorozhnikov', in *Rev. dvizh. v Omske*, p. 60.

[6] 'Stepnoy kray' (10 Dec. 1905), cited in *Rev. dvizh. v Omske*, pp. 68-9.

and a workers' sub-committee was formed under the Omsk Committee of the RSDLP. The Omsk Committee appealed to the troops to join the strike and their leaflet to the soldiers pointed out that the interests of troops, the revolutionary nation and the working class were the same[1]. The railways did not stop work completely, movements were controlled by workers' committees and troop trains were let through[2]. At the meeting of the railwaymen on 7 December 1905, speakers emphasised the importance of the trade-unions and the eight-hour day, one speaker calling on the workers to join the RSDLP[3]. In Siberia the unions were often separate from the Social-Democrats, in Krasnoyarsk the trade-unions passed a resolution that they would not join any party[4]. In Omsk, the first unions were formed in November 1905. By September 1906, the Union of Workshop and Depot Workers had a membership of 1,153, the Railway Guards' Union had 80 members and the Signalmen 60[5]. Of the two railwaymen's unions in Siberia, one was under Socialist-Revolutionary control[6].

In Omsk a 'revolutionary committee' carried out the functions of Soviets in other towns (the term Soviet was not used in Omsk). Under it were formed 'organisational commissions' – administration, sanitation and a comrades' court[7]. The committee lasted through the month of December, until on the night of 7/8 January 1906, many of the leading activists were arrested[8].

In Omsk the troops did not join the insurgents in any numbers at this time, but later some of the lower ranks refused to obey orders and a minor mutiny took place, seventeen men being arrested and a company disbanded[9]. In Omsk, the contact between party and army was not very firm. In other areas of Siberia, which I shall now briefly outline, more militant activities took place.

In Irkutsk a military-strike committee was set up in November, composed of representatives of soldiers, party organisations (Social-Democrats and Socialist-Revolutionaries) and workers from the strike committee. Its objectives were the remedy of soldiers' grouses –

---

[1] 'K soldatam', in *Omskaya org. RSDRP*, pp. 64-6.
[2] Newspaper account in 'Stepnoy kray', 3 Dec. 1905, in *Rev. dvizh. v Omske*, p. 64; and police report, *ibid.*, p. 66.
[3] 'Stepnoy kray', 10 Dec. 1905, in *Rev. dvizh. v Omske*, pp. 67-8.
[4] *Obzor Rev. dvizh.*, p. 23.
[5] *Omskaya org. RSDRP*, p. 155.
[6] A. Mil'shtein, p. 322.
[7] *Omskaya org. RSDRP*, p. 247.
[8] *Omskaya org. RSDRP*, p. 11.
[9] Police report, 'O volneniyakh v 10-m. Sibirskom Omskom polke', in *Omskaya org. RSDRP*, pp. 224-6.

better food, higher wages, quicker demobilisation, and two political demands, 'the creation of a Constituent Assembly', and 'all land to the peasants'[1]. Although they held several meetings and organised a garrison strike, the troops who had no clear aims, lost the initiative and were put out of action by loyal troops[2].

In Krasnoyarsk, two Soviets (a workers' and a soldiers' which later merged), were formed at the beginning of December 1905. It was composed of 120 men: 80 workers and the remainder soldiers. The leading group was composed of the following factions: sixteen Bolsheviks, nine Mensheviks, and six 'leftish' Mensheviks, six 'Maximalist' Socialist-Revolutionaries and three Socialist-Revolutionaries[3] – showing the almost equal representation of the Social-Democratic factions. The Soviet organised different sections which were charged with keeping order, running the railway and maintaining the local administration[4]. But these sections were not put into operation. At the end of December the insurrectionists were surrounded in their stronghold, the railway workshops, and captured[5]. The activity of the workers, Social-Democrats and soldiers was still segmental in Siberia in 1905. The role of the dissatisfied troops and their Soviet in Krasnoyarsk distinguished Siberia from the rest of Russia[6].

The full story of the Chita Soviet, the uprising and its suppression need not detain us here[7]. But the tactics put forward by the two factions illustrate the emphasis of, and the differences between, Bolshevik and Menshevik policies. The Bolsheviks advocated: 1. the formation of a Zabaykal revolutionary provisional government, 2. the concentration in Chita of all revolutionary soldiers and cossacks, 3. the fortification of the Chita mountains with cannons and turning the Chita workshops into an arsenal, 4. the destruction of the Khingan bridge (for defence purposes), 5. preparing for war and partisan activities. The Mensheviks' proposals were: 1. to fortify and mine the region and particularly the railway workshops, 2. to develop a partisan struggle in the town, 3. to break up the Black Hundred units.[8] Taken on their own the Menshevik proposals were

[1] V. Mandel'berg, Iz perezhitago (Davos 1910), p. 91.
[2] A. Mil'shtein, 'Proletariat v revolyutsionnom dvizhenii Sibirii', in Proletariat v revolyutsii 1905-07 gg. (M. 1930), p. 325.
[3] Mil'shtein, p. 329.
[4] Ibid.
[5] Mil'shtein, pp. 331-2.
[6] O. Anweiler, Die Rätebewegung in Russland 1905-1921 (Leiden, 1958), pp. 61, 71.
[7] See J. L. H. Keep, The Rise of Social-Democracy in Russia, p. 263.
[8] A. Mil'shtein, pp. 338-9.

not lacking in militancy, but they had neither the extremism nor the detailed strategy of the Bolsheviks. Mil'shtein points out that the Bolsheviks on the Chita Committee succeeded in getting accepted all their demands, except the formation of a provisional revolutionary government and the fortification of the Chita hills.

There can be no doubt that the Siberian Mensheviks when faced with decisive action faltered. This does not mean that they were counter-revolutionary. Neither in theory nor in practice did they consider themselves to be the leading forces in the revolution. In Siberia their policies were less extreme than those of their Bolshevik rivals, they were more cautious and less prepared to *lead* an uprising.

6. Summing-up

The party split between Bolsheviks and Mensheviks existed in Siberia but, perhaps due to the small size of the population, the factions worked in the same committees. The Bolsheviks had a more militant attitude to social change and tended to have relatively more support among the proletariat than the Mensheviks whose supporters were more widely based and drew on 'white collar' and other middle strata. The uprisings in Siberia took place later than in European Russia, but the upheavals were as great, if not greater. The Bolsheviks were associated with the more radical activity. The strength of the opposition to the government in Siberia was due to the political exiles – for obvious reasons, to the large numbers of settlers who had broken away from a social system in which the autocracy was legitimate, and to the railwaymen and troops whose confidence in the regime had fallen. The Social-Democrats did not seize power: they often prevaricated when chances of seizing power presented themselves, and their organisations were not prepared. Though the Mensheviks did not lead the insurrections in Siberia they joined them when they were under way. J. Keep[1] has concluded that the Siberian Mensheviks were 'unlike their colleagues in Moscow' and shrank from insurrection. This, in my view, does not give sufficient weight to the revolutionary attitudes of the Siberian Mensheviks. It is true that they 'faltered' (as Keep has pointed out), but they took part in the uprisings and supported them as did the Moscow Mensheviks.

[1] See discussion in Keep, *The Rise of Social-Democracy in Russia*, p. 264.

CONCLUSION

Short abstracts have been made at the end of each chapter: in Part One, summarising the data on social composition and support and in Part Two, showing the peculiarities of the seven areas studied. Here, it is necessary to bring out the chief features of Social-Democratic activity before and after the Second Congress and to comment on the significance of the main findings.

Though many of the local groups were still very unstable, on the eve of the Second Congress the foundations of a Social-Democratic movement had been laid in most regions of Russia. The local Committees had a small membership: a dozen or so active members, with from twenty-five to about a hundred taking a lesser part in activity. Many involved in the party's work were unclear as to its exact aims, its theory or the substance of the disagreements between different factions. Through literature received from abroad and duplicated locally, Social-Democracy was becoming known to the intelligentsia, to other middle strata and to some of the working class. The intelligentsia played a leading, but not always dominant, part in Social-Democratic activity. By 1903, some local groups had progressed no further than leading circle discussions and spreading propaganda, while others had attempted to lead strikes and had organised successful demonstrations. 'Political' activity on the eve of the Second Congress was mainly of an educative kind – circle discussions and the distribution of propaganda. 'Economistic' activity, aimed at improving conditions of work and levels of pay, was widespread and probably the Social-Democrats' most fruitful work among the working classes. Some of the Social-Democratic groups had contacts with each other and with the *émigré* organisations abroad, but most had an isolated and autonomous existence. Outside the towns Social-Democracy was weak: peasant support was minuscule and such groups as existed in the countryside were mainly in village factory settlements or formed of expatriate town workers. Police activity had succeeded in breaking up the organisation in St. Petersburg and Moscow, though it was less of a problem for the revolutionaries in other areas (for example, Baku): by exiling and deporting the revolutionary leaders, police activity contributed to spreading the movement and later became particularly important in areas of rural factory settlements. *Iskra* had attempted to join together the disparate groups and by 1903 was widely recognised as the leading organ of the party. But opposition to *Iskra* existed on organisation, tactics and on the distribution of powers between central and local bodies. Nothing like a monolithic organisation was in being before the Second Congress, though Lenin's theory of party organisation had made a large impact. Before the Second Congress there was still resistance to Social-Democratic propaganda: the Tsar was highly revered among many of the Russian factory workers who were also attracted to the police sponsored unions.

Between the Second Congress and the Duma elections of 1907, the organisation and support of the RSDLP grew considerably but unevenly. The Social-Democratic movement, inert and frustrated as a result of police action and factional squabble in 1904, during the next year mushroomed into energetic and purposeful groups which commanded a large following in the uprisings of the autumn and had much support in the Duma elections of 1907. Financial means (some Committees being able to raise £1,000 per month in 1905) were not only drawn from a few rich sympathisers, but as well from middle and working-class strata. This support lay dormant for considerable periods of time which has sometimes given the impression that Russian Social-Democracy was composed solely of a small elite of intellectuals abroad. As before the Second Congress, the appeal of the Tsar (seen as the legitimate guardian of the people's interests), and of the *Zubatovshchina* was strong among the factory workers and an effective barrier to the spread of revolutionary propaganda and activity. But his authority declined sharply in 1905, after the Gapon massacre, when the revolutionary movement rapidly expanded in membership and activity. Besides the non-party trade-union type groups, the Socialist-Revolutionaries now became important competitors to the Social-Democratic movement.

The party split was often not paralleled by two formal organisations in Russia until the autumn of 1904 (or even the spring of 1905, as in Moscow); in Siberia and other places, the two factions operated within the same organisational structure during the 1905 Revolution. For the revolutionary activist and those drawn into the revolutionary crowds during 1905, it would be wrong to emphasise factional and party divisions – except, perhaps, where national or racial differences existed. The masses, who had largely been apolitical and apathetic, were swept into revolutionary activity following the lead of the politically articulate and organised. In these conditions a movement based on a Leninist theory of organisation had a great advantage. Within the RSDLP the intensity of the factional struggles varied regionally, being stronger in the south than in the north. In practice, the 'internal democracy' of the local groups reveals no consistent differences between the factions in 1905. At the lowest levels of the party organisation, there was little conscious awareness of policy differences. Nevertheless, by the autumn of 1905, the popular image of the factions in the localities was beginning to differ. The propaganda of the Bolsheviks, especially in Moscow, advocated more extreme measures and many Social-Democratic local leaders and activists were aware of policy differences between the factions. An investigation of factional activity suggests greater militancy by the Bolsheviks. In 1905, while the Mensheviks emphasised the development of trade-union groups, the Bolsheviks were more prone to lead revolutionary activity. The Bolsheviks' attempts to seize power, often supported by the Mensheviks, were strategically wrong and failed.

Though both factions had sympathisers (as distinct from active members) from all social strata, the Second Duma elections show that the Bolsheviks were much more dependent on working class support than their more widely based Social-Democratic rivals. Current theories of 'mass society', which explain the rise of revolutionary movements in terms of the 'socially isolated members of *all* classes' are not apposite to the rise of the Bolshevik faction[1]. The leadership of both factions was predominantly drawn from the upper strata of society – the Mensheviks having more men of 'townsman' social origin and the Bolsheviks rather more of the gentry – thus confirming Lipset's hypothesis that the local leaders of radical movement come, not from the 'socially marginal' or 'deviants' but from men already having status in the community[2].

The rapid change from rural to urban forms of life causing social dislocation contributed to the growth of the Bolshevik faction: at least it had relatively more men of peasant origin among the rank and

[1] W. Kornhauser, *The Politics of Mass Society* (1960), p. 49. Kornhauser sees the Russian working class in 1904 as 'highly atomised' due to high labour turnover (p. 153). I have shown in Chapter Four (p. 113-4) that this is an oversimplification. The mainly working class support of the Bolsheviks is explained by their being 'the only revolutionary group to concentrate their agitation among the industrial workers' (p. 153). The fact that the Bolsheviks were predominantly a party with working class support cannot be explained by the tactics of 'concentrating agitation' among them: for the Mensheviks also no less sought working class support.
[2] S. M. Lipset, 'Leadership and New Social Movements', in A. W. Gouldner, *Studies in Leadership* (N.Y. 1950), p. 360.

file[1]. The Mensheviks, even in areas of very rapid growth, did not seem able to recruit the peasant urban newcomers into their ranks. Though there were no firm Social-Democratic organisations in the countryside, by 1905 there were circles in some rural areas, such as Tver and Moscow. The many town workers still linked to the village may have identified revolutionary attitudes and Social-Democracy with an urban way of life and as opinion leaders influenced their peasant peers. This has important implications for the study of communist revolutionary movements of the twentieth century. The distinction made by Barrington Moore between 'those who provide the mass support for a revolution, those who lead it and those who ultimately profit from it [who] are very different sets of people'[2] is not a good one. The Bolshevik rank and file, even in 1905, were drawn to a considerable extent from men born in and still having connections with the countryside. One should not lightly assume that 'the peasants' were a homogeneous unit supporting 'revolution' but opposing the Social-Democrats: they were fragmented and some of their number made up the Bolshevik party. The social organisation of the Russian countryside was affected by the processes of industrial-isation[3].

The local studies suggest that regional factors affected the allegiance of the peasant newcomers in the towns, who were Bolshevik in Ivanovo-Voznesensk and Socialist-Revolutionary in Moscow: the active Bolshevik membership, however, was not only drawn from peasants freshly exposed to town life. The existence of a socialist circle or of a more intangible 'tradition' of Social-Democratic activity would in itself seem to be an important factor determining later strength. Among the workers in the very large factories, at least in St. Petersburgh and Ekaterinoslav, the Socialist-Revolution-aries and not the Social-Democrats were the ones who had the most support. This phenomenon is probably explained by the industrial structure. A 'mixed' industrial structure (such as Moscow) tends to segmentalise the working class: labour-intensive unskilled in-dustries attract urban immigrants perpetuating 'islands' of peasant norms and values, whereas capital-intensive industries demanding skilled and literate workers promote a social consciousness based on a given workers' stratum. In homogeneous industrial structures (one-industry towns such as Ivanovo) immigrants are absorbed more

---

[1] This partly supports the thesis put forward by P. Selznick, *The Organisational Weapon* (1952), p. 284.
[2] Barrington Moore Jr., *Social Origins of Dictatorship and Democracy* (1966) p. 427.
[3] Cf. Barrington Moore Jr., p. xi

quickly by the urban culture and, where economic conditions are conducive, a wider class consciousness may more readily develop.

A definite regional pattern of affiliation to the Bolshevik and Menshevik factions had emerged: the Bolsheviks being concentrated in the Russian-speaking areas; the Mensheviks, being in the south and Caucasus, were composed, to a large extent, of the national minorities. This may have been started by the large number of Jews in the Menshevik elite which, once established, perpetuated itself. When considering the problems of national integration in developing societies, Almond and Coleman have pointed out that communal, ethnic, religious and racial differences are barriers to assimilation into a national society[1]. Such differences too may affect the possibility of organising a political party on a national scale. National, racial and ethnic groups with different traditions, solidarity and antagonism, provided a basis for a plural or federal political structure, which was contrary to the Bolshevik notion of an all-Russian centrally controlled socialist party. The Menshevik demand for more autonomy to local units was related to their local factional strength, to their support among the national minorities and across economic class lines. Their demands for a more decentralised form of party, for more 'democracy' in local units were closely related to the social structure of the Menshevik faction and to the political interests of its leaders.

The regional division was not only due to nationality factors, the economic structures of the regions also differed. While it has been suggested that the support for revolutionary Marxist parties is derived from workers in growing industries, and for the more moderate Social-Democrats from workers in stable industries[2], this research suggests the opposite. Bolshevik support tended to be in the economically depressed areas where the older factories were situated, whereas the Mensheviks were concentrated in areas of very rapid economic growth. It is well-known that southern Russia and the Caucasus developed rapidly after 1880. The relative rates of growth for the different regions (measured by the percentage increase in the numbers of employed workers) were – Bolshevik areas: Moscow 289%, Vladimir 288%, Kostroma 718%, Yaroslavl 380%, Perm 230%. Menshevik areas: Ekaterinoslav 41 times, Area of the Don Army 61 times, Kherson 9.7 times, Kiev 175%. (St. Petersburg's rate of growth was 500%)[3]. These figures bring out that the rapidly

[1] G. Almond and J. S. Coleman, *The Politics of the Developing Areas* (Princeton, 1960) p. 535.
[2] S. M. Lipset, *Political Man* (1960), p. 70.
[3] A. G. Rashin, *Formirovanie rabochego klassa Rossii*, (M. 1958), p. 193. The figures are calculated on 1913 figures over a base (average) of 1861-1870. See also introductory sections to chapters four, five, seven and eight of the present book.

developing areas were *less* responsive to the Bolsheviks. Indeed, one might expect areas of relative deprivation such as Moscow[1] to be more susceptible to production uncertainty and falling living standards, which would create a basis for labour unrest. This research confirms the hypothesis advanced by J. C. Davies that revolutionary outbursts are likely to occur after a prolonged period of economic and social development followed by a period of reversal[2]. It would also fit the Marxist notion that political upheavals by the working class are related to economic impoverishment.

It is also interesting to note that Bolshevism took root among the older, more 'traditional' Russian working class. In the late nineteenth century, in the Moscow and Vladimir provinces over 80% of the workers were permanently employed in factories and dependent on factory work. Whereas, in Kharkov and Kiev provinces (areas of Menshevik supremacy) only 48.78% and 42.5% respectively of the factory workers were permanent[3]. The Bolsheviks tended to be in areas of established large-scale factory production. On figures collected between 1886 and 1893, in Kiev (Menshevik), for example, 92,005 men were employed in 4,417 factories, while in Moscow 213,128 were in only 1,225 factories. Vilna had a very large proportion of permanent workers – though in very small works, on average only eleven strong[4]. As E. P. Thompson[5] has pointed out when discussing Birmingham industry in the early nineteenth century, small scale industrial enterprises tend to mute class antagonism, for in times of recession masters and journeymen are similarly affected. The more gradual social scale characteristic of such industrial areas is a general factor inhibiting political radicalism. Lipset has argued that a locality based on an 'isolated' industry tends to develop support from left-wing extremist parties[6]. The Ivanovo-Voznesensk area was Bolshevik not only because it was based on the textile industry but also because it was economically deprived. The fact that many were employed in one industry means that a crisis affects a large number of people – unlike mixed industrial areas. But economic crises linked to a dominant or 'isolated' industry do not always result in social solidarity or class consciousness. Other factors operated in Baku which prevented the development of class consciousness: it was relatively easy for the unemployed to return to their villages and national and

---

[1] See pp. 95-6.

[2] 'Towards a Theory of Revolution', *American Sociological Review*, Vol. 27, No. 1, February 1962.

[3] A. G. Rashin, *Formirovanie rabochego klassa Rossii* (M. 1958) p. 565.

[4] A. G. Rashin, *ibid.*

[5] E. P. Thompson, *The Making of the English Working Class*, (1966) p. 815.

[6] Lipset gives examples of mining, lumbering, and the docks, *Political Man*, p. 87.

racial groups existed through which discontent was articulated. The industrial structure in terms of the size and ownership of individual firms varied regionally. In Ivanovo, the textile industry – Russian-owned and vertically integrated – not only created conditions blurring differences between workers, but also uniting employers. In St. Petersburg, the industrial structure included a large number of firms in different industries and in the Donbass many were foreign-owned and foreign-managed. Such firms, with relatively more enlightened management relations, ready to negotiate with workers and more prepared (and able) to pay a 'fair wage' may have encouraged the development of a more moderate Social-Democratic party. The Bolsheviks were strongest in areas where industry was mostly Russian-owned (the central economic area and the Urals); the Mensheviks in areas where many foreign firms were being set up (the Ukraine, the Caucasus and to a lesser extent, St. Petersburg).

A corollary to the southern economic growth was the recruitment pattern of the workers drawn to the new industries and whose economic and national background affected their political behaviour. In the Donbass, many from small handicraft workshops of the western provinces either formed national Social-Democratic groups or joined the Mensheviks. Conversely, Russian-speaking industrial immigrants from the central and Ural areas tended to group around the Bolshevik faction. The 'dominant area' thesis outlined above obfuscated differences between the strata which supported the factions. The detailed examination of the social composition and support of the factions sheds some light on the character of Bolshevism as a social movement. Bolshevism at the grass roots was supported mainly by the urban proletariat, including those uprooted and new to the town. The Mensheviks had supporters across class lines. On the whole, the Mensheviks recruited more from among the better-paid and more skilled workers and less from among the poorer peasant urban newcomers – which may explain the greater emphasis they placed on 'economistic' activity. Also the support across class lines may help explain their less aggressive policy. As suggested by Lipset, conflict is promoted by parties being based on social divisions whereas 'stable democracy' is dependent on parties formed 'from many segments of the population'[1].

The leaders of Russian Social-Democracy, even in the local Committees, were of the upper social strata: the Mensheviks with a bias to the *meshchane*, the Bolsheviks to the gentry. The active participation by men of gentry origin is noteworthy: it may be one of the

---

[1] S. M. Lipset, *Political Man*, p. 31.

distinctive features of Russian Social-Democracy[1]. Social strata with high status in an autocratic regime, but socially or economically insecure, may not wish to be identified with the business and commercial groups whom they may regard as intellectually and socially inferior: to them the vision of a classless society and common cause with the proletariat both may seem more noble and equally attainable goals. At the lower levels of party organisation, I have argued, the Bolsheviks had more active workers. This was probably because the Menshevik activists were also trade unionists – activity which may have detracted them from purely 'party' political goals.

The horizontal stratification pattern of a society, the ways age or intergenerational differences affect political allegiance and activity have often been ignored. In stable societies, age differences have no significant effects on political outlook and youth may stabilise the political order[2]. In periods of change, however, youth may be more subject to opposing pressures outside the family: from the school, from new occupational groups and from political ideas which have currency in the metropolis away from home. Such was the case for many young men in Russia at the beginning of the twentieth century. The educational system did not succeed in inculcating loyalty to the autocracy: in fact schools and universities became centres of anti-Tsarist propaganda. Social 'adjustment' in many schools and higher educational institutions may often have meant participation in a school or university socialist society. There can be no doubt that few older men, born before the emancipation of the serfs, were in the Social-Democratic movement. The activists were well under thirty years of age and the Bolsheviks were significantly younger than the Mensheviks. The Menshevik elite was, on average, forty-four years old – fifteen years older than the local leaders, whereas the top

[1] According to Lipset, Michels has argued that the absence of 'upper class leaders in the German Social-Democratic Party (S.P.D) explained in part why most members of the middle class did not accept it as a legitimate opposition'. (*Political Man*, p. 31). I have been unable to find such a view expressed by Michels, though in the source cited by Lipset, Michels shows that of S.P.D. deputies in Germany (1903) only 16% were intellectuals or members of the big bourgeoisie and 18.5% were petty-bourgeoisie, R. Michels, *Sozialismus in Italien*, (München 1925), Vol. I. pp. 170-1. In Britain, the aristocracy and liberal bourgeoisie were absorbed into the Conservative and Liberal parties, relatively few took part in the Labour movement in its early days. W. Guttsman, *The British Political Elite* (1963) pp. 226-9, 236-9. Later, of course, in the 1920's the British Labour Party elite contained many of aristocratic and upper middle class background: Guttsman, p. 242.

[2] P. Abrams and A. Little, 'Young Voters and the Irrelevance of Age', *British Journal of Sociology*, Vol. xvi, No. 2 (June 1965) and R. E. Lane *Political Life* (Glencoe 1957), p. 217. In such societies educational institutions promote social stability: they 'serve democracy by increasing the lower classes' exposure to cross-pressures which reduce their commitment to given ideologies and make them less receptive to extremist ones'. Lipset, *Political Man*, p. 65.

Bolsheviks, whose average was thirty-four, were only seven years older. Unlike the Menshevik organisational structure, the Bolshevik was more open. The young Bolsheviks were able to advance rapidly to positions of authority – which may help explain the faction's more radical activity. I am not suggesting that *all* youth in Russia was Social-Democratic, but that significant groups of young men felt ideologically bound to the ideals of Social-Democracy – and Bolshevism. Such young men, having once formed their political attachment, keep it for life, carrying forward the political views of their youth[1]. Paradoxically, once a significant break has been made with tradition, a new tradition is created and this itself becomes a dominant value or ideology and may remain so for a considerable time after its original causes have disappeared.

The relationships between the members of political parties have been classified by Tönnies and Duverger in terms of *Gemeinschaft* and *Gesellschaft*[2]. It has been argued that Marxist (particularly Communist) parties are social groups based on the principle of *Gemeinschaft*. The Great Russian national basis of the Bolsheviks at this time fits well into this typology: community solidarity based on race, religion and language – even though explicitly rejected by many of the articulate leaders of the Social-Democrats – provided a cement which reinforced Social-Democratic ideology, bound together the assorted status groups and gave the Bolsheviks a homogeneity which their rival faction lacked. Nationalism, a dividing force of the international socialist movement, was also one of the main dividers of the Russian. National antagonisms, the strength of local ties, the binding force of language and tradition kept together the Bolsheviks and allowed for the easy assimilation of other Russians into their ranks. The Mensheviks, being more mixed nationally and socially, were subject to competition from purely nationalist parties and nationally-based socialist groups.

The implications of this study for theories seeking to explain radical and communist behaviour are that 'mass' theories underestimate the importance of social class and economic conflict as factors contributing to the rise of Bolshevism, which was not characterised by support from many social strata but was based mainly on the working class being subject to economic crises. Marxian theories,

---

[1] K. Mannheim, 'The Sociological Problem of Generations', in Kecskemeti, *Essays on the Sociology of Knowledge*, (N. Y. 1952), pp. 306-9.
[2] See particularly, R. Heberle, 'Ferdinand Tönnies' Contribution to the Sociology of Political Parties', *American Journal of Sociology*, No. 61, (1955-56), p. 213; M. Duverger, *Political Parties* (1959) p. 124.

however, while rightly emphasising economic and property relations, give insufficient weight to group ties based on nationality, language, cultural tradition and age. The nature of the economic framework, party organisational structure, many forms of group solidarity besides that based on class have to be taken into consideration to explain the rise and division of Social-Democracy in Russia.

APPENDIX

1. Education

PRIMARY defined as: *prikhodskoe nachal'noe uchilishche, narodnoe uchilishche.* 'Factory school' has been included in primary unless it indicates clearly trade-training when it has been included in secondary.

SECONDARY defined as: *gorodskoe uchilishche, real'noe uchilishche, gimnazium, remeslennaya shkola.* Commercial schools, technical evening schools and midwifery courses are included in secondary. Educated 'at home' is counted in secondary.

HIGHER EDUCATION includes University and institute courses. Military and agricultural academies and dental schools are included here too. Attendance at the above establishments is the determining factor: whether attendance was satisfactory or completed is ignored.

2. Occupation

Intelligentsia includes writers, university teachers, professionals (doctors, army officers), higher state servants. Agricultural smallholder includes 'landowners'. Technologist includes chemists, agronomists, engineers. *Sluzhashchi* includes all clerks. Clergy includes Rabbis. The general worker category includes men who are not more precisely defined (e.g. as 'factory workers'). The classification involves overlapping groups, e.g. a mechanic may be employed in a factory or on the railway. Factory-type skills are included in the factory/mill workers' division (*slesar'*, *tokar'*) regardless of place of work. 'Railway' skills only (guard, engine-driver, fireman) are put under railway workers. Handicraftsmen include blacksmiths, shoe-repairers, carpenters, joiners, bookbinders, seamstresses and musicians. 'Others' (a small proportion of the total) include soldiers (other ranks), a masseuse, cigarette-sellers, washer-women. Lower-medical includes midwives, nurses and hospital assistants. Some entries have two occupations, e.g. a teacher turned railway clerk. In such cases the last occupation is shown, or the most permanent. In cases of men working in the town and periodically returning to the village, the town occupation is used.

3. Geographical Division

MOSCOW and ST. PETERSBURG include town and province. WEST includes Poland and Estlyandiya, Pskov, Kurlyandiya, Kovno, Vitebsk, Grodno, Vilna, Minsk, Mogilev, Smolensk provinces. CENTRAL includes Novgorod, Tver, Yaroslavl, Kostroma, Vladimir, Nizhni-Novgorod, Kaluga, Tula, Orel, Ryazan,

Tambov provinces. SOUTH AND SOUTH-WEST include Volyn, Bessarabia, Podol'sk, Kiev, Kherson, Tavrich (The Crimea), Ekaterinoslav, Don Area, Kharkov, Poltava, Voronezh, Kursk and Chernigov provinces. The CAUCASUS includes Kuban and Stavropol and all provinces to their south-east. CENTRAL ASIA AND SIBERIA include all provinces to the east of Vologda, Perm, Orenburg and Ural'sk. URALS AND NORTH is defined as Archangel, Vologda, Vyatka, Perm, Ufa, and Orenburg provinces. VOLGA includes Astrakhan, Ural'sk, Samara, Saratov, Penza, Simbirsk and Kazan provinces.

4. *Position in Organisation*

TOP CAUCUS as defined on pp. 28-30. LOCAL LEADER, attended Party Congress (II-V Congress of RSDLP), Conference or meeting of any regional bureau and *otvetstvenny* propagandist, organiser or agitator, secretary or chairman of party group, member of the executive committee of a Soviet of Workers' Deputies, *'rukovoditel''* or *'lider'*. ACTIVIST is propagandist, orator, agitator, member of a local Soviet, member of an armed detachment. RANK AND FILE are any entries which say that participant was a member of a Social-Democratic group. Many were men arrested by the police for 'taking part in' Social-Democratic activity, or being 'on the business of' Social-Democracy, or distributing or carrying the leaflets of the Social-Democrats.

BIBLIOGRAPHY

A. UNPUBLISHED SOURCES

AKUBZHANOVA, Z. A. *Kavkazski Soyuz RSDRP (1903-1906 gg.).* Candidate of Science Dissertation (Tbilisi, 1962).

GADZHINSKI, D. D. *Promyslovye i zavodskie komissii v Bakinskom neftepromyshlennom rayone v gody pervoy russkoy revolyutsii.* Candidate of Science Dissertation (Baku, 1962).

Inter-University Project on the History of the Menshevik Movement.

Anan'in, E. A. *Iz vospominaniy revolyutsionera 1905-1923 gg.* (N.Y. 1961).

Aronson, G. *Revolyutsionnaya yunost': vospominaniya, 1903-1917* (N.Y. 1961).

Khinoy, M. *U istokov men'shevizma* (N.Y. 1960).

Khinoy, M. *V podpol'nykh tipografiyakh tsarskoy Rossii* (N.Y. 1960).

KEEP, J. L. H. *The Development of Social-Democracy in Russia 1898-1907.* Ph.D. Thesis (London, 1954).

MOYZHES, R. L. *Politicheskoe vospitanie Peterburgskogo proletariata v kanun pervoy russkoy revolyutsii 1903-1905 gg.* Candidate of Science Dissertation (Leningrad, 1960).

SHMELEVA, I. A. *Bor'ba Moskovskikh rabochikh protiv Zubatovshchiny.* Candidate of Science Dissertation (Moscow, 1962).

SHUKMAN, H. *The Relations between the Jewish Bund and the RSDRP 1897-1903.* D. Phil. Thesis (Oxford, 1961).

SLUSSER, R. M. *The Moscow Soviet of Workers' Deputies of 1905: Origin, Structure and Politics.* Ph. D. Thesis (Columbia University, 1963).

Socialist-Revolutionary Brochures (1902-1905). Helsinki University Library, Box A-117-A.

WILDMAN, A. K. *The Proletarian Prometheans: the Young Social-Democrats and the Workers' Movement 1894-1901.* Ph. D. Thesis (Chicago, 1962).

YUKHNEVA, N. V. *Rabochee dvizhenie v Peterburge v 1901 g.* Candidate of Science Dissertation (Leningrad, 1962).

1. Newspapers

Bor'ba, 1-10 (Moscow, Nov.-Dec. 1905).
Golos proletariya (organ Vyborgskogo rayona RSDRP), 1-2 (St. Petersburg, 1906).
Iskra (RSDRP), 1-112 (Zurich, Munich, Geneva, 1900-1905).
Izvestiya Moskovskogo Soveta rabochikh deputatov, 1-6 (Moscow, Dec. 1905).
Izvestiya soveta rabochikh deputatov, 1, 3, 5 (St. Petersburg, Dec. 1905).
Nachalo, 1-16 (St. Petersburg, Nov.-Dec. 1905).
Nash golos, 1 (St. Petersburg, Dec. 1905).
Novaya Zhizn', 1-28 (St. Petersburg, Oct.-Dec. 1905).
Proletari, 1-26 (Geneva, 1905).
     Reprint, edited by M. Ol'minski (M.L. 1924-25).
Rabochi golos, 1 (St. Petersburg, 1905).
Rech' (St. Petersburg, Feb. 1906 – Oct. 1917).
     Issues of Jan. and Feb. 1907 consulted on Second Duma elections.
Rus' (St. Petersburg, Jan. 1906 – May 1909).
     Issues of Jan. and Feb. 1907 refer to Duma elections.
Severny golos, 1-2 (St. Petersburg, Dec. 1905).
Sotsial-demokrat, 1-16 (Geneva, 1904-1905).
Vpered, 1-18 (Geneva, 1905).
     Reprint, edited by M. Ol'minski (M.L. 1924-25).
Vpered, 1-4 (Moscow, Dec. 1905).

2. Documents

Bol'shevistskaya organizatsiya i sestroretskie rabochie v 1905 g. (*Sbornik*), Ed. A. Matveev
     and V. Tarasov (M.L. 1926).
Doklady sotsial-demokraticheskikh komitetov vtoromu s'ezdu, RSDRP, Ed. N. Angarski
     (M.L. 1930). This book contains the full texts of the local committees'
     reports to the Second Congress with notes and commentaries. The following
     have been found particularly useful:
     'Doklad organizatsii *Iskry*'. (Commentary by N.K. Krupskaya); 'Petersburgski
     raskol', (Commentary by E. D. Stasova); 'Doklad o Moskovskom S. D.
     dvizhennii', (Commentary by B. I. Nikolaevski); 'Yuzhnogo rabochego',
     (Commentary by B. I. Nikolaevski); 'Doklad Donskogo komiteta', (Commen-
     tary by V. I. Nevsky); 'Doklad delegata Severnogo Rabochego soyuza',
     (Commentary by A. M. Stopani and O. A. Varentsova); 'Doklad Tverskogo
     komiteta', (Commentary by B. I. Nikolaevski); 'Doklad Sibirskogo Soyuza',
     (Commentary by B. I. Nikolaevski); 'Doklad Batumskogo komiteta RSDRP',
     (Commentary by B. I. Nikolaevski).
Dokumenty i Materialy: I s'ezd RSDRP (M. 1958).
Gosudarstvennaya duma v Rossii (*Dokumenty i materialy*), Ed. F. I. Kalinychev (M. 1957).
Istoriya Ekaterinoslavskoy sotsial-demokraticheskoy organizatsii, 1889-1903 (Dokumenty),
     Ed. M. A. Rubach (Ekaterinoslav, 1923).

Iz istorii revolyutsii 1905 goda v Moskve i Moskovskoy gub. (Materialy i dokumenty), Ed. V. V. Simonenko and G. D. Kostomarov (M. 1931).

Iz proshlogo (Sbornik materialov po istorii Bakinskoy bol'shevistskoy organizatsii i i Oktyabr'skoy revolyutsii v Azerbaydzhane), Vol. 2 (Baku, 1923-1924).

Khrestomatiya po istorii pervoy russkoy revolyutsii 1905 g., Ed. S. N. Belousov (M.n.d.).

Krasny arkhiv, 1-106 (M. 1922-1941). This journal contains innumerable documents from government archives on the revolutionary movement. Most are preceded by a commentary (cited below) which helps indicate the contents.

Vol. 1 (1922). A. M. Pankratova, 'Novoe o Zubatovshchine' (p. 289).

Vols. 11-12 (1925). M. Pokrovski, 'Nachalo proletarskoy revolyutsii v Rossii' (p.v).

Vol. 56 (1933). Numerous documents on strikes and workers' activity in 1903 (p. 138-).

Vol. 59 (1933). M. Nevski, 'K istorii sozyva II s'ezda RSDRP' (p. 3).

Vol. 59 (1933). Correspondence of social-democrats from police files (pp. 39-66).

Vol. 62 (1934). Material on *Iskra* 1901-1903 (pp. 140-162).

Vol. 62 (1934). Material on the 1905-07 Revolution (p. 167-).

Vol. 68 (1935). A. M. Pankratova, 'K istorii bor'by za III s'ezd partii' (p. 18-).

Vol. 73 (1935). A. M. Pankratova, 'Dekabr'skie dni v Donbasse v 1905 g.' (p. 91).

Vol. 75 (1936). Material on the student movement (1901) (p. 83).

Vol. 76 (1936). 'Rabochee dvizhenie na zavodakh Peterburga v Mae 1901', Commentary by M. Syromyatnikova (p. 49).

Vol. 82 (1937). Documents on disturbances on May Day (1900-1903) in St. Petersburg, Poltava, Kiev, Ivanovo, Tiflis, Yaroslavl, Moscow, Baku and Tver (pp. 167-191).

LENIN, V. I. *Sochineniya* (4th Edition, Moscow 1951-1954). The following articles are the most relevant to the subject:

Lenin, V. I. 'S chego nachat'' (Vol. V).

Lenin, V. I. 'Chto delat'' (Vol. V).

Lenin, V. I. 'Pis'mo k tovarishchu o nashikh organizatsionnykh zadachakh' (Vol. VI).

Lenin, V. I. 'K voprosu o dokladakh komitetov i grupp RSDRP obshche partiyno-mu s'ezdu' (Vol. VI).

Lenin, V. I. 'Shag vpered, dva shaga nazad' (Vol. VII).

Lenin, V. I. 'Dve taktiki sotsial-demokratii v demokraticheskoy revolyutsii' (Vol. IX).

Lenin, V. I. 'Nashi zadachi i sovet rabochikh deputatov' (Vol. X).

Lenin, V. I. 'O reorganizatsii partii' (Vol. X).

Lenin, V. I. 'Rabochaya partiya i ee zadachi pri sovremennom polozhenii' (Vol. X).

Lenin, V. I. 'Gosudarstvennaya duma i sotsial-demokraticheskaya taktika' (Vol. X).

Lenin, V. I. 'Russkaya revolyutsiya i zadachi proletariata' (Vol. X).

Lenin, V. I. 'Takticheskaya platforma k ob'edinitel'nomu s'ezdu RSDRP' (Vol. X).

Lenin, V. I. 'O sozyve ekstrennogo partiynogo s'ezda' (Vol. XI).

Lenin, V. I. 'Izbiratel'naya kampaniya rabochey partii v Peterburge' (Vol. XI).

Lenin, V. I. 'Sotsial-demokratiya i vybory v dumu' (Vol. XI).

Lenin, V. I. 'Vybornaya kampaniya sotsial-demokratii v Peterburge' (Vol. XII).

Lenin, V. I. 'Vybory po rabochey kurii v Peterburge' (Vol. XII).

Lenin, V. I. 'Bor'ba S.D. i S.R. na vyborakh v rabochey kurii v S. Peterburge' (Vol. XII).

Lenin, V. I. 'Nekotorye dannye o vyborakh po rabochey kurii na yuge Rossii' (Vol. XII).

Lenin, V. I. 'Reorganizatsiya i likvidatsiya raskola v Peterburge' (Vol. XII).

Lenin, V. I. 'Vybory v dumu i taktika russkoy sotsial-demokratii' (Vol. XII).

Vol. XXXIV (pp. 1-322) contains correspondence from 1895-1907.

Leninski sbornik, 1-   (M. 1924 -)

Vol. VI. Lenin, V. I. 'Sostav vtorogo s'ezda'.

Vol. XI, Lenin, V. I. 'Sostav organizatsii Iskry na s'ezde'.

Listovki bol'shevistskikh organizatsiy v pervoy russkoy revolyutsii 1905-1907 gg., Vols. 1-3 (M. 1956).

Listovki Kavkazskogo soyuza RSDRP 1903-05 gg. (M. 1955).

Listovki Moskovskikh bol'shevikov v period pervoy russkoy revolyutsii (M. 1955).

Listovki Peterburgskikh bol'shevikov 1902-1917 gg., Vol. 1 (1902-1907) (L. 1939).

LYADOV, M. N. 'Londonski s'ezd RSDRP v tsifrakh', in Itogi Londonskogo s'ezda (St. Petersburg, 1907).

MARX, K. 'Classes'. Capital, Vol. III (M. 1959).

MARX, K. AND ENGELS, F. 'The Communist Manifesto'. Selected Works, Vol. I (M. 1958).

Materialy po istorii Ekaterinoslavskoy S-D organizatsii bol'shevikov i revolyutsionnykh sobytiy 1904-05-06. (Shortened in footnotes to Ekat. Mat. (1924)) (Ekaterinoslav, 1924).

Materialy po istorii professional'nogo dvizheniya Tverskoy gubernii 1883-1917 gg., Ed. A. Dokuchaev (Tver, 1925).

Nachalo revolyutsionnogo dvizheniya v Turkmenii v 1900-1905 gg. (Sbornik), Ed. A. G. Solov'ev (Ashkhabad-Moscow, 1946).

Obzor revolyutsionnogo dvizheniya v okruge Irkutskoy sudebnoy palaty za 1897-1907 (St. Petersburg, 1908).

Omskaya organizatsiya RSDRP v gody pervoy russkoy revolyutsii (Omsk, 1956).

Pervaya konferentsiya voennykh i boevykh organizatsiy RSDRP (1906).

'Pervaya obshcherusskaya konferentsiya partiynykh rabotnikov'. Otdel'noe prilozhenie k No. 100 'Iskry' (Geneva, 1905).

Pervaya perepis' naseleniya 1897 g. (St. Petersburg, 1905), Vols. I, II.

Pervaya Russkaya revolyutsiya v Peterburge (Sbornik No. 2, Fabriki i zavodi), Ed. Ts. Zelikson-Bovrovskaya (M.L. 1925).

1905 v Peterburge. Vol. I. Sotsial-demokraticheskie listovki (L. 1925).

Peterburgski i Moskovski Sovety rabochikh deputatov 1905 goda (v dokumentakh), Eds. L. Galler and N. Rovenskaya (M. 1926).

PROKOPOVICH, S. Soyuzy rabochikh i ikh zadachi (St. Petersburg, 1905).

Proletarskaya revolyutsiya (R.K.P. kommissiya po istorii Oktyab'skoy revolyutsii), 1-113 (M. 1921-31, 1933-40). This journal contains leaflets, letters, memoirs and interpretive articles on revolutionary activity. Some of the most useful articles are listed under the relevant headings in this bibliography.

'Prepiska Guseva s Leninom', No. 3 (1921); 'Perepiska Ekaterinoslavskoy i Luganskoy organizatsiy s N. Leninym i N. K. Krupskoy', No. 4 (51), 1926; 'Perepiska N. Lenina i N. K. Krupskoy s Kavkazskoy organizatsiey', No. 5 (40), 1925;

'Perepiska: A. Stopani – Lenin/Krupskaya', No. 40 (1925).

Protokoly: chetverty (ob'edinitel'ny) s'ezd RSDRP (M. 1959).

Protokoly: pyaty (Londonski) s'ezd RSDRP (M. 1963).

Protokoly: vtoroy s'ezd RSDRP (M. 1959). The following documents on local organisations are included:

'Doklad sotsial-demokraticheskogo Soyuza gornozavodsk.rabochikh yuga Rossii'; 'Doklad Bakinskogo komiteta'; 'Otchet Tul'skogo komiteta'; Doklad Donskogo komiteta'; 'Doklad Tverskogo komiteta'; 'Doklad o Moskovskom sotsial-demokraticheskom dvizhenii'; 'Peterburgski raskol'; 'Doklad Kievskogo komiteta'; 'Doklad delegata Severnogo Rabochego Soyuza'; 'Doklad Batumskogo komiteta RSDRP'; 'Doklad Sibirskogo Soyuza'.

Protokoly: treti s'ezd RSDRP (M. 1959). Including the following documents:

'Doklad Tsentral'nogo komiteta'; 'Otchet izdatel'stva Vpered'; 'Doklad komiteta biblioteki i arkhiva'; 'Doklad Peterburgskogo komiteta'; 'Iz otcheta Tverskogo komiteta'; 'Otchet Rizhskogo komiteta. Partiynaya rabota v Rige (1903-05)'; 'Otchet Severnogo komiteta'; 'K otchetu Ural'skogo Soyuza RSDRP'; 'Doklad III s'ezdu RSDRP o deyatel'nosti Kavkazskogo Soyuza za 1903-05 g.'; 'Kratki konspekt dlya doklada na III partiynom s'ezde Bakinskogo komiteta RSDRP'; 'Doklad Voronezhskogo komiteta RSDRP'; 'Otchet Ekaterinoslavskogo komiteta RSDRP; 'O postanovke raboty sredi intelligentsii'; 'Izveshchenie ob obrazovanii organizatsionnogo komiteta i o sozyve III ocherednogo s'ezda RSDRP'; 'Pis'mo chlena Ekaterinoslavskogo bol'shevistskogo komiteta III partiynomu s'ezdu o Ekaterinoslavskoy partiynoy organisatsii'; 'Pis'mo Nikolaevskogo komiteta III partiynomu s'ezdu'; 'Rezolyutsiya rabochikh i sudoremontnykh zavodov g. Nikolaeva o sozyve tret'ego s'ezda'.

Rabochee dvizhenie v godi pervoy russkoy revolyutsii (Dokumenty) (Baku, 1956).

Resheniya yuzhno-russkoy uchreditel'noy konferentsii RSDRP avgust 1905 g. (Geneva, 1905).

Revolyutsiya 1905-7 gg. v Rossii: dokumenty i materialy, Ed. A. M. Pankratova (M. 1955-).

Nachalo pervoy russkoy revolyutsii: yanvar'-mart 1905 g.;

Revolyutsionnoe dvizhenie v Rossii vesnoy i letom 1905 g.: aprel'-sentyabr';

Vserossiyskaya politicheskaya stachka v oktyabre 1905 g.;

Vysshiy pod'em revolyutsii 1905-7 gg.: vooruzhennye vosstaniya: noyabr'-dekabr' 1905 g.

Revolyutsionnoe dvizhenie v Zabaykal'e 1905-07 gg. (sbornik) (Chita, 1955).

Sbornik dokumentov i materialov: treti s'ezd RSDRP (M. 1955).

Sibirski soyuz RSDRP, Ed. E. Yaroslavski (M. 1935).

Sostav vsesoyuznoy kommunisticheskoy partii (bol'shevikov), Ed. E. Smitten (M.L. 1927).

STALIN, J. V. Works (English edition, 1954-).

Vol. 2. 'The London Congress of the RSDLP (Notes of a Delegate).'

TROTSKY, L. D. 1905 (3rd Russian ed., M. 1925).

TROTSKY, L. D. *Permanent Revolution* (English ed., 1962).
TROTSKY, L. D. *Results and Prospects* (English ed., 1962).
TROTSKY, L. D. *Our Political Tasks* (1904).
TROTSKY, L. D. *Istoriya revolyutsii* (Berlin, 1917).
TROTSKY, L. D. *The Soviet and the Revolution* (1908). (English ed. Ceylon, 1954).
Vserossiyskaya perepis'chlenov RKP (b) 1922 goda, No. 4 (M. 1923).

3. *Memoirs*

ALADZHALOVA, N. N. *Iz bol'shevistskogo podpol'ya (vospominaniya)* (Tbilisi, 1963).
BABUSHKIN, I. V. *Vospominaniya, 1893-1900* (M. 1951).
BARANSKI, N. N. *V ryadakh Sibirskogo sotsial-demokraticheskogo soyuza* (Novonikolaevsk, 1923).
Dekabr'skoe vosstanie v Moskve 1905 g., Ed. N. Ovsyannikov (M. 1919).
DIANIN, S. *Revolyutsionnaya molodezh' v Peterburge* (L. 1926).
Dinamo 25 let revolyutsionnoy bor'by (M. 1923).
Dvatsat'pyat' let Bakinskoy organizatsii bol'shevikov (sbornik) (Baku, 1924).
XXV let RKP (b). *Vospominaniya Ivanovo-Voznesenskikh podpol'shchikov* (I.-V., 1923).
FRUNZE, M. V. 'K istorii sotsial-demokratii v Ivanovo-Voznesenskoy gubernii'. *Sobranie sochineniy*, Vol. I (M.L. 1929).
GARVI, P. A. *Vospominaniya sotsialdemokrata* (N.Y. 1946).
GOLUBEV, V. S. 'Stranichka iz istorii rabochego dvizheniya'. *Byloe*, No. 12 (St. Petersburg, 1906).
Iskrovski period v Moskve, Ed. O. Pyatnitski (M.L. 1928).
    Milyutin, N. 'V Moskovskoy S-D organizatsii 1902 g.'
                'Vospominaniya I.A. Teodorovicha.'
KHRUSTALEV-NOSAR', G. S. 'Istoriya soveta rabochikh deputatov', in N. Trotsky (et al), *Istoriya soveta rabochikh deputatov St. Peterburga* (Spb. 1906).
KONDZHARIYA, V. Z. *Moi vospominaniya* (Sukhumi 1959).
KUYBYSHEV, V. V. *Izbrannye proizvedeniya* (M. 1958).
Letopis' revolyutsii (Zhurnal vseukrainskogo istparta, Kharkov, 1922-27).
    Merinkov, I., Andronov, S. et al (Memoirs). 'Bryanski zavod v 1905 g.', Nos. 3-4 (1926).
    Kogan, E. 'Iz istorii selyanskogo dvizheniya na Ekaterinoslavshchine nakanune 1905 g.', No. 5 (1926)
    Kramer, S. 'Yanvarskie dni 1905 g. v Ekaterinoslave i Donetskom basseyne', No. 1 (1925).
    Ravich-Cherkasski, M. 'Moi vospominaniya o 1905 g.', Nos. 5-6 (1925).
    Skubitski, T. 'Rabochee dvizhenie na Dneprovskom zavode (1895-1905)', No. 6 (1926).
    Yaroslavski, E. 'Posle Stokgol'mskogo s'ezda v Ekaterinoslave', Nos. 3-4 (1926).
MANDEL'BERG, V. E. *Iz Perezhitago* (Davos, 1910).
MARTOV, YU. O. *Zapiski Sotsialdemokrata* (Berlin, 1922).
MEL'KUMOV, A. *Materialy revolyutsionnogo dvizheniya v Turkmeniya 1904-19 gg.* (Tashkent, 1924).
MITSKEVICH, S. I. *Revolyutsionnaya Moskva* (M. 1940).

Moskovskie pechatniki v 1905 g., Ed. A. Borshchevsky (M. 1925).

Moskovskie tekstil'shchiki v gody pervoy revolyutsii 1905-07 (Sbornik), (1929).

Moskva v dekabre 1905 g., Ed. P. V. Kokhmansky (M. 1906).

Pervaya Russkaya revolyutsiya v Peterburge (Sbornik No. 1), Ed. Ts. Zelikson-Bovrovskaya (M.L. 1925).

Proletarskaya revolyutsiya (R.K.P. Kommissiya po istorii Oktyab'rskoy revolyutsii), 1-113 (M. 1921-31, 1933-40).

Baranski, N. 'Ob oktyabr'skikh dnyakh 1905 g. v Tomske', No. 5 (52) (1926).

Enukidze, A. 'Istoriya organizatsii i raboty nelegal'nykh tipografiy RSDRP na Kavkaze za vremya ot 1900 po 1906 god', No. 2 (14) (1923).

Leman, M. 'Iz proshlogo Kavkazskikh bol'shevistskikh organizatsiy', No. 40 (1925).

Makharadze, F. 'Partorganizatsiya Zakavkaz'ya nakanune i posle II s'ezda', No. 2 (1933).

Nelidov, N. 'Tov. Makar (V.P. Nogin)', No. 7 (30) (1924).

Samoylov, F. N. 'Pervy sovet rab. deput. v 1905 g.', No. 39 (1925).

Smirnov, A. P. 'Sametki o Tverskoy organizatsii', No. 12 (47) (1925).

'Stat'i i vospominaniya', No. 4 (51) (1926).

Varentsova, O. 'Severny Rabochi Soyuz', No. 9 (1922).

Vasil'ev-Yuzhin, M. 'Moskovski sovet rabochikh deputatov v 1905 godu i podgotovka im vooruzhennogo vosstaniya', Vol. 4 (39) (1925) and Vol. 5 (40) (1925).

Put' k oktyabryu (Sbornik statey, vospominaniy i dokumentov), Ed. S. Polidorov (M. 1923).

O rabochem dvizhenii i S-D. rabote vo Vladimirskoy gub. v 1900-kh. godakh, Part II (Vladimir, 1925).

Rabochie o 1905 g. v Moskovskoy gubernii (Sbornik vospominaniy), Ed. E. Popova (M.L. 1926).

Rabochie Trekhgornoy manufaktury v 1905 g. (Abbreviated to *R.T.m.*) (M. 1930).

Rabochie zavoda 'Serp i molot' (b. Guzhon) v 1905 g. (M. 1931).

RAEVSKI, A. *Bol'shevizm i men'shevizm v Baku v 1904-05 gg.* (Baku, 1930).

O revolyutsionnom proshlom Peterburgskogo metallicheskogo zavoda 1886-1905 (Sbornik) (L. 1926).

SAMOYLOV, F. N. (Ed.) *Ivanovo-Voznesensky sovet rabochikh deputatov 1905 g. v dokumentakh* (M.L. 1935).

SAMOYLOV, F. N. *Pervy sovet rabochikh deputatov* (M. 1935).

SAMOYLOV, F. N. *Vospominaniya ob Ivanovo-Voznesenskom rab. dvizh*, Part I (1903-05) (M.L. 1922).

SCHWARZ, SOLOMAN M., *The Russian Revolution of 1905* (Chicago 1967).

SHERTERNIN, S. P. *Rabochee dvizhenie v Ivanovo-Voznesensk za pos. 15 let* (Geneva, 1900).

'1905' god (Collection of essays, memoirs and documents), *Krasnaya letopis'*, No. 1 (12) (1925).

1905 god v Ivanovo-Voznesenskom rayone, Ed. O. A. Varentsova (Ivanovo-Voznesensk, 1925).

1905 god v Moskovskoy gubernii (sbornik), Ed. E. Popova (M. L. 1926).

1905 god v Tverskoy gubernii (Tver 1925).

TROTSKY, L. *My Life* (N.Y. 1930).

TSVETKOVA, S. *Na barrikadakh, 1905 g. (po vospominaniyam rabotnitsy)* (M.L. 1926).
VARENTSOVA, O. A. AND BAGAEV, M. A. *Za desyat' let* (Ivanovo-Voznesensk, 1930).
VASIL'EV-YUZHIN, M. I. *Moskovski sovet rabochikh deputatov v 1905 g.* (M. 1925).
Zamoskvorech'e v 1905 g. (Sbornik dokumentov), Ed. Morozov-Vorontsov (M. 1925).

C. PRINTED SOURCES: SECONDARY

1. Works of Reference

BAZILEVICH, K. V. *Atlas istorii SSSR*, Pt. II (M. 1949).
Bol'shaya sovetskaya entsiklopediya, 1st edition, Ed. O. Yu. Shmidt (M. 1926-48); 2nd edition, Ed. S. I. Valilov (M. 1950-1960).
Bol'shevistskaya periodicheskaya pechat' 1900-1917 (M. 1964).
BROKGAUZ, F. A. AND EFRON, I. A. *Entsiklopedicheski slovar'* (Spb. 1905-07).
Deyateli revolyutsionnogo dvizheniya v Rossii: bio-bibliograficheski slovar', Ed. V. Vilenski-Sibiryakov (M. 1927-33).
Digest of Krasny Arkhiv (Vols. 31-106), Ed. Leona W. Eisele (University of Michigan, 1955).
Entsiklopedicheski slovar' Russkogo Bibliograficheskogo Instituta Granat (M. 1910-1948). See Vol. XLI (*Prilozhenie*) for biographies of members of the Duma.
KAMENEV, L. B. *Sotsialisticheskie izdaniya* (Guide to literature in Russian on S.D. from 1898-1905) (Paris, 1913).
NECHKINA, M. V. *Bibliografiya po istorii proletariata v epokhu tsarizma: feodal'no-krepostnoy period* (M.L. 1935).
NEVSKI, V. *Materialy dlya biograficheskogo slovarya sotsial-demokratov*, Pt. 1 (M.P. 1923).
Pervaya Russkaya revolyutsiya: ukazatel' literatury, Ed. G. K. Derman (M. 1930).
Rossiya: polnoe geograficheskoe opisanie nashego otechestva, Vols I-XIX, Ed. V. P. Semenov-Tyan'-Shanski (Spb. 1899-1913).
SHILOV, A. A. *Chto chitat' po istorii revolyutsionnogo dvizheniya* (P. 1922).
Sibirskaya sovetskaya entsiklopediya, Vols. I-III (M. 1929).
ZALESKI, E. *Mouvements Ouvriers et Socialistes. La Russie*, Vol. 1 (Paris, 1956).

2. Russian Language Sources

ABDURAKHMANOV, A. A. 'Pervy Bakinski Sovet rabochikh deputatov' in *Trudy Azerbayzhanskogo filiala IMEL pri TsK KPSS*, Vol. XIX (1955).
ALEKSANDROV, P. K. *Ocherk rabochego dvizheniya v Tverskoy gubernii 1885-1905* (Tver, 1923).
AMAL'RIK, A. S. 'Razmeshchenie stachechnikov v Evropeyskoy Rossii v 1905 g.' *Istoricheskie Zapiski*, No. 52 (1955).
BALABANOV, M. *Ocherki po istorii rabochego klassa v Rossii*, Pt. I (Kiev, 1924).
BLINOVA, EL. ET AL. *Iz istorii revolyutsionnogo dvizheniya vo Vladimirskoy gubernii (1905-07)* (Vladimir, 1955).
Bol'sheviki vo glave vserossiyskoy politicheskoy stachki v oktyabre 1905 g. (M. 1955).

226

BRANDENBURGSKI, YA. G. *Delo Peterburgskogo komiteta* (Kharkov, 1923).

BUBNOV, A. S. 'V.K.P. (b)'. *Bol'shaya sovetskaya entsiklopediya*, Vol. XI (1930) (pp. 386-544).

CHERNOVA, E. *Ivanovo-Voznesenski proletariat* (M. 1955).

EKZEMPLYARSKI, P. M. *Istoriya goroda Ivanovo* (Ivanovo, 1958).

EKZEMPLYARSKI, P. M. *Ocherki po istorii rabochego dvizheniya v Ivanovo-Vosnesenske* (Ivanovo-Voznesensk, 1924).

ESAIASHVILI, V. G. *Ocherki istorii kommunisticheskoy partii Gruzii*, Pt. 1 (Tbilisi, 1957).

GAVRILOV, B. *Moskovskie bol'sheviki v bor'be za armiya v 1905-1907 gg.* (M. 1955).

GELLER, A. AND ROVENSKAYA, N. *Peterburgski i Moskovski sovet rabochikh deputatov 1905 g.* (M.L. 1925).

GORDON, M. *Professional'noe dvizhenie v epokhu pervoy russkoy revolyutsii 1905-07 gg.* (L. 1926).

GORIN, P. *Ocherki po istorii sovetov rabochikh deputatov 1905 g.* (M. 1925).

GRINEVICH, V. *Professional'noe dvizhenie rabochikh v Rossii* (St. Petersburg, 1908).

GULIEV, A. N. *Bakinski proletariat v gody novogo revolyutsionnogo pod'ema* (Baku, 1963).

IBRAGIMOV, Z. *Revolyutsiya 1905-1907 gg. v Azerbaydzhane* (Baku, 1955).

IL'IN-ZHENEVSKI, A. 'Kak Iskra zavoevala Peterburg'. *Krasnaya letopis'*, No. 4 (15) (1925) (p. 216).

Istoriya kommunisticheskoy partii sovetskogo soyuza, Vol. 1 (M. 1964).

Istoriya Moskvy, Vol. V (M. 1955).

Istoriya rabochego klassa Leningrada, Vol. 2 (L. 1963).

KATS, A. AND MILONOV, YU. *1905* (M.L. 1925).

KOZLOV, T. S. *zachatki bol'shevizma v revolyutsionnom dvizhenii Turkmenii (1904-1916 gg.)* (Ashkhabad, 1928).

KOZ'MINYKH-LANIKH, I. M. *Fabrichno-zavodski rabochi Vladimirskoy gubernii (1897 g.)* (Vladimir, 1912).

KOKUSHKIN, I. *Dve revolyutsii* (M.L. 1925).

KONDRAT'EV, V. A. 'Iz istorii izdaniya dokumentov o deyatel'nosti sovetov rabochikh deputatov 1905 g.' *Arkheograficheski ezhegodnik za 1957 g.* (M. 1958).

KRETSOVA, F. D. *Bol'sheviki vo glave pervoy russkoy revolyutsii (1905-07* (M. 1956).

KUZ'MICH, A. *Moskovskaya organizatsiya na II S'ezde RSDRP* (M. 1963).

LYASHCHENKO, P. N. *Istoriya narodnogo khozyaystvo S.S.S.R.*, Vol. 2 (1952).

MARTOV, YU.O., MASLOV, P., POTRESOV, A., ET AL. *Obshchestvennoe dvizhenie v Rossii v nachale XX-go veke*, Vols. 1-4 (St. Petersburg, 1909-14).
The following articles have been found most useful:
Vol. I.   Kol'tsov, 'Rabochie v 1890-1904 gg.'
            Egorov, 'Sotsialdemokratiya 1900-1904'.
Vol. III.   Yu. Martov, 'Sotsialdemokratiya 1905-1907'.
Vol. IV.ii. F. Dan, 'Vtoraya Duma'.

MERKUROV, G. S. 'Sovety v pervoy russkoy revolyutsii'. *Pervaya russkaya revolyutsiya 1905-07* (M. 1955).

MIL'SHTEIN, A. 'Proletariat v revolyutsionnom dvizhenii Sibirii'. *Proletariat v revolyutsii 1905-07 gg.* (M. 1930).

Ocherki istorii Leningrada, Vol. III (L.M. 1956).

PANKRATOVA, A. M. *Pervaya Russkaya revolyutsiya 1905-1907* (M. 1951).

PANKRATOVA, A. M. 'Tekstil'shchiki v revolyutsii 1905-07 gg.' *Proletariat v revolyutsii 1905-07 gg.* (M.L. 1930).

PAZHITNOV, K. A. *Polozhenie rabochego klassa v Rossii* (St. Petersburg, 1906; second edition M. 1925).

PETROV, V. A. *Ocherki po istorii revolyutsionnogo dvizheniya v russkoy armii v 1905 g.* (M.L. 1964).

PLATOV, V. S. *Revolyutsionnoe dvizhenie v Tverskoy gub.* (Kalinin, 1959).

POGOZHEV, A. V. *Uchet chislennosti i sostava rabochikh* (St. Petersburg, 1906).

POKROVSKI, M. N., ED. *1905 Istoriya*, Vols. I-III (M.L. 1925-27).

POLEVOY, YU. *Iz istorii Moskovskoy organizatsii VKP(b) (1894-1904 gg.)* (M. 1947).

POTOLOV, S. I. *Rabochie Donbassa v XIX veke* (M. 1963).

POZNER, S. M. *Boyevaya gruppa pri TsK RSDRP 1905-07* (M.L. 1927).

POZNER, S. M. *Pervaya boyevaya organizatsiya bol'shevikov 1905-07* (M. 1934).

Proletariat v revolyutsii 1905-07 gg. (M.L. 1930).

Proletarskaya revolyutsiya, 1-113 (M. 1921-31, 1933-40).

Balashov, S. 'Rabochee dvizhenie v Ivanovo-Voznesenske', No. 39 (1925).

'Kanun revolyutsii 1905 g. na Kavkaze' 1 (48) (1926).

Leman, M. 'Iz proshlogo Kavkazskikh bol'shevistskikh organizatsiy', 5 (40) (1925).

Morokhovets, E. 'Krest'yanskoe dvizhenie 1905-07 gg. i sotsial-demokratiya', 4 (39) (1925).

Morokhovets, E. 'Proletariat i krest'yanstvo v epokhu pervoy revolyutsii', 5 (52) (1926).

Moshinski, I. 'K voprosu o S.D. (Donetskom) Soyuze Gornozavodskikh rabochikh', 5 (65) (1927).

Nevski, V. I. 'Dekabr'skaya zabastovka 1904 g. v Baku', No. 25 (1924).

Nevski, V. I. 'Yanvar'skie dni 1905 g. na Kavkaze', No. 27 (1924).

Nevski, V. I. 'Yanvar'skie dni 1905 v Ekaterinoslave i Donetskom basseyne', No. 15 (1923).

Taratuta, V. 'Kanun revolyutsii 1905 g. na Kavkaze', 1 (48) (1926).

Vetoshkin, M. 'Bol'sheviki i Men'sheviki v 1905 g. na Dal'nem Vostoke', 4 (51) (1926).

PYASKOVSKI, A. V. *Revolyutsiya 1905-1907 gg. v Turkestane* (M. 1958).

RASHIN, A. G. *Formirovanie rabochego klassa Rossii* (M. 1958).

ROZENBLYUM, K. *Voennye organizatsii bol'shevikov 1905-1907 gg.* (M.L. 1931).

SHELYMAGIN, I. I. *Zakonodatel'stvo o fabrichno-zavodskom trude v Rossii 1900-1917 gg.* (M. 1952).

SHESTAKOV, A. *Krest'yanskaya revolyutsiya 1905-07 gg. v Rossii* (M.L. 1926).

SHIPULINA, A. V. 'Ivanovo-Voznesenskie rabochie nakanune pervoy russkoy revolyutsii. Usloviya ikh trud i byta'. *Doklady i soobshcheniya instituta istorii*, No. 8 (M. 1955).

SMIRNOV, A. *Kak proshli vybory* (St. Petersburg, 1907).

SOF'EV, V. 'Gornorabochie v 1905-07 gg.' *Proletariat v revolyutsii* (M. 1930).

SOF'EV, V. '1905 v Baku'. *Proletariat v revolyutsii* (M. 1930).

SPEKTOR, S. *Moskovskie tekstil'shchiki v gody pervoy revolyutsii (1905-07 gg.)* (M. 1929).

SPIRIDOVICH, A. I. *Istoriya bol'shevizma* (Paris, 1922).

STEPANOV, V. N. 'Dokumenty Leninskoy Iskry'. *V.I. KPSS*, No. 1 (1961).

STOPANI, A. M. *Neftepromyshlenny rabochi i ego byudzhet* (M. 1924).

SVERCHKOV, I. D. *Na zare revolyutsii* (M. 1922).
TOMSINSKI, S. G. *Bor'ba klassov i partiy vo vtoroy gosudarstvennoy dume* (M. 1924).
1905: armiya v pervoy revolyutsii (M.L. 1927).
'U istokov partii: materialy o sotsial-demokraticheskikh organizatsiyakh v Rossii nakanune II s'ezda RSDRP'. *V.I. KPSS*, Nos. 3, 9 (1963).
VARZAR, V. E. *Statistika stachek rabochikh na fabrikakh i zavodakh 1906-1908* (St. Petersburg, 1910).
ZELIKSON-BOBROVSKAYA, TS. *Tovarishch Bauman* (M.L. 1928).
ZLATOUSTOVSKI, B. V. *Stachechnoe dvizhenie v Ivanovo-voznesenskom rayone 1905-1906 gg.* (Ivanovo-Voznesensk, 1928).
ZOTOV, M. A. 'Iz istorii bor'by V.I. Lenina za partiyu posle II s'ezda RSDRP'. *V.I. KPSS*, No. 2 (1961).

3. *Non-Russian Language Sources (Place of publication is London unless otherwise stated)*

ANDERSON, C. A. 'A Footnote to the Social History of Modern Russia'. *Genus* (Rome), Vol. XII, No. 1-4 (1956).
ANWEILER, O. *Die Rätebewegung in Russland 1905-1921* (Leiden, 1958).
BENDIX, R. *Max Weber: An Intellectual Portrait* (1960).
BENDIX, R. 'Social Stratification and Political Power'. *American Political Science Review*, No. 46 (1952).
BENDIX, R. *Work and Authority in Industry* (N.Y. 1956).
BENDIX, R. and Lipset, S.M. 'Political Sociology' in *Current Sociology*, Vol. VI (Paris, 1957).
BENNEY, M. ET AL. *How People Vote* (1956).
BERELSON, B. *Content Analysis* (Chicago, 1952).
Bulletin for Labour History, No. 10 (Spring, 1965).
COBBAN, A. *The Social Interpretation of the French Revolution* (1964).
DAHRENDORF, R. *Class and Class Consciousness in Industrial Society* (1959).
DAN, T. *The Origins of Bolshevism* (1964).
DEUTSCHER, I. *The Prophet Armed* (1954).
DUVERGER, M. *Political Parties* (1959).
FUTRELL, M. *Northern Underground* (1963).
GEYER, D. *Lenin in der russischen Sozialdemokratie: Die Arbeiterbewegung im Zarenreich als Organisationsproblem der revolutionären Intelligenz, 1890-1903* (Köln, 1962).
HAIMSON, L. H. *The Russian Marxists and the Origins of Bolshevism* (Harvard University Press, 1955).
HAMMOND, T. T. 'Lenin on Russian Trade Unions under Capitalism 1894-1904'. *A.S.E.E.R.*, Vol. 8 (Dec. 1949).
HAMMOND, T. T. *Lenin on Trade Unions and Revolution 1893-1917* (N.Y. 1957).
HEBERLE, R. 'Ferdinand Tönnies Contribution to the Sociology of Political Parties'. *American Journal of Sociology*, No. 61 (1955-56).
HEBERLE, R. *Social Movements* (N.Y. 1951).
KEEP, J. L. H. *The Rise of Social Democracy in Russia* (1963).
KEEP, J. L. H. 'Russian Social-democracy and the First State Duma'. *S.E.E.R.* (Dec. 1955).

KORNHAUSER, W. *The Politics of Mass Society* (1960).

LANE, R. E. *Political Life* (Glencoe, 1957).

LASSWELL, H. D. ET AL. *Language of Politics* (N.Y. 1949).

LEVIN, A. 'The Fifth Social-Democratic Congress and the Duma'. *Journal of Modern History*, Vol. XI, No. 4 (Chicago, 1939).

LEVIN, A. *The Second Duma* (Yale University Press, 1940).

LIPSET, S. M. *The First New Nation* (1964).

LIPSET, S. M. *Political Man* (1960).

LIPSET, S. M. 'Social Stratification and Right-wing Extremism'. *British Journal of Sociology*, Vol. X, No. 4 (Dec. 1959).

LIPSET, S. M. and Zetterberg, H. 'A Theory of Social Mobility'. *Transactions of the Third World Congress of Sociology* (1956).

MANNHEIM, K. 'The Sociological Problem of Generations'. Kecskemeti (Ed.) *Essays on the Sociology of Knowledge* (N.Y. 1952).

MARTOV, JU. O. *Geschichte der Russischen Sozialdemokratie* (Berlin, 1926).

NOWAKOWSKI, S. 'Aspects of Social Mobility in Post-war Poland'. *Transactions of the Third World Congress of Sociology*, Vol. III (1956).

PIPES, R. 'Russian Marxism and its Populist Background: The Late Nineteenth Century'. *Russian Review*, Vol. 19, No. 4 (Oct. 1960).

PIPES, R. *Social Democracy and the St. Petersburg Labor Movement, 1885-1897* (Harvard University Press, 1963).

PLAMENATZ, J. *German Marxism and Russian Communism* (1954).

RADKEY, O. H. *The Agrarian Foes of Bolshevism* (N.Y. 1958).

REX, J. *Key Problems of Sociological Theory* (1961).

RUDÉ, G. *The Crowd in the French Revolution* (1959).

SCHAPIRO, L. *The Communist Party of the Soviet Union* (1960).

SELZNICK, P. *The Organizational Weapon* (1952).

SLUSSER, R. M. 'The Forged Bolshevik Signature: A Problem of Soviet Historiography'. *Slavic Review*, Vol. XXIII, No. 2 (June 1964).

THOMPSON, E. P., *The Making of the English Working Class* (1966).

TREADGOLD, D. W. *The Great Siberian Migration* (Princeton, 1957).

TREADGOLD, D. W. 'Russian Expansion and Turner's American Frontier'. *Agricultural History*, Vol. 26, No. 4 (Oct. 1952).

UTECHIN, S. V. 'Who Taught Lenin'. *Twentieth Century*, Vol. CLXVIII (1960).

UTECHIN, S. V. 'The 'Preparatory' Trend in the Russian Revolutionary Movement in the 1880's'. *St. Antony's Papers*, No. 12 (1962).

VENTURI, F. *The Roots of Revolution* (1960).

WEBER, M. 'Class, Status and Party', in R. Bendix and S. M. Lipset, *Class, Status and Power* (1954).

WILDMAN, A. K. 'Lenin's Battle with Kustarnichestvo'. *Slavic Review*, Vol. XXIII, No. 3 (Sept. 1964).

WOLFE, B. D. *Three Who Made a Revolution* (1956).

INDEX